How to Produce CREATIVE ADVERTISING

Proven Techniques & Computer Applications

Ann Keding ·· Thomas Bivins

NTC Business Books
a division of *NTC Publishing Group* • Lincolnwood, Illinois USA

Library of Congress Cataloging-in-Publication Data
Keding, Ann
  How to produce creative advertising: proven techniques and
computer applications / Ann Keding and Thomas Bivins
    p. cm.
   Includes index.
   ISBN 0-8442-3481-8. (hardbound); 0-8442-3482-6 (softbound)
   1. Advertising. 2. Advertising—Data processing. 3. Advertising copy.
4. Advertising layout and typography. 5. Media Planning
I. Bivins, Thomas   II. Title.
HF5823.B53 1990
659.1—dc20   90-60194

Published by NTC Business Books, a division of NTC Publishing Group
4255 West Touhy Avenue
Lincolnwood (Chicago), Illinois 60646-1975, U.S.A.
©1991 by NTC Publishing Group. All rights reserved.
No part of this book may be reproduced, stored in a retrieval system,
or transmitted in any form or by any means,
electronic, mechanical, photocopying, recording or otherwise,
without the prior permission of NTC Publishing Group.
Manufactured in the United States of America.
1 2 3 4 5 6 7 8 9 BC 9 8 7 6 5 4 3 2 1

Contents

Introduction   vii

PART ONE
The Creative Process

Chapter 1   What It Takes to Create Great Advertising 3
   How to Accomplish Something You Can Revel in 4
   Looking for Inspiration 4
   The Apprentice Craftsperson 5
   So Which Skills Will You Have to Acquire? 5
   Push up Your Sleeves and Get to Work 7

Chapter 2   Defining the Problem and Knowing the Consumer 8
   Define the Problem: Know the Product or Service 8
   Define the Problem: Choose Your Target Audience 10
   Define the Problem: Know the Consumer 11
   How to Conduct Research on Your Own 15
   Find New Marketing Opportunities through Creative Research 15

Chapter 3   Strategy Can Be Creative 17
   Make Sure Your Strategy Is on Target 18
   Strategy Should Tell the Truth 18
   Thinking Through a Strategy 19
   Positioning Your Product 22
   Structuring Your Strategy: Creative Blueprints 23

Chapter 4 Ideas, Large and Small 27
What Makes an Idea Great? 28
    Guard Your Ideas 32
    The Difference between a Single Idea and a Campaign 32
    What Holds an Advertising Campaign Together? 33
    Should a Campaign Be Single Medium or Multimedia? 38
    Do Creative Ads Sell? 38
    Winning Recognition for Creative Work 40

Chapter 5 Print Ads: A Writer Writes 41
    Clustering: A Tool to Make Writing Easier 41
    Before You Start to Write: The Copy Platform 42
    Next, the Headline 43
    Using Slogans and Logotype 45
    Body Copy 46
    The Lead 47
    Tracking: Crafting the Copy 48
    The Close and the Call-to-Action 49
    Using Subheads 49
    Grammar: Respect the Rules 50
    Playing with Words 50
    A Word on Style 51

Chapter 6 Print Ads: The Elements of Art Direction 53
    What Does the Art Director Do? 53
    Visuals: The Power of Sight 54
    Art Direction: What It Entails 55
    Ad Design 56
    The Mechanics of Layout 57
    Typography 59
    Selecting Illustrations and Photography 61
    Use of Color 63
    Two Principles of Great Advertising 64

Chapter 7 Creating Broadcast Advertising 65
    Television Advertising 66
    Radio Advertising 75

Chapter 8 How to Sell Your Ideas 81
    Sell to Yourself Before You Sell to Anyone Else 82
    Selling to Others 82
    Making a Presentation to Colleagues 83
    Selling to a Client: Sales Presentations 85
    Learn How to Take Criticism 86

Chapter 9 Putting Together and Using a Portfolio 87
    What Should Be Represented in a Junior Portfolio? 87
    Compiling a Portfolio 88
    Showing Your Portfolio 90
    The Job Search 90

PART TWO
Computers: The Added Ingredient

Chapter 10 Word Processing 97
    How to Choose a Word-Processing Program 97

Chapter 11 Typography 100
    Digital Fonts 101
    Using Computer Type 103
    A Word About Style 106
    Display Type 106
    Kerning 107
    Initial Caps 108

Chapter 12 Photography 109
    A Brief Glossary of Terms 110
    The Method 111
    The Process 113

Chapter 13 Illustration 123
    Illustration Programs 123
    Scanned Art 127
    Clip Art 127

Chapter 14 Layout 130
    The Advantages of Computer Layout 131
    Formats 134
    Creating Thumbnails on the Computer 136
    Creating Roughs on the Computer 139
    Creating Comprehensives on the Computer 139
    Preparing the Mechanical 142
    Adding Color 144

Chapter 15 Printing 146
    Pre-mechanical Printing 147
    Printing the Finished Piece 151
    Color Printing 152

Appendix: Setting Up a Desktop Publishing System   157

Colophon: How This Book was Put Together   163

Glossary   168

Index   177

Introduction

Most people who have created great advertising could correctly say their success had nothing to do with the tools they used and had everything to do with dedication to their craft. It was a passionate commitment that drove them to master the skills needed to create something special out of the ordinary.

A good many advertising craftspeople are reluctant to consider a personal computer *essential* to the process of putting together any form of advertising. There are several reasons for this reluctance: a belief in the value of art directors acquiring hands-on production skills; a belief that copywriters should stay out of the realm of advertising art; uncertainty about changing tools; and a desire to maintain control over one's work. These craftspeople want the human element to remain central to the creative process. Using a keyboard and a screen to shape an idea, some feel, distances them from their work. In the realm of problem solving and ideas, they feel a personal computer just isn't necessary. Roy Paul Nelson, author of *The Design of Advertising*, states that he would never advocate learning the mechanics of design on a computer. He believes working on the board is essential to the proper development of an art director's skills.

The aim of this book is twofold: first, to show you how to improve your skills and craft better advertising by emphasizing the problem solving process behind the creative process; and second, to give you a few ideas about how your personal computer can help. In Part One, author Ann Keding tackles the concept of creativity in advertising and in Part Two, Tom Bivins introduces the computer as a key production tool. It is our hope that you will not only learn how to do your work more efficiently, but that you will be motivated to bring that essential human element, inspiration, to all of it.

Creative solutions come from spontaneous connections made between unrelated ideas and events. Quite clearly, the state-of-the-software indicates that there is none that completely fits this definition of the creative process. The thought of using a personal computer to produce something creative seems contradictory. However, there are many ways in which a personal computer can help you with the technical process of putting advertising together after you have done the mental work necessary to come up with a worthy idea. Learn to consider your computer as an efficient tool in the creative process. Perhaps the most significant benefit it offers is time savings. As anyone in the advertising industry knows, saved time always can be fit into a busy work schedule. With a computer, multiple layouts and designs can be tried quickly and easily. Editing becomes a snap. In Part Two of this book you will learn how using a computer can make life easier for you.

Why Focus on Print?

Print has been called the queen of advertising. Most advertising craftspeople agree that it is the most challenging medium when it comes to the discipline of concept development. Print advertising is emphasized throughout this book because through print you will learn to judge more quickly whether or not you have created good advertising .

Excellent print advertising results when a unique perspective or thought is expressed in language that stimulates understanding beyond the edges of the words that carry it. In print, an idea is openly displayed and its quality can be easily identified. A brilliant execution does not cover up a mediocre idea. It often highlights it. In print, there are no quick cuts or slow dissolves to distract us from a poor idea. There is no melodious voiceover and no musical score. Learn to apply the principles presented in this book to print advertising first, then with practice transfer them to broadcast, and your broadcast work will be the better for it.

Why the Computer Has Made Such a Difference

Probably the single most revolutionary invention of the last century has been the computer. Scarcely 50 years ago, a computer able to do the simplest calculations took up an entire room. Today, even the most complex work can be accomplished at a desk. When the microcomputer became commonplace, only a very few years ago it seems, life changed for millions of people. For the publishing industry, however, the most significant change followed invention of the hardware itself. The microcomputer changed the way we did nearly everything. Page layout software programs changed the way we think about and execute publications, in particular.

One of the earliest, some say the first, page layout programs was *PageMaker*, invented by Paul Brainerd and a handful of friends. Its original target audience was newspaper publishers. When that audience proved to be basically unreceptive, Brainerd turned to business. As it turned out, page layout software revolutionized the way organizations thought about in-house publication. What once had to go through the traditional writing, editing, typesetting, pasteup, and printing processes could now be done in a few very simple steps.

Although it took several long years before "desktop publishing" caught on, today it is sweeping the country. Advertising agencies (and freelancers) were quick to realize the potential of desktop publishing in the creation of print ads and related publications. Art directors, designers, illustrators, and layout artists all have benefitted from the computer.

What the new software and the increasing sophistication in hardware allow for is the involvement of fewer "middlemen" in the layout process. To some, this is a blessing, to others, a curse. Everyone with a computer and the necessary software is producing his or her own layouts—with or without the background needed to do so.

As Paul Brainerd (now president of Aldus Corporation) once quipped, "A desktop publishing program won't make you a designer." What the revolution in computer publishing has done is to provide copywriters, art directors, and layout artists with another tool to better accomplish their respective jobs. Without the knowledge and experience gained through a study of the basics of writing, design, and layout, even the best computer hardware and software won't help you.

The computer has made a tremendous difference. Word processing programs, once cumbersome and nearly impossible to work with, allow us to write, delete, move whole blocks of copy between files, index, outline, and perform myriad other tasks that once took hours and days to accomplish on a typewriter. The computer has allowed copywriters to facilitate their work through on-line interchange of information (or exchange of disks). Editors can now edit on-screen, and the designer and artist can see their work come to life before their eyes and instantly delivered into their hands as fast as a laser printer can print. Working together, account executives, copywriters, designers, and artists have made the most of this revolutionary tool, but they haven't done so without countless hours of training in the basics of their professions.

No book can teach you how to create great advertising. What this book will do is show you a thorough, professional, and creative approach to solving advertising problems, with and without computer technology.

NOTES

[1] Nelson, Roy Paul, *The Design of Advertising*, 6th ed., Wm. C. Brown, Dubuque, Iowa, 1989.

Part One

The Creative Process

Creative Advertising

Defining the Problem

Creative Strategy

Ideas

Writing

Art Direction

Broadcast

Selling Your Ideas

Portfolios

Chapter 1

What It Takes to Create Great Advertising

Great advertising is a *lightning quick* method of communication that delivers a *persuasive* and *memorable* sales message to a chosen audience. Remove these qualities, *lightning quick* and *memorable*, and you have a definition of ordinary advertising. Let's amplify the definition of great advertising. *Lightning quick* means that the complete strategy and message has been refined as much as possible. Meaning is grasped at a glance. No lengthy interpretations are necessary. The message drives home the most important point to be remembered, instantly. *Memorable* advertising presents information in a provocative or unusual way or recounts the familiar with a twist.

Original advertising uses ideas in a fresh way to convey its message. We may have seen the picture or heard the words before, but the juxtaposition of these elements causes us to pause and think of the product differently. For example, a phrase commonly used to indicate commitment is "you have our word" or "you have our word on it." This sentence—"You have our word on it"— over a photograph of a plump orange with the Sunkist logo clearly stamped on it makes a powerful statement to consumers about Sunkist oranges.

The first time this new combination surfaces is the only time it is considered original. Any similar use that follows is considered derivative, whether or not intentional.

Tough standards?

That's not the half of it. Not only must the message be conveyed in a fresh way, it has to be a well-thought-out distillation of an advertising strategy. Much thinking and planning is involved in the development of that strategy. Returning to the Sunkist example, the strategy here was to communicate to the target audience that the Sunkist name was synonymous with freshness and quality. The creative execution chosen delivers that strategy dramatically.

How to Accomplish Something You Can Revel in

There is absolutely no greater feeling on earth than that of hitting on a *great* idea. People who strive for excellence in a craft report that they experience physiological reactions when they receive inspiration—cold chills, tearing eyes, uncontrollable laughter, and more. This combination of enlightenment and physiological experience seems to be so forceful that people will work long weary hours, never letting up, to achieve it. Their eyes are glazed over and they seem slightly frenzied. Rollo May has described this period in the creative process as one that is exemplified by a high "degree of absorption, the degree of intensity."[1] It is this often unreasonable level of commitment that helps creative people arrive again and again at a point of inspiration.

One could say that these people simply have high standards and know the difference between the exceptional and the ordinary. We would argue that each of us intuitively knows the difference between a good and a bad idea and something inside clicks when we come up with a great one.

Copywriters and art directors encouraged to revel in their accomplishments take more risks. They also create more original and memorable work than those who don't revel. The risks they take reflect a willingness to expose their inner selves, to express a point of view, no matter how farfetched it is. Often, the best creative people are those whose perspectives are so unusual that they transform ordinary ideas into those that are unique.

Looking for Inspiration

Unique connections between seemingly unrelated pieces of information can result in ideas that are inspired. In advertising, creative inspiration means presenting a familiar product in a way that causes people to begin to think about it differently, or presenting a new product in a way that causes people to see how it can help them. Research often paves the way for inspiration. In advertising, the work leading up to the creative process is called the "prewriting" phase. During this phase, it is important to collect and absorb a multitude of different data. These data are then processed through a filter—the sum total of your experiences and observations. Ideally, the solution that comes forth in the form of an idea is unique to you.

Sometimes people go only halfway in the process of preparing to arrive at a creative solution, and it shows. When several people come up with similar solutions because no one had enough information to increase the opportunity for the unusual, these solutions come from the surface, not from a deeper creativity.

Even after the most resourceful information gathering, there is no guarantee of an inspired solution. But the chances are greater. No one knows exactly what happens between the research stage and the appearance of a magical solution. There isn't even any certainty that what happens once will happen again. What is known is that great ideas don't hang around waiting for someone to reach up and grab them. They save themselves for the dedicated. They are there for those who won't give up until they fully understand everything about the problem they have set out to solve.

If the path toward inspiration could be marked, the roadsigns might read as follows:

- Gather information
- Store the information in a file
- Forget about the problem and go on to some other activity
- Return to the problem

Remember to be humble when the muses reward you with a brilliant solution.

The Apprentice Craftsperson

In the Middle Ages, craftspeople organized themselves into guilds and invited those who wished to learn their craft to join them as apprentices. Oddly enough, nearly six centuries later, in an industry known for its progressiveness and need to stay on the cutting edge of cultural changes, junior writers and art directors are taken on in much the same way.

People majoring in English, political science, history, mathematics, or psychology are brought into advertising to be trained as copywriters. Occasionally, a writer with very little formal education but with obvious talent is hired. The same is true for art directors. Some have a formal education, others do not. Once they are selected, they are assigned to the creative departments to begin their initiation into this side of the business.

When advertising is viewed as a craft, it is easy to see that there is good reason for an "apprenticeship" system. Craftspeople develop skills slowly. They learn by trial and error and amass a reservoir of experience from which to draw when new problems present themselves. As their skills improve, they are given more and more challenging assignments.

It makes little difference what the education and training of an advertising apprentice is. All that matters is that he or she show a spark of talent or the ability to think through a problem. A mathematics major is as likely to have these unpolished abilities as someone who majored in English. Majoring in advertising, though it does not guarantee you a successful career in the industry, does provide one advantage: you can learn the principles of advertising and may be able to discern where your talents best fit. Though the increasing number of advertising programs available means that the level of skill required to enter as an apprentice has risen, there is, however, always room for talented beginners.

So Which Skills Will You Have to Acquire?

Advertising is a unique business, because when done well, it calls for a special synthesis of business and analytical skills and creative and artistic abilities.

Copywriters and art directors need to develop the following skills:

- The ability to *think strategically*, that is, to reason through a marketing or advertising problem;

- The ability to *transfer* that *thinking* into a powerful idea that will move the person who sees it into action;

- The ability to *execute* that idea *provocatively* so that it will be remembered. (Copywriters learn to write copy that sells and art directors learn to execute advertisements that attract people's attention.); and

- The ability to *make judgments* in order to evaluate effectively their work and that of others.

Tenacity Separates Great Craftspeople from the Not-So-Great

An essential attribute of those who create good advertising is the tenacity with which they stick to any advertising problem until they arrive at a satisfactory solution. Because so much relies on *informed* judgment, one has to focus on the problem the advertising is to solve until every bit of relevant information has been collected.

Problem solving in advertising means understanding the truth about the relationship between the consumer and the product. The truth about that relationship is present in the information you gather and in the intuitive judgments you make after you have gathered *all* of the necessary information. Great ideas come to those who keep at it.

After Tenacity Comes Passion

Unfortunately, solving the advertising problem only leads to an understanding of what needs to be communicated. Often, it doesn't provide a clue about how to say it.

That's when passion takes over. If you are passionate about great advertising, you will never settle for anything less than the best. You become ruthlessly critical of your work, rejecting derivative ideas while searching for those that present the truth so stunningly that no one can escape noticing it.

There are times when you come up with a great idea and find out later that it has been used before. Discovering this after the fact can be heartrending. If you make such a discovery during the creative problem solving process, and if you want to be truly original, it is your obligation to cast this idea away and move on to a fresh one.

To create work that you are proud of, that earns the respect and admiration of your colleagues, and that persuades prospects to buy requires commitment, passion, and a single-minded quest for excellence. If you are willing to consider one hundred ideas before you find one that measures up, congratulations, you have the endurance it takes to be great.

Teamwork Works

Doyle Dane Bernbach, the agency that changed the look of advertising in the late 1950s and early 1960s, recognized that it is often the magical relationship between copywriter and art director that inspires great advertising. Bill Bernbach noticed that people create better solutions to advertising problems when they work in teams of two. Until that time, it was customary for the copywriter to come up with the idea and then pass it on to the art director, who drew a picture to illustrate it. Today's advertising craftspeople wouldn't think of working in this way.

Ideally, teamwork means that each member of the team has as much control over the work as the other. The copywriter and art director work together to form an advertising concept or idea. The art director may articulate the headline just as often as the copywriter. And the copywriter may come up with the idea for the visual. Each brings unique skills and abilities, so every team is different and has a particular chemistry. The final effort is a product of people working together.

There is some division of labor

Writing the copy is the responsibility of the copywriter; the layout is the responsibility of the art director. To maintain a successful working relationship with your partner, it is important to ask your teammate for his or her opinion about your work—good or bad—as you progress. In a healthy team relationship, each member of the team can give and take constructive criticism, so the final product is the best work possible.

The team relationship, therefore, requires good communication skills. Honesty, loyalty, and commitment all help solidify a feeling of trust. Partners who trust each other are willing to risk sharing the silly ideas along with the good ones—and, often in advertising, it is the silly ideas that work best.

Self-confidence, too, is important in the team relationship. If you don't believe in your ability to come up with original ideas, you'll never be able to sell those ideas to your teammate, and that's the first sale you have to make.

What if you and your teammate don't get along? Sometimes you have to part ways. You should try to resolve the problems first, however. Just as in other personal relationships, the problems that occur in one partnership can plague you in those that follow. So, stop and take a hard look the first time you run into a problem. Even if you feel you are not to blame, do all you can to resolve the situation. Working through communication problems will bring you closer together and improve your work.

Push up Your Sleeves and Get to Work

The approach to improving your advertising skills, covered in Part One of this book, emphasizes the importance of creative thinking during every phase of the advertising process. Bring creativity to the research phase of your work and you stand a better chance of uncovering some hidden fact that becomes the theme for a campaign. During strategy development, creativity can move the spotlight from a traditional target audience to a new, unexpected one. Or it can be the force behind the discovery of a benefit with universal appeal. Creative thinking challenges you to bring unique perspectives to everything you do. It spawns ideas that grab you by the lapels and demand your attention, language that enchants, and visuals so inspired you wonder how you ever imagined them.

The aim of Part One, then, is to help you understand how creativity works in advertising. You will also learn how to use and control your natural talents so that when you come up with a great advertising idea, you can make the most of it. The skills we help you develop will bring discipline and direction to the ways in which you approach each advertising assignment. In the chapters that follow, you will be encouraged to think creatively about everything from problem solving and generating ideas, through translating thoughts into advertising, to selling your ideas, giving presentations, and finally, finding a job.

NOTES

[1] Rollo May, "The Nature of Creativity" in *Creativity and Its Cultivation*. Address Presented at the Interdisciplinary Symposia in Creativity, Michigan State University, ed. Harold H. Anderson, New York: Harper & Row, 1959, pp 58-59.

Chapter 2

Defining the Problem and Knowing the Consumer

A preliminary step in creating great advertising is to define the problem the advertising is meant to solve. Advertising problems are varied. They can be straightforward, *no one knows the product exists*. Or they can be much more involved, *persuade a battered woman to call a hotline for assistance when she doesn't believe anyone can help her*. Defining the problem is the first stage of producing an effective advertisement, and is accomplished through the process of information gathering. You may have a hunch about an advertising problem before you begin, but by the time your research is finished, you will either have data to confirm that hunch or you will have discovered a more pressing problem that advertising can solve.

The research you carry out has two objectives: to help you know the product or service you are advertising; and to help you know the consumer your advertisements will target.

If you work in an advertising agency, the account executive who hands you your assignments may have the advertising problem fairly well defined. But once in a while, through your sleuthing you may find that another problem, if solved, will allow for even more sales or responses. A discovery like this is good enough reason to review the strategy the account executive has given you each time you receive an assignment. Making this effort is not a waste of your time. Someone else can't run five miles a day to help you prepare for a marathon. Inspired creative solutions require that you put in the necessary mileage on the information-gathering phase of the problem solving process.

Define the Problem: Know the Product or Service

Research is the first step for anyone who wants to create effective advertising. Here, research means an exhaustive examination of the advertising problem from every imaginable angle. The more resourceful you are during this phase, the better your chances are of coming up with a unique solution.

Your first resource is the client. For many reasons, junior-level copywriters and art directors don't always have access to the client whose product or service they are advertising. It is up to you to convince the account executives who control your information flow of your need to visit the client. There is no substitute for being there. You need to see how the product is made, or talk to the people who perform the service. If you are there in person, some seemingly insignificant piece of information or some nuance from those who know the product or service best may catch your attention and spark the greatest campaign the client has ever run. Without a field trip to the client, you risk losing that opportunity.

As you begin looking for more sources of information, remember that your sources are only limited by your imagination. In larger advertising agencies, stacks of papers and reports from the research department should be available to you. Take time to read and absorb all the information you can get your hands on. Next, go to the library and look in the reference section and in encyclopedias under the categories that describe your product or service. Have the reference librarian complete a current literature search on the topic in newspapers and magazines. Better still, learn how to do it yourself. Knowing how to use a library's resources is a key research skill.

Talk to people. If you can't talk to the client, talk to consumers. Go wherever the product is sold and talk to retailers. Talk to your mother, your uncle, your aunt. Then talk to your creative partner.

In addition to finding out all you can about the product, you will need to keep abreast of the culture or environment in which it will be sold. To do this you must read the newspapers, go to movies, plays, museums, attend concerts, listen to Willie Nelson, U2, Herbie Hancock, Sly and Robbie, or Bad English. Watch *Saturday Night Live*, *Miami Vice,* and *L.A. Law*. Try out new radio stations, and watch public broadcasting programs. If you are committed to the goal of creating great advertising, you must become a cultural sponge. The more you know about what's going on around you, the better prepared you will be to create a message that communicates your product or service effectively, and that stands out amidst the deluge of messages your customers receive through the media each day.

Find Out Why the Client Is Advertising

Before the creative work begins, therefore, resourceful research can help you understand your product. It will also help you understand exactly what underlies your client's desire to advertise. Defining an advertising problem can be as easy as telling people that your client has a ton of fresh lettuce to unload or as complicated as telling them about running shoes for dogs. In the first example, you're reminding people about a product they already know, in the second—a *low profile* category—you have to educate people about the product and about the category.

Before you start, then, find out why your client wants to advertise. It may be to increase sales in the short term, to promote a daily or weekend special, to improve and build upon a quality image, or to introduce a new and innovative product or service. Each may require a different approach.

All of these aims, and others, can be achieved through advertising. In fact, wherever a business problem can be solved or a business objective reached by presenting a clear message, advertising can help. Remember, though, that advertising can't solve problems that result from poor product or service quality, or from incorrect pricing, or inadequate distribution. In fact, advertising will only draw more attention to these problems once consumers hear about the product and either have trouble finding it or are disappointed when they do. The information you have gathered during the research stage of each project will help you understand every aspect of the product—good or bad—and will help you focus your ideas accordingly.

Define the Problem: Choose Your Target Audience

Imagine your marketing target as a series of concentric circles. On the periphery are the people who have no interest in your product because it would be of little or no use to them. At the center of the circles are those people for whom it would be most relevant.

Consider, for example, a diaper service that launders and delivers cloth diapers. This is a business that once flourished but declined rapidly with the advent of disposable diapers. Now that people are being actively encouraged to choose environmentally safe products, let's assume diaper services are enjoying a revival. What is your target market? People who are not parents would not have much interest in knowing anything about diapers. These people stand on the periphery or outside the periphery of your target. Parents or expectant parents, are, of course, at the center. Others, such as grandparents and other relatives, and purchasing agents for hospital nurseries and day-care facilities may be somewhere near the center.

Placing your prospects within the circle in this way is helpful when you're deciding to whom to direct your messages. The people most likely to buy are at the center and your communication should be directed at them.

Can you Reach All Audiences with the Same Message?

It is often difficult to create a message that will reach all the members of your audience and move them to buy. To continue the same example, like parents and expectant parents, hospital purchasing agents are consumers. They read newspapers and magazines, see outdoor boards, television, and other advertising media. But purchasing agents may not read the *same* magazines or watch the *same* television shows expectant parents watch. They may be older or younger and have completely different interests. They also have different *motivations* for purchasing the same product, and are looking for different benefits. A prompt, reliable service with soft diapers to keep a newborn dry is key, but of equal importance would be a price break on large volume orders.

Think through each assignment as it has been presented to you and see if the facts make sense. It could be that your client, or the agency executive who assigned the project to you, knows exactly how advertising can solve a particular marketing problem, but do not rest until you have come to the same conclusions. Consider all recommendations in the light of the information you have. Approaching the problem with a fresh pair of eyes and thinking it through for yourself gives you the opportunity to find a unique angle that others have overlooked.

A Brilliant Technique for Bright Ideas

James Webb Young, whose long and illustrious career as a copywriter began at J. Walter Thompson, suggests one method of closing in on an idea. He highlights the value of extensive research. In *A Technique for Producing Ideas*, Young recommends that as you return from each fact-finding mission, you take time to write each piece of information you collect on an index card.[1] That's right. Each fact belongs on a separate card. As you continue to collect bits and pieces of information, add them to your box of cards. After you have completed the search, close the box and keep it closed for as long as you can afford. A week is probably best. Then, return to the file, review it, and write down your best ideas as they begin to emerge.

Define the Problem: Know the Consumer

In its strictest sense, the goal of advertising is to communicate information about a product, service, or institution to interested people. Given that goal, anyone who creates advertising must be aware of *who* is going to be interested and *what* these people want to hear.

People who see and hear advertising have varying degrees of interest in its message. Those most interested respond when it tells them something useful about a product, or how a product will solve a problem they have.

It is obvious, then, that to communicate successfully to more than one audience about a product, you need to consider the benefits relevant to each and focus on these. If your client's budget is limited, you may have to recommend reaching one audience before you can target the others. It is through consumer research that you can uncover all the facts you need to know about your audience before making decisions such as these. You need to find out, for example, which audience is most likely to generate most sales. Or you may have to concentrate on discovering a creative use of media to stretch the client's budget. Before you can begin, you need to understand as much as you can about each of your target audiences. You need consumer research.

How to Build a Dossier on a Million People at Once

Defining target audiences is as much a craft as coming up with creative executions that deliver a brilliant idea. Research into *demographics* and *psychographics* can give you the specific information you need to tailor your message to them.

Demographics include descriptives such as gender, age, income, education, family size, and region of residence. Psychographics refer to attitudes, behaviors, and lifestyles. A measurable attitude, for example, could be the degree of liking for a product; a behavior, how often the product is purchased; and a lifestyle, how people who buy the product spend their leisure.

One way of finding target audience information for the product or service you are researching is through syndicated research studies, published by such companies as Mediamark Research, Inc. (MRI)[2] or Simmons/Target Group Index.[3] Both are nationally known research companies.

Companies like these report the demographics of your audience through surveys of several thousand people who buy products from the various product or service categories, such as health and beauty aids, dairy products, snack foods, fruit, automobiles, insurance, banking, and credit cards. From the data they collect, they describe the consumer who uses each product or service. These data are presented in table form.

Simmons/TGI has also begun reporting some psychographic data, focusing on values, attitudes, and lifestyles (VALS).[4] The Yankelovitch Monitor[5] is another syndicated company that offers a similar service, and tracks trends in people's attitudes toward time, money, the future, family, self, institutions, and other lifestyle aspects.

Values, Attitudes, and Lifestyles (VALS)

VALS, now the most widely used commercial psychographic-research program, grew out of a study that examined the way in which a person's needs influenced his or her attitudes and behavior toward consumption of products or services. Originally, this research categorized people according to nine basic life-styles: Belongers, Emulators, Achievers, I-Am-Me's, Experientials, Societally Conscious, Survivors, Sustainers, and Integrateds.

VALS makes a distinction between inner- and outer-directed people. The three outer-directed types are the Belongers, Emulators, and Achievers. Belongers, the largest VALS group, are stable, hard-working, blue-collar, conforming individuals. Emulators are more ambitious and more status conscious than Belongers, and they envy the life-style of the group just ahead of them, the Achievers. Achievers are successful business people and professionals. Seeking success, they know what they want and make it happen.

The three inner-directed VALS categories are quite different. The I-Am-Me's are generally young, highly individualistic, and egocentric. A small group, they may mature into Experientials with a major focus on choices that emphasize new experiences. When a person in this group becomes concerned with society as a whole, he or she moves into the Societally Conscious group. The members of this group tend to be knowledgeable and concerned about social causes, such as the environment. The Societally Conscious is the largest of the inner-directed groups. Its members earn a good deal of money, but their life-styles emphasize simplicity.

Survivors and Sustainers function marginally in society. They are made up of people with limited resources. For example, survivors could include the elderly or poor who may feel trapped by poverty with little chance of escape. Sustainers also struggle at the edge of poverty, but they have not given up.

The ninth and smallest group includes those psychologically mature individuals known as the Integrateds. These people combine the best qualities of the inner- and outer-directed groups. They have the power and drive of the Achievers and the sensitivity of the Societally Conscious. They have achieved balance in their lives.

These categories can help you decide which people may be interested in the product or service you are trying to sell, and the reason why. For example, both an Achiever and a Societally Conscious individual might be interested in purchasing a Mercedes automobile, but for different reasons. The Achiever may choose the car as much for status as for performance, while the Societally Conscious person may choose it solely because of its reputation for durability. (An Emulator would, perhaps, buy an American or Japanese import styled to imitate the Mercedes.)

VALS 2

Because these categories were criticized as being too restrictive and not easy to apply, VALS took another look at these segmentations and came up with revised classifications.

In the VALS 2 segmentation (see **Exhibit 2.1**), people are divided into three basic categories: those who are principle oriented, status oriented, and action oriented. People in these categories are divided into eight subcategories: Fulfilleds, Believers, Actualizers, Achievers, Strivers, Strugglers, Experiencers, and Makers.

These subcategories take into consideration the resources consumers can draw upon, such as their education, income, health, energy level, self-confidence, and degree of consumerism. Simmons Market Research Bureau now uses these subcategories in their reports, which are available in the business or reference section of most libraries.

Some clients and agencies do their own psychographic research instead of subscribing to syndicated sources. This is not surprising, as the categories of these syndicated services have been criticized for being superficial, overrated, and not particularly helpful in predicting consumer behavior. They can even be seen as restrictive if you ignore the fact that people may move in and through two or three of them. Usually, one category is dominant for a person, but it is not uncommon for several categories to overlap. Nonetheless, psychographic research can be a useful tool in the creation of an advertising message.

VALS 1	VALS 2
Integrateds	**Actualizers**
Inner-Directed	**Principle-Oriented**
Societally Conscious	Fulfilleds
Experientials	Believers
I-Am-Me's	
	Status-Oriented
Outer-Directed	Achievers
Achievers	Strivers
Emulators	
Belongers	**Action-Oriented**
	Experiencers
Need Driven	Makers
Sustainers	
Survivors	**Strugglers**

Exhibit 2.1
VALS psychographic classifications of consumers. Source: Advertising Age, *February 13, 1989. Reproduced with permission of* Advertising Age.

Consumer Buying Patterns

How often people buy your product or service and how much they buy when they make a purchase are other things to consider.

For starters, how frequently will your prospects be making their purchase(s)? Every day (the daily newspaper), once or twice a week (yogurt, soda), or once every three to five years (automobiles)? You'll also want to think about how much the product costs. Is the price in line with similar product offerings? Too high? Too low? Finally, how many other products like yours are vying for your prospects' attention?

While you are developing advertising you need to have a clear picture in mind that gives you the following information:

- How often a consumer considers your product
- Where your product fits in relation to similar products that meet your prospects' needs
- Whom the competition is addressing with their advertising
- What the competition is saying to your prospects and others
- How your product is priced in relation to the competition

Thinking in this way helps you *identify with* consumers. Here, you begin to understand the complex selection process consumers experience when faced with many choices. You become aware of the multitude of distractions that work to get your prospects' attention. And you can see how powerful a message has to be in order to get through the clutter.

Do Those Who Already Use Your Product Deserve More of Your Attention?

Your consumer research should take into account the differences that exist between heavy, medium, and light users in a product or service category in which you advertise. You should also be aware of how *nonusers* differ from *users* and *potential users* and should have a clear idea which group you will target.

Heavy users are those who purchase and/or consume your product or service most often. Traditionally, heavy users account for a disproportionate amount of the volume. For example, 17 percent of all beer drinkers are heavy users, and they account for 88 percent of all beer sold.

In the research stage, you should assess the potential of your target audience. Can your advertising convert medium users to heavy users or move light users up to the medium use frequency?

The relevance of the frequency-of-use factor depends to some extent on what your product or service is. It is more relevant to a package of yogurt, for example, than to a racing bicycle (though dyed-in-the-wool cyclists often own any number of sophisticated bicycles and bicycle parts).

Imagine that your advertising strategy is to persuade light users to buy your product more often. It follows that what you say to a light user will differ from the message you convey to the heavy user. For example, think how you might sell the sports cable network, ESPN, to someone who watches only the Super Bowl, and how you might sell it to someone who has two television sets, one tuned to professional football and the other to the World Series.

How to Conduct Research on Your Own

If your product is a typical consumer product, it is easy enough to find demographic and psychographic information through the syndicated media resources already mentioned. Most agencies will, in fact, purchase syndicated information to help them plan media strategies. If you are working alone or for a small agency, you may find these resources in the reference section of a university library or in the business section of a larger municipal library.

However, if, for example, your client manufactures something as unheard-of as a polarotor—the microwave collector on a satellite dish—you won't find the answers you need in a syndicated source. If you don't have access to a research department, you will have to conduct product and consumer research on your own. You will need to collect first-hand and secondary information using all the branches of research covered in this chapter. You'll talk to people who use the product. You can ask your client to furnish a list of names so that you can choose a random sample and conduct a few telephone interviews. Or you can ask your client for a list of dealers' names so that you can spend some time in a retail outlet, watching people as they go about selecting a product in the same category. Observing people as they make purchase decisions can be eye-opening. Talking to them after they have made a decision can give you some great advertising ideas.

A good book for guidance on conducting a small survey is *Fundamentals of Advertising Research*, by Alan Fletcher and Tom Bowers.[6]

Find New Marketing Opportunities through Creative Research

To bring creativity into the research process, you must be willing to leave no stone unturned and to see your product and your customers from every imaginable angle. Ask questions whenever you see gaps in the information you have gathered. If you cannot see any gaps, then question any and all assumptions you have made. Remember, assumptions are dangerous—things are not always as they appear.

Look at every problem as though it is an opportunity in disguise. The copywriter or artist who has learned to research each assignment from a number of different perspectives will not only produce advertisements that stand out, but will open new market opportunities for the product. Here is an example to illustrate how this can work.

You are creating the advertising for Rent-a-Wreck Rental Car Company. The first problem the advertising has to solve is to let people know your rental car company exists. The more competition there is in your local area, the more complex the problem becomes. The advertising must not only inform people of Rent-a-Wreck's presence, it must give them a reason to choose this company over all of the others.

Your research shows that a low daily or weekly rate, the number of free miles allowed, the selection of models available, and the ease of pick up and return of the automobile all have differing degrees of interest to different people. Since the only difference between cars at Rent-a-Wreck and those at Hertz or Avis is that yours are two years older and therefore cheaper, you know that the key benefit that your company offers is low price. Through detailed fact-finding you discover that consumer attitudes toward your client are mixed—they like the low price, but are uncomfortable with the image that the name Rent-a-Wreck conjures. Once you have uncovered this information, the purpose of advertising becomes twofold: to inform potential customers of your low price, and to clear up this *mistaken identity*. Your advertising will tell people that you offer all the benefits other car companies offer and that they will not receive clunkers when they rent from you. Your cars are only two years older than those rented by your competitors and are just as reliable—and your rates are better. Informing people of these facts becomes a persuasive strategy.

This example serves to show that by depending on the directions your research takes, you can present your client as a provider of low-cost transportation, or, perhaps, of exotic transportation for a weekend soiree, as a service that offers a climate-controlled atmosphere for traveling in smog-filled cities, or that offers a safe and comfortable ride for a large family. The point is that once you have identified customer needs, there is no limit to the number of ways an advertising problem can be turned into a marketing opportunity.

NOTES

[1] James Webb Young, *A Technique for Producing Ideas*, NTC Business Books, Lincolnwood (Chicago), 1975.

[2] Mediamark Research Inc., 341 Madison Avenue, New York, NY 10017.

[3] Simmons Market Research Bureau, Inc., 219 East 42 Street, New York, NY 10017.

[4] VALS Program, SRI International, 33 Ravenswood Ave., Menlo Park, CA. 94025.

[5] *The Yankelovitch Monitor*, Yankelovitch Clancy Shulman, 8 Wright Street, Westport, Conn. 06880.

[6] Alan D. Fletcher, and Thomas A. Bowers, *Fundamentals of Advertising Research,* 3rd ed., Wadsworth Publishing Company, Belmont, 1988.

Chapter 3

Strategy Can Be Creative

You'll be pleased to learn that you've already covered most of what goes into making up a strategy. *Strategy* sounds ominously important, like some great secret to successful marketing that's waiting to be discovered. In fact, it is not a secret, it is much more straightforward than that. Strategy is the guiding hand that holds all elements of the ad or ad campaign together. It can inspire, shape, control, measure, and target ideas.

In advertising, strategy simply refers to sound, innovative problem solving aimed at defining your target audience, your competition, your product/service benefits, and the message you wish to convey. *Webster's Dictionary* defines strategy as the science of planning and directing military operations. It is more broadly defined as a skill in managing and planning. How does this rather aggressive language describe what we do in advertising? What we want to seize by strategic planning isn't a plot of land or a waterway, it's a few precious seconds of someone's time—a fiercely guarded commodity. When you consider the task is to have your message be the *one* that is remembered among the 1,000 to 1,500 advertisements the average family is subjected to each day, you know you need a plan and that your plan must be aggressive.

Webster goes on to define a *stratagem* as a trick, a plan, or any ruse used to deceive an enemy in war. In advertising, if tricks are considered at all, they involve drawing your prospects' attention away from your competitors so that they focus on the product you are advertising. The best way to do that is with clever and memorable advertising. That's the only trick with which this book is concerned.

Learn to look at strategy development as an ongoing process. Ideally, in advertising, strategy is worked out before the creative work is attempted and its purpose is to guide the creative team as they work out the ideas and execution that will make the advertising succeed. But, as often happens once copywriters and art directors get to work, ideas emerge that are strong enough to change the direction of the assignment. This means that some aspect of the strategy must change. When strategy development is viewed as a process which is, by nature, changeable, creativity and responsiveness become an even more vital aspect of successful advertising.

Make Sure Your Strategy Is on Target

To follow through an advertising strategy requires that you understand your target audience so well that you can adopt its point of view. Imagine you are a potential customer for the product or service you are advertising. Your desire to buy stems from a particular need. Before you make a choice, you will consider every alternative product or service that might satisfy that need. Once you have looked at your product amidst all the others that could serve the same purpose, ask yourself which is the benefit your product offers that is most likely to make you buy. Focus primarily on those features or qualities that make your product stand up against the competition and that are most relevant to the target audience.

Do this systematically. Examine each competitor in the same product or service category. See what benefits each offers and how it compares with your own brand. Whenever your product has an advantage—or a disadvantage—make a note of it. This will help make a stronger case to present to your prospects. Analyze all factors that you, as a customer, would consider in making a similar purchase decision: price, quality, reliability, novelty, versatility, guarantees, and so on. By the end of this process, you should have a clear idea of what needs your product satisfies and where it stands in relation to other products. You should be able to tell anyone who asks what its strengths and weaknesses are. You should know each competitor, from the market leader to the newest arrival.

Because of this strong analytical aspect, many people think that the strategy phase of advertising is more of a science than an art. But some of the greatest strategies ever developed have come from people who, after gathering all of the information they could, followed their intuition and judgment when it came to the final call. This is the creative element of strategy development: once you have all the facts at hand, it is time to let your imagination and instincts take over.

Strategy Should Tell the Truth

When you're offering an uninvited message to thousands of people at once, it's impossible to anticipate with absolute precision how many of them will respond to it. It stands to reason, however, that more people will respond to a message that rings true. Strategy is a way of finding the truth about a product and telling it.

One of the most often discussed campaigns in advertising history is Doyle Dane Bernbach's handling of its Avis account (see **Exhibit 3.1**). In the 1960s, when Bill Bernbach, the creative power behind the agency, was given the Avis account, he decided that the best strategy for the client was to acknowledge the truth: they weren't the market leaders. But this simple statement of truth was followed by another powerful statement. The headline and copy read:

> *Headline:* Avis is only No. 2 in rent-a-cars. So why go with us?
> *Copy:* We try harder.

Its impact was immediate.

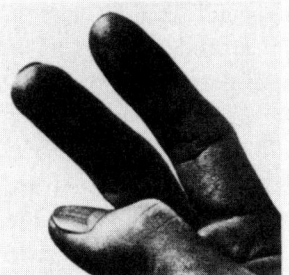

Avis is only No.2 in rent a cars. So why go with us?

We try harder.

(When you're not the biggest, you have to.)

We just can't afford dirty ashtrays. Or half-empty gas tanks. Or worn wipers. Or unwashed cars. Or low tires. Or anything less than seat-adjusters that adjust. Heaters that heat. Defrosters that defrost.

Obviously, the thing we try hardest for is just to be nice. To start you out right with a new car, like a lively, super-torque Ford, and a pleasant smile. To know, say, where you get a good pastrami sandwich in Duluth.

Why?

Because we can't afford to take you for granted.

Go with us next time.

The line at our counter is shorter.

Exhibit 3.1
Doyle Dane Bernbach's Avis Campaign. Reproduced with permission of Avis, Inc.

Thinking through a Strategy

Let's imagine that we have been asked to create an advertising campaign for a travel company called Nature Expeditions International (NEI). A brochure already produced by the company shows the exact nature of these trips. A vacationer could choose a photo-safari in Kenya, a wilderness trek across the Himalayas, a spiritual journey through Nepal, or penguin-watching in the Galapagos Islands. The lengths of the trips vary from one week to four or five, and the cost averages around $1,000 a week, not including airfare.

Also, the tours are led by college professors who are knowledgeable about the specific destinations. They are either cultural anthropologists, biologists, linguists, or have some other relevant scholarly interest in the areas where they will be taking their clients.

The first question we need to ask is who might be interested in these trips. Would your first guess be anyone with a few thousand dollars to spend? No? You're right. Some people with that much money would prefer to take a cruise or some similar luxury vacation. But we can assume that our target will be in a similar income range to those with an interest in a cruise, since both vacations cost about the same. (We just discovered a demographic.)

One way to discover more about the people who like this sort of trip is to speak to people who have taken one and who would be willing to take one again. Imagine that we made a few calls and discovered that the people who fall into this category are quite proud of the fact that they don't "fritter their time away lying on some beach in Hawaii or Mexico." They are proud that they have chosen an adventurous, educational vacation. (This is an attitude toward leisure, a psychographic.) We have also found out that most of the patrons of these trips are *well educated* and *over the age of 35*. (We've just discovered two more demographics.)

We will have to guess that people likely to be interested in these trips will be similar to those who have already taken them. Right away, that eliminates most people interested in luxury cruises.

We've considered the target audience and the benefit that NEI offers it. The primary benefit is not the "getaway" aspect of a vacation but rather "the promise of adventure."

What's left to consider but the competition? When this author originally worked on this project, NEI was a one-of-a-kind company, offering a unique vacation experience. That made things easier. The campaign the copywriter and the art director created for this company, was based upon this tagline or theme:

> *Go on an adventure. Not a vacation.*

The campaign was a small-space, all copy campaign (see **Exhibit 3.2**).

Today, with so many companies offering similar trips, competition is a major consideration. We would have to do more research to find a point of difference.

This example serves to demonstrate two other points. First, an advertising strategy is obviously greatly affected by the stage of development of products or services within the relevant category. In a new category, the first company to advertise has the task of educating everyone about the category. Later, when the category is saturated with direct competition, a company has the task of positioning itself just to be noticed. Of course, that task is easier for a name that's more familiar (market leaders). But both market leaders and market followers are just trying to reach their audience with the right message.

The second point illustrated here is that when there is a significant point of difference between competitors, say so. That's news. And you can't do any better. Your work becomes more difficult when there isn't anything substantial that differentiates your product from another. Then it is your job is to create advertising that emphasizes the minor differences that exists or, better yet, creates a difference in your prospects' minds.

NO TOURIST ATTRACTIONS.

GO ON AN ADVENTURE.
NOT A VACATION.

Nature Expeditions International
P.O. Box 356 Eugene, OR 97403 Ph. (503) 484-1072

NO FANCY DINNERS.

GO ON AN ADVENTURE.
NOT A VACATION.

Nature Expeditions International
P.O. Box 356 Eugene, OR 97403 Ph. (503) 484-1072

NO MAI TAIS.

GO ON AN ADVENTURE.
NOT A VACATION.

Nature Expeditions International
P.O. Box 356 Eugene, OR 97403 Ph. (503) 484-1072

NO BEACH CHAIRS.

GO ON AN ADVENTURE.
NOT A VACATION.

Nature Expeditions International
P.O. Box 356 Eugene, OR 97403 Ph. (503) 484-1072

Exhibit 3.2
An "adventure" campaign for Nature Expeditions International. Art Director: Caron Perkal—Copywriter: Ann Keding. Reproduced with permission of Nature Expeditions International.

Positioning Your Product

Imagine that you are working on a new high-fiber breakfast cereal. You begin to look over the competition and ask yourself, "What is my prospect going to consider doing or buying instead of this product?" More sleep? Toast or a bagel? Other cereals? Hot? Cold? Which cold cereals? Sleep and other breakfast food choices are considered indirect competition. Other cereals are considered category competition, and other fiber cereals would be direct competition.

Then ask yourself, in relation to these and other alternatives, where your product stands. At this time, conduct a thorough inventory of your product's attributes. Next, compare your list with the attributes of products in direct competition and begin looking at the advertising claims each competitor has made. As well as discovering what benefit or attribute advantage you may have over the competition, you will find out what qualities of the product are not being claimed by your competitors. If you find such a space or *niche* in the market, you can claim it. This is called *positioning* your product. Essentially, it means selecting *one* thing to tell consumers about your product that—in the minds of consumers—is new and will differentiate it from others in the same category.

In a saturated market, the obvious benefits that can be claimed about a product are most likely already being said by your competitors. So, the task becomes discovering the claim that is not so obvious. This is, for example, what the marketers of Seven Up did when they took a look at the crowded cola market and positioned the drink as the "un-cola."

Let's practice. By itself, you know your high-fiber cereal probably won't hold much appeal to the best established consumer group—the diehard Wheaties eater. For one, the Wheaties customer is buying an image of health and fitness. For your product to appeal to this prospect, your advertising will have to promise even more vitamins and nutrients—a better fitness deal.

Can it do that? If it can't, look for another possibility.

How much will this product appeal to a consumer group that is not established—the non-breakfast eater? If you decide to target the non-breakfast eater, your advertising has to work the hardest of all. Your task will be to persuade non-breakfast eaters to change their daily habits and routines and to eat breakfast! Ever tried that?

Once you have a better understanding of the range of choices available to your prospects, you begin to get a clearer picture of what you have to do to make a sale. You also have a better idea about what to say in your advertising.

Consider the cereal category, again. Consumer research in the category tells us that nine out of ten breakfast-eaters in the U.S. eat cereal. Among those nine, some people eat cereal every day and some eat cereal once a month. They can be categorized into light, medium, or heavy users. Toast or eggs might be alternatives the light user could choose. But a heavy user? No way. That person eats cereal seven times a week, or more.

Now consider this. Research shows that people who eat cereal eat more than one brand. They, in fact, keep from three to five brands of cereal in their cupboards. You decide that this is the best group for your product to target. So the first challenge is to get your new cereal in the cupboard. What will it take to do that?

Just as before, you must look closely at your product and examine all its benefits to see which one might be missing from all of your competitors' offerings. You must consider what your target audience wants. Again, you are looking for the truth so you can tell it. In a category such as ready-to-eat cereal with over 100 brands, finding a new truth can be a challenge. When a category is overdeveloped like this one, and if there's no news about your product, it's up to you to create the news or, in other words, create a new position.

Kellogg's did this for Sugar Frosted Flakes. The cereal was losing market share. Other cereals were nudging it off the kitchen shelf. Kellogg's attacked the problem with a two-pronged strategy. They targeted adults with a campaign that positioned Sugar Frosted Flakes as the "kid's" cereal adults love. The message inherent in this campaign was that "it is O.K. for adults to eat a kid's cereal."

At the same time, Kellogg's conducted a Tony the Tiger Promotion targeted to children in major cities around the country. During the promotion, Tony the Tiger would show up at neighborhood supermarkets, hand out balloons, and have his picture taken with children. Meanwhile, large boxes of Sugar Frosted Flakes would be handed to Mom and Dad for purchase. Later, the children would register for a bicycle drawing. If their names were drawn, then Tony himself would go to their homes and check to see if they had Sugar Frosted Flakes on their shelves. If they did, the children won new bicycles.

This is an example of advertising and promotion working together to create excitement and get the product into consumers' cupboards. In the campaign targeted to adults, the benefit was taste. In the promotion to kids, the benefit wasn't inherent in the product at all.

What if most products in a category are similar? Which benefit do you claim? You claim the benefit that holds the most promise for your prospect.

Once the persons to whom you're aiming your message try your product, then they'll know if it lives up to the claim you have made. Hence, the claim must not only be believable, it must be honest.

So, tell the truth. There's an old saying that applies as much to advertising as it does to any other realm of life, "Never make a promise you don't intend to keep."

Structuring Your Strategy: Creative Blueprints

People in advertising speak of the *creative blueprint* in the same way as an architect may speak of house plans. This metaphor is accurate, because it is the creative blueprint that gives each advertising assignment or campaign its structure and form. Without it, creating advertising would be like building a house without a plan. The builder could add a room here, a room there, and the resulting house might look lopsided or, even worse, it might collapse. The same thing can happen to advertising—without a thorough plan, it can fall apart.

Using a creative blueprint can help you get closer to a great idea. It is the plan that describes how the advertising strategy is to be executed. You should prepare a creative blueprint only after you have fully researched your product and its target audiences, and after you have thought through the strategy which your advertisement will follow. In written form, the blueprint will help you synthesize all the information you have gathered and you will be ready to work out ideas.

Here's a list of the elements your blueprint can include.

- Product Description—a summary of what the product or service is, what it offers people, and how they might use it.

- Target Audience—a summary of each relevant audience. This can be broken down into primary and secondary audiences. Known demographics and psychographics should be given for each.

- Competition—a summary of other products or services that might be selected instead of yours. This should include direct and indirect competition.

- Problem Advertising Is to Solve—a summary of the research findings that identify the communications problem to be solved by advertising. For example, is lack of awareness the problem? Or, is the problem too much competition and barely identifiable product differences?

- Advertising Objective—a statement declaring what the advertising will accomplish. For a new product introduction, an example would be: increase awareness to 20 percent.

- Features/Benefits—a summary of product or service features with their attendant benefits. Rank them in order of importance: the most important one will become the central point of your advertising.

- Positioning—a statement claiming a place for the product or service in the minds of the target audience.

- Tone/Manner—a statement describing the feeling the advertising will convey. For example, the tone of an awareness-building campaign for a funeral home might be characterized as "sensitive, caring, personal" while the tone for a cemetery might be "solid, trustworthy, having a long tradition."

- Premise/Blueprint Statement—a sentence or two that synthesize all of the above information and communicate just what should be said in the advertising.

The steps don't have to be followed in any particular order. All that matters is that by using a blueprint like this you become accustomed to the thinking process necessary to come up with ideas that generate good advertising.

How the Blueprint Works

Look at the sample blueprint that follows. The assignment is to create a battered women's hotline public service advertisement that will appear in local newspapers and on local transit kiosks.

Creative Blueprint for Los Angeles Battered Women's Hotline

- Product Description: The L.A. Battered Women's Hotline is an emergency telephone service offering assistance to women living in physically abusive relationships.

- Target Audience: Los Angeles area women living in physically abusive relationships.

- Competition: The choice, in competition with a telephone call to the hotline, is no action at all.

- Problem Advertising Is to Solve: Women living in a physically abusive relationship often share a feeling of hopelessness. The abuse syndrome is characterized by physical abuse, remorse on behalf of the abuser, and an unrealistic belief or wish held by the abused that each time will be the last. Women living in this syndrome are most likely isolated, which further reinforces a sense of helplessness. The problem the advertising is to solve is to make it easier for them to reach out for help.

- Advertising Objective: The advertising will increase awareness of the hotline among Los Angeles area women living in physically abusive relationships. This increased awareness will also result in an increase in hotline calls because women seeing the advertising will be stirred to action by it.

- Features/Benefits: Twenty-four hours a day, women in distress or crisis can call the hotline and receive help from specially trained volunteers.

- Positioning: Fight back. You don't have to accept this way of life.

- Tone/Manner: Strong, assertive, action-oriented.

- Premise/Blueprint Statement: Call the L.A. Battered Women's Hotline and get help. You can end the cycle of physical abuse.

The advertising objectives are to increase *awareness of the hotline* among Los Angeles area women living in physically abusive relationships and *to break through a woman's denial and encourage her to use the hotline* for help. Notice that it isn't the objective of the advertising to addres the societal problem of women who suffer abuse, beyond getting them to telephone the hotline. Solving the societal problem is the responsibility of the client, the hotline staff of volunteers.

In this case, the competition is not a rival organization, but a competing attitude and behavior. This is the strongest possible competition. The advertising will ask women to go against an established pattern of behavior, and patterns of behavior, even painful ones, are difficult to break.

What about the tone of the ad? Physical abuse is a subject that triggers strong emotions in people. The object of the advertising is to empower women to make a change. Some alternatives might leave them feeling ashamed or embarrassed, and, even worse, some might not impact them at all. The challenge is to discover a tone that will cut through a woman's veil of denial and give her reason to believe she will find help if she called the hotline. It had to fall somewhere in between hostility and hopelessness. It can't be too strong or too weak.

We finally arrive at the premise and summary statement of the creative blueprint, from which the ideas and creative execution of the advertisement will stem. The one simple statement the Los Angeles Battered Women's Hotline wanted to communicate was Call the hotline and find the help you need to end the abuse.

Now look at the advertisement that the creative team working on the L.A. Battered Women's Hotline finally came up with (see **Exhibit 3.3**). Notice, in particular, how this advertisement answers each of the points included in the blueprint.

The first task was to decide what portion of the premise statement to show in the visual. By making the visual a photograph of a telephone, the creative team showed women exactly what action to take. It also avoided having to use the word telephone or "call" in the headline. The logo and telephone number became a significant part of the design, telling battered women who and where to call.

Exhibit 3.3
Advertisement for battered women's help hotline. Art Director: Caron Perkal—Copywriter: Ann Keding. Reproduced with permission of Los Angeles Commission on Assaults Against Women.

This left the headline the single task of telling the battered woman she could do something to end the abuse. The final ad uses a highly creative headline that, when combined with the visual, zooms in on the target audience and communicates the message: "Beat him to the punch."

The strategy, as summarized in the creative blueprint, is the guiding hand that holds all elements of this ad together. Understanding strategy is central to producing ideas that are in tune with the client's overall purpose and with consumer needs. It is strategy that keeps single ads and campaigns on target and disciplines the creative work.

Chapter 4

Ideas, Large and Small

In the beginning, every advertising assignment can be thought of in terms of its strategy. But once the creative team gets to work the elements of this strategy will synthesize and form something else. We can call the result of this synthesis an *idea* or, more frequently, a *concept*.

The advertising concept differs from a marketing or product concept, both of which come into the picture long before advertising begins. An advertising concept is simply a form of communication shorthand—it quickly transmits all the thinking behind a strategy into a single thought. The means by which this thought is executed, while not a part of the concept itself, must also be meticulously considered. It carries the message and must facilitate the communication and not get in the way. In the very best conceptual print advertising, the visual and headline depend upon one another completely. Remove the headline and the visual becomes obscure, remove the visual and the headline does the same. This interdependence between the word and the picture is also true of the best television advertising. This chapter will concentrate on how ideas or concepts can be generated, and how they can be executed successfully.

You'll find that people who work in advertising use the term *concept* loosely. You might, for example, hear a copywriter or art director complain, "It doesn't have a concept." What they mean is that there is no idea there. Or you may hear, "It's not conceptual enough." That is, the idea isn't very strong. Or "He's not very good at concept," meaning that the person is not a strategic thinker, or worse, he is not very smart. You might even hear an account executive ask, "Where's the concept you promised I could show the client today?" meaning "Where is the ad?"

In the context of this book, however, a concept is an idea presented as a single message that addresses all elements of the strategy at once. Within a hard-working or highly developed concept you will find information directly communicated to the target audience that tells them the benefit they will derive from choosing this product or service along with the action they are being asked to take. The product's position in relation to the competition will be clearly stated or inferred. A good concept will also carry the tone best suited to the client. And finally, for both print and television, a good concept displays an interdependence between the picture and the word.

Let's examine an advertisement piece by piece, so that we can look for the concept behind it and see how this has been executed. Look at the award-winning ad for Zero Pet Population Growth, shown in **Exhibit 4.1**.

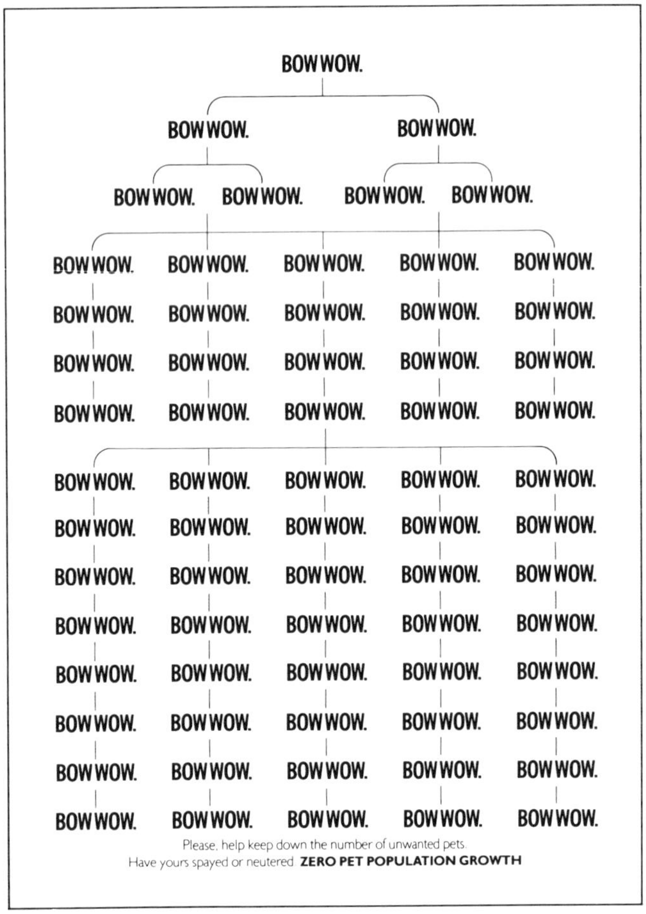

The strategy here is to persuade dog owners to have their pets spayed or neutered—instead of not having them spayed or neutered—because of the proliferation of unwanted pets.

From the synthesis of this information the creative team who worked on the assignment came up with an advertising concept: to demonstrate that geometric progression works for animal births just as it does for humans.

The execution chosen to convey this message was through a depiction of a family tree. But one could have chosen any number of executions or ways to display this idea, such as littering the family tree with pictures of puppies, pictures of dogs' faces, photographs of family dogs, dog names, and so forth.

This creative team selected a written symbol that conveys *dog*—the expression "Bow Wow." This does more than to convey the idea of *dog*, it reminds us of a barking dog, a dog that demands our attention. It is also less personal or endearing than, for example, pictures of puppies, and therefore appeals more to pet owners' common sense, than to their sentiments. By using "Bow Wow" in a geometric tree, the advertising communicates the *problem* of unwanted animals in language every dogowner can understand.

The execution includes all elements of the communication—the use of all type (no visuals) the page layout, and the symbols—the geometric tree and the "Bow Wow" expression. The concept is the idea behind the execution—the birthrate symbolized by geometric progression of the expression "Bow Wow."

Exhibit 4.1
Zero Pet Population Growth ad.
Art Director: James Hendry—Copywriters: Richard Kelley/Bob Coburn. Reproduced with permission.

What Makes an Idea Great?

As we saw in previous chapters, ideas are born of knowledge. Once your research is complete and you have thought through each aspect of the advertising strategy, you have a better sense than anyone else involved in the project of which message delivered through which medium will reach your prospects and incite them to action.

But what is it that makes one idea better than another? One thing that makes people like a creative work, whether it is a film, a short story, or an ad, is the universality of its message. When you are working on an idea, you must ask yourself if the premise behind it is broad enough for the people in your target audience to understand. Ask yourself if the symbols chosen and words used communicate successfully across the barriers of language, age, gender, etc.? Good concepts go beyond surface word plays, they stretch the thought.

Another quality inherent in a good idea is its *freshness* and *provocativeness*. The purists among advertising craftspeople strive for ideas that have a spark of originality. If you are in doubt, the idea is probably neither fresh nor provocative. The purpose of this effort to create something original is to make people think of the product or service in a new way.

From there you need to question whether your creation is *believable* and *honest*. Does your work tell the truth about your product in a convincing way?

You will also need to consider whether or not your execution of the message is *clear*. Will people understand it right away? Keep in mind also that the medium you use determines how much time people will have to comprehend your message. For instance, people driving past an outdoor board have only a few seconds to concentrate on what they are seeing. On television they have anywhere from 10 to 30, or 60 seconds, with few exceptions. In a magazine or newspaper, people have longer to think about what you are saying, but may choose to spend no more than a few seconds looking at a print ad. Because advertisements are usually uninvited messages, you must make sure that your message is unobstructed by the execution you use to carry it. It must be *clear*.

Remember that however well-crafted or original an idea, if it is not in keeping with the advertising strategy it will not work. Ask yourself, am I speaking to the right audience? Am I talking about the most important benefit? Does my ad make this product more desirable than the competition's? Above all, ask yourself, *is it on strategy*?

Techniques That Can Generate Ideas

Brainstorming

It is not always easy to move from the premise to the idea stage. Sharing the problem can help.

Brainstorm with your partner. Set some time aside to sit down together with the single objective of coming up with a whole list of new ideas. Bounce ideas off each other, play with them, turn them around and see them from opposite perspectives. This is an opportunity for both of you to let your imaginations run riot.

Remember that authentic brainstorming means that no one evaluates one idea until all of them are out on the table. This openness and acceptance means that even the silliest idea is given a chance. In the embryonic stage, ideas are very fragile. Harsh words and negative reactions can kill them. When you're looking for gems, there is no room to lose even one, particularly when there's a chance that it might be a great one. So get your partner to agree not to criticize during a brainstorming session. It is essential to be positive and receptive toward each and every suggestion. This is one rule that is not to be broken.

Be sure to write down all ideas, serious or silly, so that after the session both you and your partner can evaluate them. By this time, the strongest have had an opportunity to catch on, so criticism isn't so deadly.

What if...?

Another method of generating new ideas is to set up a problem and imagine different ways it can be solved. "What if...?" questions work well and can stimulate exciting new ideas. Go completely off the wall. No matter how conventional the product you are working on, this is, again, a chance for your imagination to take over. For example, if you're working on a pizza account, why not ask, what if pizza came in rainbow colors? What if pizza were stewed like chicken? What if the moon were a great big pizza? Your questions don't need to make sense or follow any patterns. All that matters is that they stimulate your imagination and spark ideas that are unique to you and that will work.

Mental kindling

To come up with fresh ideas again and again, creative people need to be receptive to the limitless variety of information and impressions that abound in the world around them.

Look at the advertisements in **Exhibit 4.2**. How do you think they came into being? What knowledge and experience of the world did their creators draw on?

Exhibit 4.2

Outstanding Creative Ads. (Voting) Art Director: Hanna Mayer—Copywriter: Sande Riesett. Reproduced with permission of The Baltimore Sun. *(Llamas Tto...) Art Director: Larry Frey—Copywriter: Larry Frey. Reproduced with permission of Oregon Economic Development Department. (Cal Mag) Art Directors: Mark Erwin/Richard Kelley—Copywriters: Harry Woods/Richard Kelley—Designer: Robert Keding. Reproduced with permission of* California Magazine. *(Volvo) Art Director: Steve Montgomery—Copywriter: Mike Fineberg. © 1989 Volvo North America Corporation. Reproduced with permission.*

Exhibit 4.2 *(continued)*

> ### "What could possibly compare with whale sex?"
> Adventure Vacations. In the June issue. On newsstands now. *California* MAGAZINE

> ### "Why did they all ignore my fly?"
> Trout fishing. In the September issue. On newsstands now. *California* MAGAZINE

> ### "Meet flowing blobs of jelly with high I.Q.'s."
> Space Travel. In the August issue. On newsstands now. *California* MAGAZINE

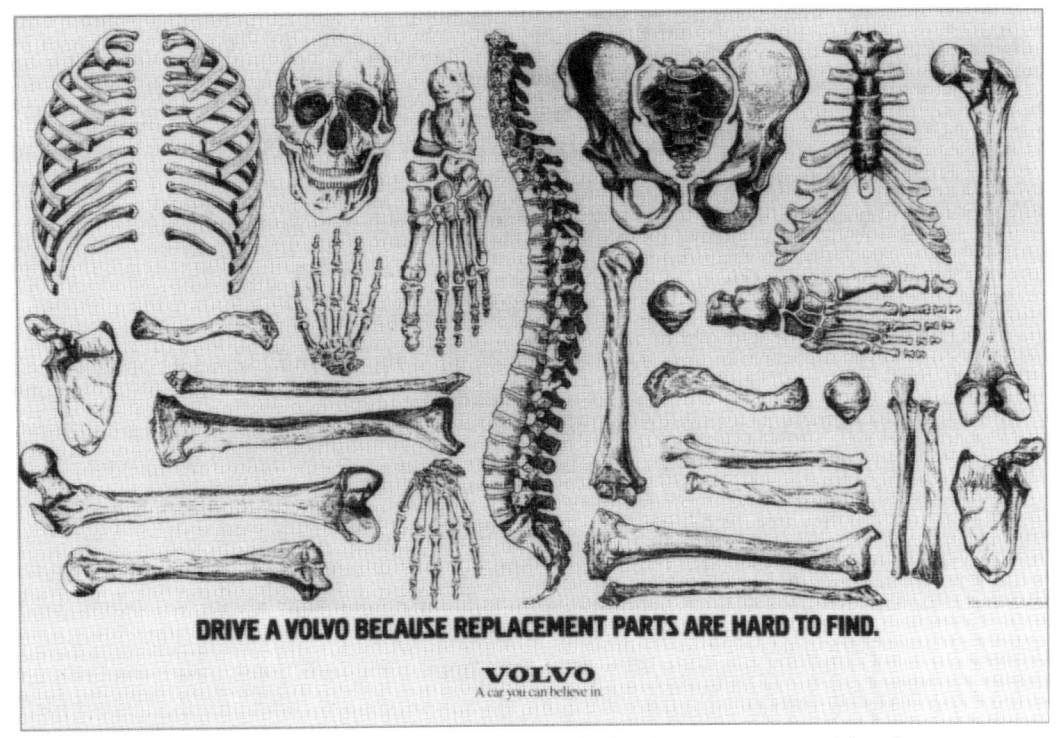

DRIVE A VOLVO BECAUSE REPLACEMENT PARTS ARE HARD TO FIND.

VOLVO
A car you can believe in.

   No cultural or environmental information is irrelevant to you. Absorb everything. Who can say when your knowledge of aborigine lifestyle in Australia will connect with an idea and produce a hard-working and award-winning advertisement for a computer your client is selling?
   Become passionate about advertising. Become passionate about life. Find out as much as you can about the world you live in. Take a night class at your local community college. Visit the museum and art galleries regularly. Read

fiction. And read poetry. Poetry will teach you the rhythm and metaphor that are at the heart of good advertising. Study art. Read comic books. Watch television. Go to plays. Spend a few hours a week browsing through your favorite book store. Study great advertising. Study every advertisement you see. Become aware. The more in touch you are with popular culture, trends, and lifestyles, the better you will be at your craft.

Doesn't that sound like a job made in heaven? Mark Twain said it best, "The secret of success is making your vocation your vacation." To become great, advertising must be more to you than a vocation. It must become an avocation, too. This means that there are very few hours in the day that you are not working toward becoming a better, more creative advertiser.

Guard Your Ideas

As an advertising creative, you are the standard bearer. No one in the agency and no one with the client you represent will care as deeply as you about the creative elements of your work that make it unique. You have a higher personal stake in its success than others.

Once you have put your ideas onto paper, you are responsible for protecting them through all the approval cycles to which they will be subjected. Your partner, your account executive, other agency colleagues, and your client will all want to see and evaluate your work. They may also want to introduce suggestions of their own.

Though such suggestions can move the idea off-track, remember to hear each one out. Constructive criticism can improve an idea and enhance those qualities that make it unique. Moreover, by witnessing the reactions of others to your work, you can better assess its worth. After all, it's your neck that's on the line if the idea is lousy, and it's you who will reap the rewards if it's great.

The Difference between a Single Idea and a Campaign

There's a common problem that develops when a junior copywriter and art director go to work on an assignment. Before they know it, they have created a wonderful ad, one of which they are very proud. The problem is that though the ad works well alone, it does nothing to reinforce the image dictated by the client's advertising strategy. Even worse, the ad is so far afield it looks as though people in a different agency created it. This is what typically happens when the creative team focuses on the immediate problem the advertising is meant to solve, and forgets that this problem may be only one facet of a broader one. Broad versus narrow application is what makes one ad a single idea, and another the first idea in a campaign.

A single ad should hold one message, and the message may or may not come from an idea that enables it to be interpreted other ways. As an example, look again at the ad for Zero Pet Population Growth (**Exhibit 4.1**). This ad holds one message with an idea behind it. Could this ad be extended into a campaign?

Let's imagine that the creative team chooses to create an ad suggesting that cats be spayed and neutered, too. They use the same layout and design but change the expression to "Meow Meow." That would work because cats are household pets, they make a recognizable sound, and their birthrate is as prolific as that of dogs.

But here, this execution seems to run aground. Think about it. It just wouldn't work the same for rats or mice or parakeets or pigs. For one, the majority of us don't hold these other creatures quite as dear or keep them as pets. Yes, rats and mice can be pets, but not often. But most people are not endeared to them. They are prolific in their reproduction. But a geometric tree with branches stating "Rat Rat" or "Mouse Mouse" would most likely inspire a call to an exterminator, not a veterinarian. Pet parakeets and pigs just don't seem to represent the same overpopulation problem. However, a solid campaign could have been continued by varying the depiction of the idea—the geometric progression of animal births—into different images.

A campaignable idea is sometimes called a *big idea* because there are many ways in which the same idea can be applied. A big idea is broad enough to inspire numerous executions. Our Zero Pet Population Growth ad is a striking example which demonstrates how an idea can make the difference between an extendable and a limited campaign. This advertisement shows us how an idea can remain the same and be presented through limitless executions of images and phrases that represent birthrate problems among favorite household pets. So, yes. It is a campaignable idea.

Every ad created should have a single idea behind it. But when should an ad be part of a campaign? If your client is only going to advertise once a year or less, a single idea is fine. However, if your client has made an on-going commitment to advertising, the answer is—as often as possible. Here's why. If a company has an image or a strategy already developed, then every advertising opportunity should remind people of it.

If you think in terms of a campaign from the start, you will do your client a big favor. For one, when you produce subsequent ads, even though they may have different sales messages, because each message in each advertisement has the same tone and each advertisement in the campaign has the same appearance, a feeling that the company is stable will be created. People who see these ads get the sense that the same people are in charge and that they know what they're selling and what they need to say.

Continuity builds confidence in the company. Advertising that is unplanned or created helter-skelter gives one the feeling that each time a different ad appears, should you drive up to corporate headquarters, you would find a sign declaring "Under New Management."

Another reason a campaign works more effectively than a single ad has to do with the lifespan of an idea. Some ideas can be shown for a nanosecond and people will never want to see them again. Others can be used again and again before people tire of them. But tire of them they will. When a good campaign has been developed, you have several opportunities before this happens to convey the same or a similar message by varying the execution.

What Holds an Advertising Campaign Together?

The best advertising campaigns are held together by the campaign concept or idea. This can be executed through a number of techniques: through the tone each

Exhibit 4.3

Campaign for Working Opportunities for Women. Art Director: David Fox—Copywriter: Joe Alexander. Reproduced with permission of Clarity, Coverdale, Rueff.

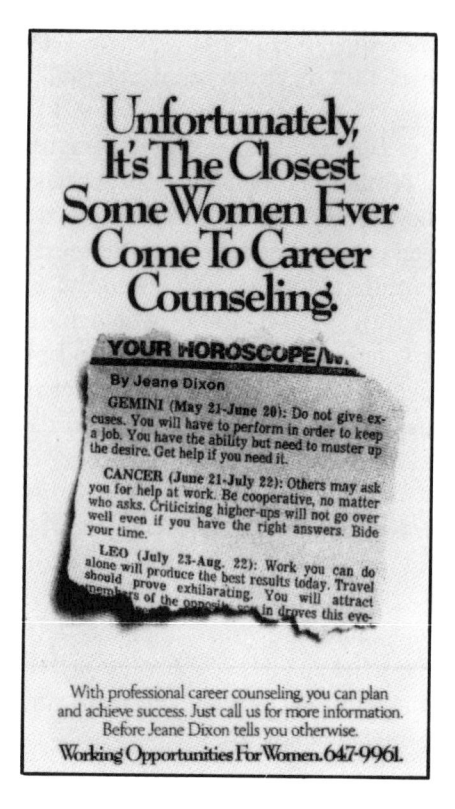

Exhibit 4.4

Continuing the campaign for Working Opportunities for Women. Reproduced with permission of Clarity, Coverdale, Rueff.

advertisement in the campaign takes, through visual continuity, through the use of a slogan or tagline, or through any combination of these.

Look at the two advertisements for the client Working Opportunities for Women, reproduced in **Exhibit 4.3**. What is the campaign idea? (Remember, first, that a strategy lies behind the idea. Here the strategy is to convince women to consider career counseling as a means of getting ahead. The idea challenges a woman to take a look at the realities she may face unless she engages in active career planning.) The key thought is *you have to take action in order to avoid a stalled career or no career.*

Now think about how this idea has been executed. The layout and design of the ads hold them together and help make them a campaign. But the idea is the most central element in the campaign. And what about the tone? These newspaper ads challenge women by showing them the unflattering stereotypes and the realities they face in working life. Here then, all three—idea, layout and design, and tone—are woven through the campaign.

Imagine that your next print assignment is to create a third ad for Working Opportunities for Women. The strategy and the tone have been established. The design and layout are in place. To follow the same theme, we know there should be a visual. Or must that be so? Could there be a way of communicating the same idea: we can help working women cope with difficulties they face. Referring back, you can see that this becomes a premise statement just like one you might have written had you thought through a complete creative blueprint.

In this assignment, the problem becomes simply to communicate that message one more time while staying in line with the campaign. You need a headline or headline and visual that will spur women to action by presenting them with similar stereotypes or work situations common to all women. Take some time and think of your own example. Now look at **Exhibit 4.4**.

It's time to ask yourself whether your headline and the one illustrated above stay within the campaign framework already established.

This example serves to demonstrate that a campaign idea based upon a strong strategy is easy for another copywriter to pick up and continue.

The manner in which a campaign maintains continuity differs from campaign to campaign. For example, if the campaign already in existence has a consistent look but the copy and ideas vary across the ads, then you may decide to take more liberties with the copy. Or, if the tone of the copy is similar in a series of ads, you would want to imitate that style.

More Campaign Examples

Look at the three advertisements in **Exhibit 4.5**. These classic ads created by Doyle Dane Bernbach for Volkswagen cars in the 1960s and 1970s have a *look* that immediately establishes a campaign feel. There is also a tone established in the copy and continued from ad to ad. The first advertisement of the series, *Lemon*, intelligently communicates that Volkswagens are well-crafted cars. The ads that follow use several different ideas to communicate a different message—that Volkswagens are inexpensive. But the tone remains the same. And though copywriters and art directors working on the Volkswagen account over the years changed, that same tone was maintained.

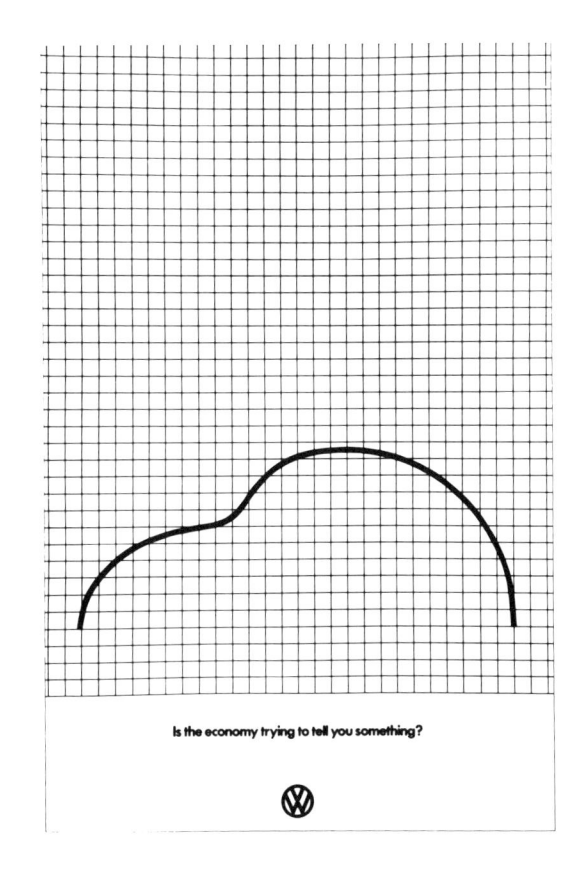

Exhibit 4.5
Early Volkswagen ads. © *Volkswagen of America, Inc. Reproduced with permission.*

Look at the later Volkswagen ads crafted by completely different creative teams (**Exhibit 4.6**).

Mass transit.

Exhibit 4.6
Later Volkswagen ads.
(Mass Transit) Art Director: Sy Lam—Copywriter: Ed Bigelow. (Rabbit the cheapest...) Art Director: Gary Goldsmith—Copywriter: Shawne Cooper. ©Volkswagen of America, Inc. Reproduced with permission.

Ra bbit

**Diesel
42mpg.
56mpg.**

As a further example, examine the award winning campaign for the Virginia Department of Waste Management, illustrated in **Exhibit 4.7**. As you can see, continuity was established through the *idea*: waste is a mounting problem. The *look* helps, too. The choice of typeface, its size, and the placement of the 1-800-KEEPITT line all maintain continuity. When it comes to the copy, all three ads use the name, *Virginia*, in the headline. While two of the ads aggressively

36 Chapter 4

challenge the false belief that there is an unfillable space for waste in Virginia, the third takes full advantage of the newspaper medium by asking someone who is reading the newspaper to think of it as waste.

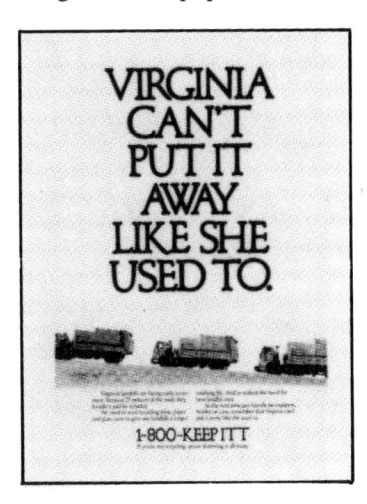

Exhibit 4.7
Campaign for the Virginia Department of Waste Management. Art Director: Nancy Heely Walker—Copywriters: Drena Decker/Richard Maume/Michael Tanner. Reproduced with permission of The Polizos Agency.

What if you were asked to create a campaign for the US Post Office? The objective of this campaign would be to encourage people to *write letters instead of making long-distance phone calls*. Suppose the theme or slogan for this campaign were: *Write, because talking is no longer cheap*.

Your task would then be to stick with this theme and create a series of three or more print ads that encourage people to write instead of call.

Your strategy is simple. It is to persuade people to write letters instead of making phone calls because it's cheaper.

Here are some possible headlines.

Write off the cost of a long-distance friendship.

Talking isn't cheap.

It may be time to hang up on your friends.

Just because good friends are worth their weight in gold, do you have to prove it to the phone company?

These examples suggest the same reason (economy) to write, not call. Another line might be, "Keep a written record of your friendship," but the benefit here is *emotional* and not *economical*. This line does not remain on strategy.

Should a Campaign Be Single Medium or Multimedia?

A campaign can be created for only one medium or it may stretch across several media. The advertising strategy usually determines which it will be.

As we saw in the previous chapter, strategy should include a definition of the target audience and the competition. It tells you who to reach and then tells you where your competition is advertising. Based on this information, you can decide where and how to target your audience. You can also decide whether to choose the same media as your competitors or alternatives.

A good idea may sometimes lend itself more to one medium than another. The Episcopal Church ads shown in **Exhibit 4.8** are a good example. Using a limited budget, they communicate very well in print what they would have to work much harder to communicate using television. In fact, bringing sound and motion to these concepts wouldn't make them any more interesting or effective.

How many pieces should appear in a campaign? At least two, preferably three different ads in each chosen medium. If you have come up with an extendable idea or creative concept, you'll be able to create dozens more.

Do Creative Ads Sell?

A major debate in advertising has developed around one question: how creative should advertising be? While advertising professionals in general agree that advertising should be creative, they don't all agree on the effect creativity has on persuasiveness, and therefore on sales.

Some believe that highly creative ideas can't be relied on to help consumers recall the brand name or product benefit after seeing the advertising. To them, all advertising should be measured against audience ratings and through recall and purchase statistics.

Others think that testing creative work is heresy. To them, creating persuasive advertising is an art. They argue that whatever it is about the advertising that moves people to buy a product is intrinsic to memorable and entertaining advertising: ads must be imaginative and entertaining to bring forth the greatest number of sales. By measuring the unmeasurable, one guarantees mediocrity.

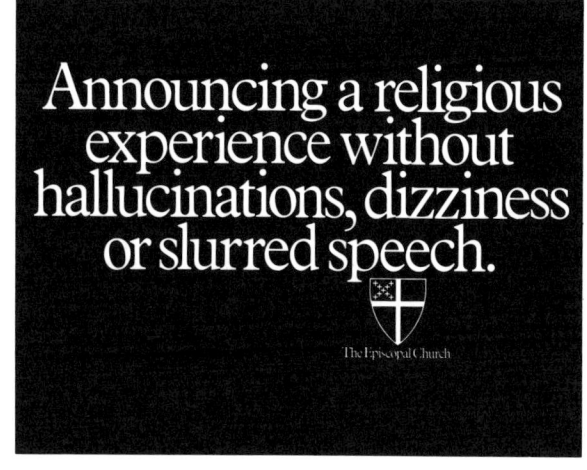

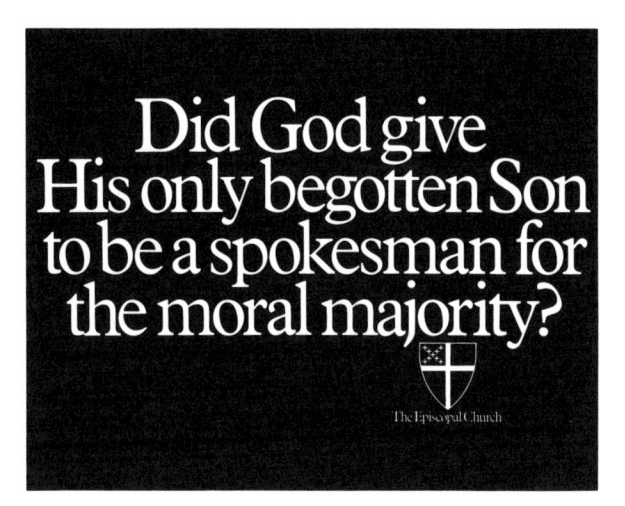

Exhibit 4.8
A Print media campaign. Art Director: Nancy Rice—Copywriters: Tom McElligott/DickThomas. Reproduced with permission of Fallon McElligott.

Agencies such as Chiat/Day/Mojo of Los Angeles, New York, and San Francisco and Fallon McElligott of Minneapolis stand firmly by the argument that creating advertising is an art. Others, such as Lintas Worldwide or Leo Burnett of Chicago agree that advertising should be memorable and provocative, but they lean toward the "what was the recall score?" method of evaluation. As agency mergers are on the increase and more and more agencies are run by people whose business expertise is finance, we can expect to see the larger agencies become less interested in the art of persuasion and more interested in ways to predict profitability.

It is interesting to note that agencies that have won top creative recognition by the CLIO'S, the One Show, the *Art Director's Annual*, and *Communication Arts* have also been listed high in *Advertising Age*'s top 100 agencies for the past two years—a listing that is based on client billing and growth. For example, among U.S. agencies, Chiat/Day/Mojo ranked 20th in 1988 and 18th in 1989 based upon domestic gross income. The agency also had 41 citations in the 1988 One Show. Fallon McElligott received 100 citations. Fallon McElligott also stormed the 1989 *Art Directors Annual* with 80 citations, and was ranked high by *Advertising Age* in 1988 and 1989.[1]

So should an ad entertain or should an ad sell? As the *Advertising Age* listing shows, it is a mistake to think that these two criteria are mutually exclusive. If the goal of advertising is to inform consumers about a product or service, and the client is paying the agency to do this, then the client's product—not the copywriter's or art director's style—should be the hero of the ad. However, to be persuasive as well as informative, the ad will be most effective if it presents that product in an entertaining and creative way.

If you are going to seize someone's time to give them a message they didn't request, you stand a better chance of being heard if you do this with a sense of humor or with drama. So what if that's entertaining? You owe it to your audience and to your client.

Winning Recognition for Creative Work

Should you create advertising with the goal of winning awards?

Awards serve a very important function in the advertising industry. They are the source of industry-wide recognition, which matters a great deal to the creators, agencies, and clients of the ads that win them.

In 1987, Bob Kahn conducted a study, the results of which highlight the importance of recognition as a motivating factor among creative people in advertising. In the study, recognition ranked higher among creatives than among other advertising industry employees —higher than money, and higher than perceived status symbols, such as office size or decor. The only factors considered more important in motivating creativity were getting ideas accepted, and working in a supportive work environment with fewer approval cycles.[2]

Industry-wide recognition is especially valuable as it is the means by which creative people can be judged by their peers. Those who treat the opportunity to win awards as one of their goals are working to meet standards of excellence set by those who know the advertising business best.

NOTES

[1] *Advertising Age*, March 26, 1990, pp. 5-14; *The One Show,* in association with The One Club for Art & Copy, Inc., 1989, 3 West 18th Street, New York, NW 10011; *The 68th Art Directors Annual,* for The Art Directors Club Inc., 1988, 250 Park Avenue South, New York, NY 10003.

[2] "What Motivates Creatives?" *Adweek*, November 9, 1987, p. 73.

Chapter 5

Print Ads: A Writer Writes

Writers write. Whole volumes have been written that describe the feelings writers experience as they face a blank page, or, in this day and age, a blank computer screen. Fearfulness, unworthiness, and blankness are all states of mind that this author can recall. It is feelings like these that have prompted many successful writers to say that while they do enjoy having written, they don't enjoy writing.

Everyone agrees that writing is not easy, though scholars who have studied the process offer a few valuable pointers. Before we look in detail at the skills involved in advertising copywriting, let's look at what author Henriette Klauser has to say about writing in general, and at a technique anyone can learn to get started on that blank page.

Clustering: A Tool to Make Writing Easier

In *Writing on Both Sides of the Brain: Breakthrough Techniques for People Who Write*, Klauser introduces a technique called *clustering* as a process for collecting and organizing your thoughts before you begin to write.[1] A more traditional method of ordering data and ideas would be to outline the subject systematically and logically, i.e., using *linear* thinking. Clustering is a *nonlinear* process that Klauser recommends for all writers, creative or otherwise. It enables one to gather scattered information or information that is not obviously related and organize it so that it *is* related. Because clustering is not systematic or linear, it allows the writer's imagination to select random, seemingly unconnected thoughts and thought patterns and introduce these into his or her writing. The result is faster organization and a greater opportunity for the unusual, the hallmark of creativity.

Let's see how clustering works. To begin, choose a topic and give yourself from five to ten minutes to complete the actual clustering task. Take a blank sheet of paper and set your timer. Write the name of the topic by hand in the middle of the page. It might read something like "chapter on writing." Circle that topic. From there you will branch off with as many thoughts as come to you triggered by that topic. Draw branches from the center of the page to the outer edges in any direction you please. Branches can have offshoots. There is no particular form a clustering tree must take, it depends upon where your thoughts take you. While you are quickly writing down all of the bits of information that come to mind, you can twist and turn the page any way you please. You can jump from branch to branch. This activity is nonlinear.

During the process it's likely you will run into a blank, and will think you have run out of ideas. Leave a blank, dangling line. If the idea does not come to you while you are drawing the line, then skip over it and onto the next idea. Let your imagination—not your logic—lead the way.

Once the timer stops, immediately take another sheet of paper or go to your word processor and begin writing. Don't think. Just write. This is the magic of clustering. It is a way of letting the right-side of your brain—where psychologists believe the creative work is done— do all of the work for you.

Clustering works especially well in writing advertising copy. It encourages the free association of unrelated ideas, and that is what creating good advertising is all about.

Before You Start to Write: The Copy Platform

As we have seen in earlier chapters, there is much thinking that must be done before you begin to write any form of advertising. No matter which medium you are creating for, you must first complete your research. Next, the research is synthesized into an advertising concept, which is in line with the strategy that has been worked out for the advertising assignment.

Remember the creative blueprint used in **Chapter 3** to help you think through an advertising problem? The first step in the writing process is to develop from the statement of strategy that the blueprint summarizes, and from your research and advertising concept, a basis for the copy you will write. This takes the form of a *copy platform*—a synthesis of all the research and thinking you did to solve the advertising problem at hand. Your clients, your account executive and anyone else involved in the advertising process should be able to read the copy platform and see where you are going.

The copy platform isn't very long. Some agencies ask that it be written on one page, others allow two or three. It begins with a description of the product or service you are advertising, your target audience, and the competition. Next comes a clear statement defining the advertising problem. This is followed by a statement outlining the advertising objectives, and by a list of features (or selling points) that the consumer will perceive as benefits. The copy platform concludes with a statement that describes your product positioning, and a statement regarding the tone the advertising should take.

If the copy platform is well thought out and clearly written, it will serve as a road map for your clients—it will show them how you plan to tackle the advertising problem and will help them begin their own problem solving process.

Next, the Headline

Since headlines and visuals emerge along with and are intrinsic to the idea for the advertising, we touched upon writing headlines in the previous chapter. By the time you write a headline, the creative blueprint and the copy platform have given some structure to the advertising problem and certain parameters will have been defined. Each member of the creative team knows and understands the message that needs to be communicated. The next challenge is to discover the language and—if you have decided to include one—the visual that can best communicate that message.

To adhere rigidly to the parameters set out in the copy platform doesn't always promote the kind of creativity that results in award-winning or breakthrough work. The trick to writing good, relevant, well-targeted headlines is to relax and let your imagination flow, without getting too far afield or wasting too much time on tangents. Again, you can use the same brainstorming technique outlined in the previous chapter to come up with the best headline.

In an effective advertisement, the headline can have the task of communicating to its target—at a glance—part or all of the ads meaning. The headline is the first piece of copy your audience will see and should do its best to convey the message.

Make Sure Your Headline and Visual Complement Each Other

Before we deal with headlines in detail, here is a generally accepted rule on how headlines in an ad should interact with the visuals used.

Every time you work on an advertisement, ask yourself whether your headline and visual work together to communicate the message. This can be tested by looking at each part separately. If the sales message is not clear when either the headline or the visual is studied separately, but becomes crystal clear when the two are put together, then the concept is working as hard as it can. Both the headline and the visual are adding something to the communication.

As a further check, you should not be able to remove either element without disturbing the meaning of the ad. They should complement each other.

Good advertising craftspeople avoid letting the headline and the visual repeat each other. Remember, in advertising the time and space you have to convey your message are limited. Your audience can easily turn the page or switch channels. The "see and say" approach is, in most cases, a waste of time and space.

Sometimes, you will hit on a headline that is so strong that you feel no visual is necessary. If you are sure the concept is best expressed in words alone, skip the visual.

Types of Headlines

Besides working with the visual to offer a complete selling idea, headlines are the quickest way to get the reader into the ad. They can attract attention, tell prospects what the ad is about, and lead them into the body copy.

You can use different types of headlines to do different things in an advertisement.

Headlines can *command* the reader to take an action as in **Exhibit 5.1**. They can *reason* with the reader as in **Exhibit 5.2**. They can ask the reader a *question*, and invite a response as in **Exhibit 5.3**. They can give the reader *news* about the product as in **Exhibit 5.4**. Or they can inform the reader of the *primary benefit* of using the product as in **Exhibit 5.5**.

Exhibit 5.1
A headline that commands. Art Directors: Mary Mentzer/Mike Fornwald—Copywriters: Mike Fornwalds/Mary Mentzer. Reproduced with permission of Beans & Barley Restaurant.

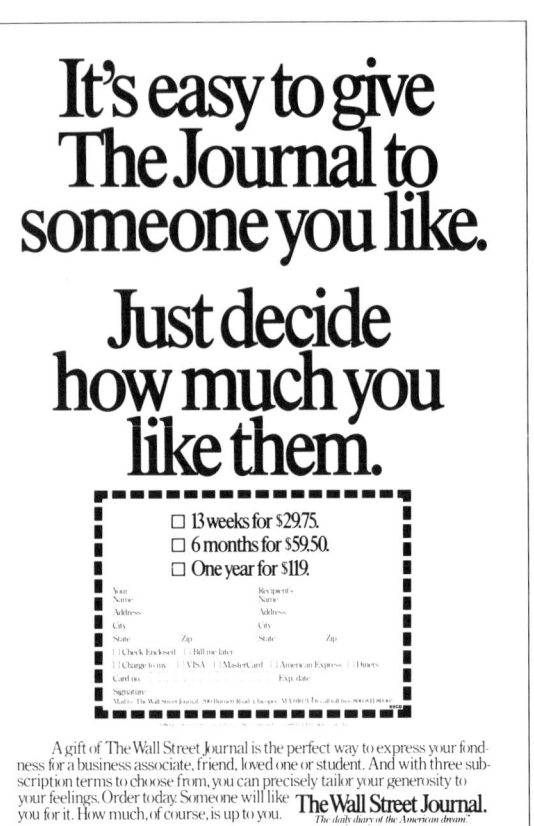

Exhibit 5.2
A headline that reasons. Art Director: Tom Lichtenheld—Copywriter: Rod Kilpatrick. Reproduced with permission of The Wall Street Journal.

In each of the examples given, the headlines are provocative enough to grab the reader's attention. However, if you remove the visuals from the ads that have them, you might be left wondering exactly what is meant. As we saw above, the sales message is only complete when the two, headline and visual, are seen together. Notice that each of the examples uses a subject and verb while using different styles of sentence structure—they make sense gramatically. Notice, too, that each has a period (or a question mark) at the end. This simple device makes the reader stop and think before going on to read the body copy.

Blind headlines

A blind headline is one that, even when combined with a visual, doesn't complete the sales message. The reader is forced to the body copy for a more complete explanation. In general, blind headlines are not a good practice for the same reason *it is* good practice for headlines and visuals to work together. The problem is that blind headlines rely on the body copy to convey the message, and often prospects do not get as far as reading the body copy. When the headline is

Exhibit 5.3

*A **headline that asks a question**. Art Director: Rob Dalton—Copywriter: Rod Kilpatrick. Reproduced with permission of The Wall Street Journal.*

Exhibit 5.4

*A **"news" headline**. Art Director: Mark Johnson—Copywriter: Tom McElligott. Reprinted with permission from Porsche.*

obscure and the visual doesn't complete the message, you are taking a great risk. Your prospects have not been "hooked" and they can quickly lose interest. Blind headlines risk never getting close to a sale.

Using Slogans and Logotype

Slogans and logotype are an important part of the sales communication, in both print and broadcast advertising.

Slogans, sometimes called taglines, are sentences or phrases used consistently whenever a product is advertised. They can be used to connect ads in a campaign or to focus on the advertisers image or market position. Each time prospects are exposed to the advertising, the slogan reminds them of

Exhibit 5.5

*A **headline that informs**. Art Director: Michael Fazende—Copywriter: John Stingley. Reproduced with permission of Fallon McElligott.*

Print Ads: Writing 45

what your product represents. Here are some examples of hard-working slogans. Notice how well they position the product in the prospect's minds.

> **The daily diary of the American Dream.** (The *Wall Street Journal*)
>
> **Don't leave home without it.** (American Express)
>
> **What becomes a legend most.** (Blackgama Mink)
>
> **Does she or doesn't she?** (Clairol Hair Care)
>
> **Member of the F.D.I.C. and the Human Race.** (People's Bank of California)
>
> **Because so much is riding on your tires.** (Michelin)

The logotype or signature cut (sig cut) is the special lettering style, typeface or design used, for example, in a clients trademark, brand name, and company name. Logotypes appear in all advertisements and serve to bring continuity and instant recognition to the advertising. The giant *M*, for example, used by the fast food chain McDonalds is a logotype. Recall how critical the logo was to the message in the public service announcement for the Los Angeles Battered Women's Hotline (see **Exhibit 3.3**). Look back, too, at **Exhibits 5.1** through **5.5** and notice how logotypes are used. A clearly placed logo can allow more flexibility when creating a headline. With a good logo, it's possible to exclude the client or product name from the headline.

Body Copy

How Long Should Body Copy Be?

The amount of information a consumer needs to make a purchase decision varies from product to product and from service to service. The length and amount of detail you include in your body copy should reflect your assessment of the consumers' need.

A general rule of thumb is that the more expensive the product or service, the more information and detail the customer needs. Expensive purchases are usually planned purchases. This means that your prospect is going to consider any information that's available before making a purchase decision. Giving your prospect enough information and making it readily accessible is important for planned purchases. Another rule is that convenience and impulse purchases don't require long, logical arguments or, it follows, much copy. For these, the purpose of the advertisement is to help your prospect remember the product next time the impulse purchase is made. Image purchases, for different reasons, may not require much copy either. But they do require a strongly developed and easily identifiable image, either in the visual or words.

A Few Guidelines to Follow When Writing Body Copy

No book can teach you everything about writing good advertising copy. That comes with hard work and experience. What we can do, however, is give you a few pointers that will help you stay on track and evaluate the copy you have written.

Never write a word of body copy until you have a strong idea and a headline. There is no use writing copy until your concept has been worked out fully. Only then will you be able to decide what else needs to be said to complete the sale.

Don't waste any ideas. When you are working out ideas and headlines never throw any of your work away. If you keep a list of all the lines and phrases you and your partner toss about at different stages of the project, you will have several pages of them when you are finished. Keep this list close at hand, so that if you get stuck or go off track when writing body copy you can refer back to it for fresh ideas and new direction.

Emphasize the benefits. Body copy usually concentrates on the benefits a product or service offers customers. Once you have listed all of the features of your product and have thought of them as benefits, arrange the important ones in a hierarchy, from most important to least important. This ranking quickly shows you which benefit to discuss first, second, third, and so forth. Selecting the number of benefits to discuss takes some experience and depends on any number of factors: is the product a new innovation? How crowded is the market? Are all the benefits you claim unique to your product? Once again, there are no rules, just judgment. And good judgment has to be developed.

Once you have selected the benefits you want to emphasize, ordering your copy is quite easy. Determine which benefit would make people most want to purchase your product, and use that benefit as the main selling point in your ad. The benefits that remain are all possible copy points. Look them over again and determine which need to be elaborated on in order to make the sale, and which do not need to be included at all.

Keep body copy conversational. Imagine that you are having a conversation with someone you know well. Pay close attention to the rhythm of the words you choose. To check for rhythm and conversational tone, read your copy out loud. Don't skip this step—it's important both for broadcast and for print ads.

Select your transition words very carefully. Use them to begin paragraphs. Look through the examples of print ads in this book and pick out the transitional words or phrases you think are most effective. You'll notice that the word *and* is not often used to begin a paragraph. It is a weak transitional word, best used to introduce an afterthought or minor point. It is, however, effective when connecting sentences within paragraphs.

The Lead

The lead-in sentence immediately follows the headline and is the first line of body copy. It should connect the idea put forth in the headline and visual with the information to be expanded upon in the body copy. It invites customers to read further and find out more about the product.

There are two things not to do with the lead line: don't repeat the headline word for word, and don't begin a lengthy narrative explaining *what you meant to say and didn't* with the headline and visual. Remember, when space and time are at a premium, it's vital that each sentence says something new.

Look back at the headline in the ad for a sports radio station in **Exhibit 5.5**: "No other radio station has the balls we do." Consider also that to complete the sales' message, the visual shows balls representing 12 different sports. In this example, the lead-in sentence works to *lead* the reader quickly in the intended direction: "Whatever your game is, nobody has the up-to-the-minute coverage or in-depth analysis we do."

Tracking: Crafting the Copy

The term *tracking* refers to the way in which the ideas in the body copy are connected. Ideas should follow a logical sequence and be so solidly connected that you cannot remove one of them without destroying the flow of the writing. If you can remove a sentence without disrupting the advertisement, then leave that sentence out altogether.

Good tracking means that each claim should lead into the next, paragraphs should be short, sentences simple, and the language clear. How well does the example in **Exhibit 5.6** measure up?

This is an ad for Gorham sterling silver. The lead sentence acknowledges the humor set up in the headline and prepares you for the sell. The second sentence is completely straightforward and gives you a fact that supports Gorham's *credibility*. The third sentence subtly reminds you that the Gorham name is credible because it shares the attribute of longevity with fine sterling silver. The copy then repeats this point twice more but does it differently each time. The sixth sentence yields three facts about Gorham that support the longevity claim, and so forth.

Tracking not only means presenting thoughts in a logical and meaningful order, it means using language to connect them so precisely that nothing can be added or taken away. When copy tracks, every sentence connects to the one before it. Each new thought is dependent upon the last.

For practice, take out the second sentence and read the copy aloud. Doesn't this seem like a lead that takes much too long to deliver its message? Now, leave in the second sentence but remove the third, the fourth, and so on. The advertisement no longer works. When you do this, you find that essential thoughts are missing.

As an example of a shorter advertisement that tracks well, look at the ad for Waterford Crystal in **Exhibit 5.7**.

Exhibit 5.6
Tracking body copy. Art Director: Woody Kay—Copywriter: Ernie Schenck. Agency: Pagano, Schenck & Kay. Reproduced with permission of Pagano, Schenck & Kay.

The headline tells you that Waterford has inspired poetry. This leads smoothly into the body copy, which confirms the point by sharing a line of the poetry with you and by telling you just when it was created. The last line of body copy reminds you that it is the ability to inspire that sets Waterford apart from its competitors.

Tracking begins with the lead sentence and continues as a thread of thought that holds your whole piece of copy together. It is important to note that this thread is tied to the concept. So whatever idea is communicated by the visual and the headline must be carried throughout the body copy. The first line of the copy grounds the reader in the main thought communicated by the concept and may sometimes begin to give relevant sales or product information.

The next paragraphs should get right to the facts, or copy points, as they are called, and give them in order of importance. These interior paragraphs contain any persuasive information you have that helps make the sale. Facts from consumer research, product taste tests, or the existence of a guarantee are examples of facts that could become persuasive copypoints.

The Close and the Call-to-Action

Close to the end of the copy, give the reader a call-to-action. Tell them what you want them to do. That could be anything from "Remember Johnson's, the foremost name in floor wax" to "Call 1-800-123-4567 and order yours now."

Look for calls-to-action in the advertising examples given in this chapter. Notice how the ads that use them sign off with a closing reference to the concept on which the ad is based.

Using Subheads

You are most likely to use subheads if you are writing a collateral piece or brochure rather than a print ad. Collateral pieces are usually much longer and you have more space to present detailed information.

When using subheads, the same principles of tracking apply. The idea embodied in the headline and visual must be continued throughout the piece. It should be picked up and displayed in subheads dividing longer sections of the body copy. This means that the concept should be strong enough for several logical references to be made to it without changing the original meaning. **Exhibit 5.8** is an example of a brochure that establishes and maintains a central concept throughout.

Exhibit 5.7
Short body copy. *Art Director: Jerry Whitley—Copywriter: Bill McCullam. Agency: Ammirati & Puris. Reproduced with permission of Waterford Wedgewood USA, Inc.*

Exhibit 5.8

Continuing a concept throughout a brochure. Art Director: Susan Fukuda—Copywriter: Ann Keding. Reproduced with permission of Dessert of the Month Club.

Grammar: Respect the Rules

Use language correctly. Sometimes copywriters break rules of syntax and grammar. Good copywriters follow grammatical rules, they don't break them. They use correct verb tenses, parallel construction, and correct punctuation and spelling. If your grammar isn't the best, consult a book like *When Words Collide*[2] or *Words Into Type*.[3]

There are some cases, however, when rules of grammar and syntax are broken to make a point. Look, for example, at the advertisement for Pounce Pesticide in **Exhibit 5.9**. As you can see, the body copy for this ad misuses the principles of grammar. But in this instance, using poor grammar in the body copy sets off the use of double entendre in the headline and visual. The ad is a success.

Playing with Words

To pun or not to pun? According to Walter Redfern's amazingly thorough work on the subject, *Puns*, puns are language on vacation. Redfern writes that within a pun, "ambiguity is celebrated."[4] While wit is the juggling of ideas, he says, puns require the juggling of words.

Puns work because of the double meanings that can coexist in words. They allow us the duplicity of language.

In advertising, since space and time are limited and economy is essential, puns are highly popular. Two meanings for the price of one word or phrase. Look back at the Volkswagen ad with the headline *Mass Transit* to see how this pun is used (**Exhibit 4.6**). But beware when you create a headline with a double

Exhibit 5.9
Writing in the vernacular.
Reproduced with permission of
FMC Corporation.

meaning—you must consider all possible interpretations. It's safe to assume that every possible meaning will find someone to interpret it, so be sure that all of them are desired.

A Word on Style

A writer's style can be seen simply as the way in which he or she sees the world, communicated through the choices made to represent that unique perspective in writing. Style is reflected in the words, phrases, and images used to express ideas. A writer with a distinct "style" trusts the choices he or she makes and does not emulate others.

To develop style, a writer needs to take risks. It takes courage to communicate to others that which is deep within yourself. It is always easier to avoid criticism by remaining conventional or anonymous. But to play safe in this way can mean that your work is lost in mediocrity. To write with style you need to discover what is honestly yours and avoid mimicking others. Then you need the courage to share what you discover. Each expression reveals an inner world. Our style is a means of externalizing all that is going on inside us.

But to what extent does this understanding of style apply to advertising copywriters? Good writing, no matter what the style, should be natural and easy; it shouldn't feel artificial or contrived and its hallmark should be clarity. The key purpose of advertising is to sell a product. The copywriter is speaking on behalf of a client. In advertising, therefore, style is best when it is clear, subtle, and unobtrusive. The copywriter's style should not compete with the tone established for the product or the message. It should work to enhance both. Remember, too, that the ads you write will often be part of an ongoing campaign that communicates a client's image. Copywriters who have their own style *and* who can imitate others are always in demand.

NOTES

[1] Henriette Anne Klauser, *Writing on Both Sides of the Brain: Breakthrough Techniques for People Who Write,* Harper & Row, San Francisco, 1987.

[2] Lauren Kessler and Duncan McDonald, *When Words Collide: A Journalist's Guide to Grammar and Style*, Wadsworth Publishing Company, Belmont, 1984.

[3] Marjorie E. Skillin and Robert M. Gay, *Words Into Type*, 3rd ed., Prentice Hall, New York, 1974.

[4] Walter Redfern, *Puns,* Basil Blackwell Publisher Ltd., Oxford, 1986.

Chapter 6

Print Ads: The Elements of Art Direction

The research and problem solving skills required of art directors are much the same as those required of copywriters. The approach taken depends less on job description than on a person's unique accumulation of experiences and perceptions.

When it comes to the execution of the creative concept, however, the copywriter and art director have distinctly different responsibilities. A copywriter's task is to work the message into the language of the headline and body copy of the advertisement. An art director's task is to work the same message into the visual or into the way the advertisement looks.

What Does the Art Director Do?

Whether creating an advertisement for print or television, the art director is as responsible for the idea or concept as the copywriter. Together they come up with as many ideas as it takes before they find one that successfully communicates the sales message they have in mind. After that, the art director is responsible for the whole visual presentation of the advertisement. For print, that includes how the words are arranged in the ad, the size and style of type chosen, the decision to use photography or illustration, the style of the photography or illustration, the use of color, and the arrangement, size, and proportion of the elements of the ad. For television—which we will look at in a later chapter—the art director and copywriter share responsibilities for the visualization of the concept, writing the words and supervising production of the commercials.

Visuals: The Power of Sight

Describe a sunrise. Which sense is most important in recreating the experience? It is sight. Sight is powerful. It is lingering. It is memorable.

Information that comes to us through sight allows us to make sense of our world. Without vision, much of the aesthetic pleasure of learning about the world is lost. Through sight we can experience humor, tragedy, boredom, beauty, ugliness. All of these can be communicated without a word.

Visual communication is a powerful form of shorthand. It conveys information, detail, and emotions in a flash. We see a dollar sign and we know it stands for money. We see a stop sign and know we must stop or take the consequences. We can look at a man in a suit and decide that he is dressed for business or for a formal occasion. Additional visual detail, such as a briefcase or a champagne glass with the suit will tell us which.

Visual symbols such as these transmit information quickly—information it would take much longer to convey in words alone. In advertising we are searching for the most rapid and forceful way possible to communicate a specific message. The immediate impact that visuals convey make them one of the most valuable tools we have.

Visuals can be anything from a cartoon drawing to a full-color photograph. Visuals can be illustrations, photography, all typography, computer-generated art, or any special photographic or film effects. They can be as simple as a line drawing or as complicated as an x-ray of the human body. The subject matter is only limited by your imagination and by your ability to make it work well alongside your message. If changing the face on the Statue of Liberty to that of Madonna is the clearest and most effective way to say what you need to say, then your only challenge is to find an illustrator who can do it to your liking.

What Else Do Visuals Tell Us?

In *The Design of Advertising,* Roy Paul Nelson classifies visuals by the impact they have on us. Visuals, he says, affect us in any of three ways, through *logic, surprise,* or *vagueness.*[1]

A logical impact is one that appeals to our common sense. To illustrate, let's consider an ad that is *not* logical. Imagine a visual of a mail carrier delivering an unwrapped package. For most people, packages come through the mail wrapped, not unwrapped. The ad in question asked the customer to order the product by mail and used an illustration of the postman holding the unwrapped product in his hands to do so. The visually illogical implication was that the mail carrier would assist you by unwrapping your package for you. This ad loses appeal because it defies common sense. The point is, ads should be visually logical. Your prospects should not have to work out the message for themselves. The visual you choose should do that for them.

A surprise visual has an impact that is unexpected. Surprise visuals either have an unusual twist or present a completely unexpected response to a customer need. The ad in **Exhibit 6.1** has both of these elements of surprise.

Vague visuals rely on ambiguity to deliver a message. They work through symbols that represent a particular message, and usually do not provide specific information. A raised glass of champagne, for example, stands for celebration. A rose can imply romance. A shirt thrown over one sweaty shoulder can stand for a laborer at work.

Exhibit 6.1
Surprise Visuals. Art Director: Bob Barrie—Copywriter: John Stingley. Reproduced with permission of Prince Foods.

Once you master each of these elements—logic, surprise, and vagueness—and can incorporate them into your visuals, the immediate impact of your advertisements will be stronger.

Taking Responsibility for the Symbols You Use

The use of social stereotypes to convey ideas in advertising is a two-edge sword. On the one hand, a stereotype can communicate a whole range of ideas and evoke reactions quickly, but on the other, your prospects may find the use of stereotypes socially unacceptable or offensive.

If you choose, for example, to feature Italians—stereotyped as emotive and passionate—because you want to create an image of passion for your product, think out the implications of your choice carefully. Should you exaggerate a perceived cultural trait like this? What will it mean to people who are Italian? Do they enjoy the portrayal or do they find it embarrassing?

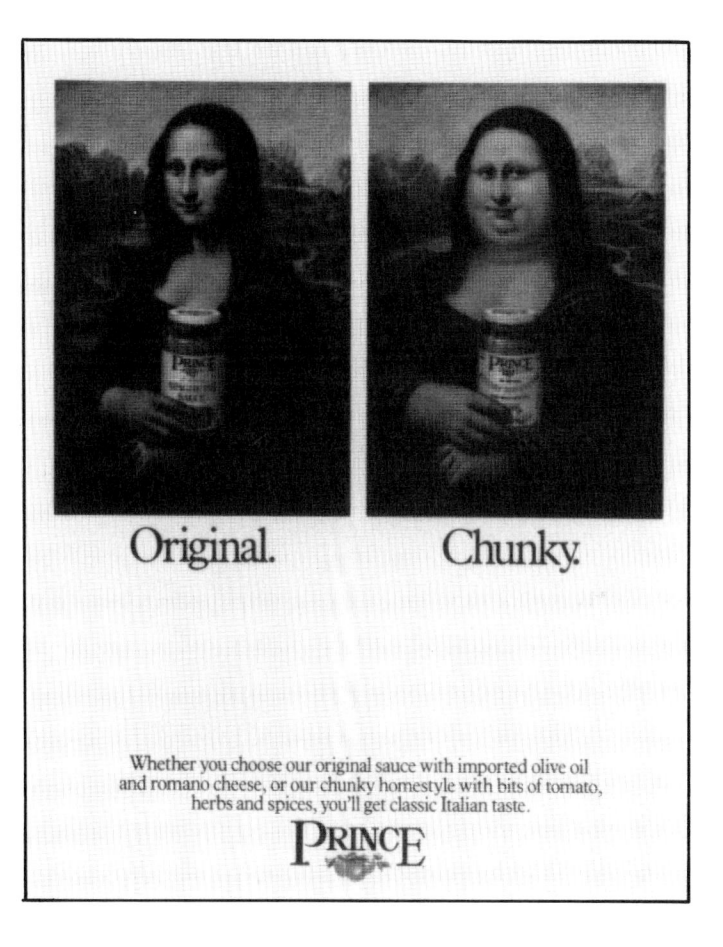

Social stereotypes that portray people in positions of powerlessness or as second class citizens are more obviously unacceptable. Whether, for example, you portray women as sex objects or in the role model of homemakers, or whether you present racial minorities in positions of servitude or underachievement, you risk alienating part of your audience. You may also risk associating your client with socially irresponsible attitudes, and are perpetuating stereotyped images in society.

Art Direction: What It Entails

Print media includes everything from outdoor billboards to newspapers and magazines, from collateral pieces such as brochures and sales promotion pieces to full direct mail kits.

Once the idea for the visual that will carry the advertising message is in place, the art director of a print advertisement takes charge of:

- Ad design
- Ad layout: the mechanics
- Selecting typography
- Selecting illustrations and photography
- Use of color

We will look at each of these in detail.

Ad Design

In *The Design of Advertising*, Roy Paul Nelson describes the relationship between ad design and ad layout, two elements of art direction that are often confused.[2] Design is the artful use of space and art to complete a communication, he says. Layout is the physical act of fitting it all together.

Simplicity is often heralded as the key to successful design. The purpose of advertising is to communicate a message with clarity and with impact. To complicate or obscure a design, to make it too elaborate or unnecessarily complex reduces its impact and, it follows, its effectiveness within an advertisement.

Simplicity along with the following elements of design, thoughtfully applied, will add to the effectiveness of an advertisement. These elements are balance, proportion, sequence, unity, and emphasis. According to Nelson:

- The design must be in balance.
- The space within the ad should be broken up into pleasing proportions.
- A directional pattern should be evident.
- A unifying force should hold the ad together.
- One element, or part of the ad, should dominate all the others.

All of these principles will be integrated into a well-designed ad, although one may be more dominant than the others.

Balance can be formal (symmetrical) or informal (asymmetrical). An ad in formal balance is designed so that every pattern on one side of the ad is repeated on the other. The ad for WFAN Sports radio, **Exhibit 5. 5**, is an example. An ad with informally balanced elements has optical balance. That is, from top to bottom or from side to side, elements may be placed slightly off center but create a sense of balance nonetheless. The ad for Gorham silver, **Exhibit 5.6**, is an example.

Proportion is the use of sizes and space in each element of an ad. It applies to the width of the ad in relation to the depth; the width of an element within an ad to the depth of that element; the amount of space between elements; the amount of color in proportion to non-color; and the amount of light area in proportion to the dark area. Proportion can be mathematically conceived, using a 3:2 or, better, a 5:3 ratio of width to depth. In a well-designed ad, proportion of the elements is varied enough to make the ad lively and interesting. Nelson reminds us that nature is the best place to look for inspiration regarding proportion.

Directional pattern or *sequence* refers to the purposeful arrangement of elements by the designer in order to guide the reader through the ad. In western culture, people read from left to right and from top to bottom. Using this already

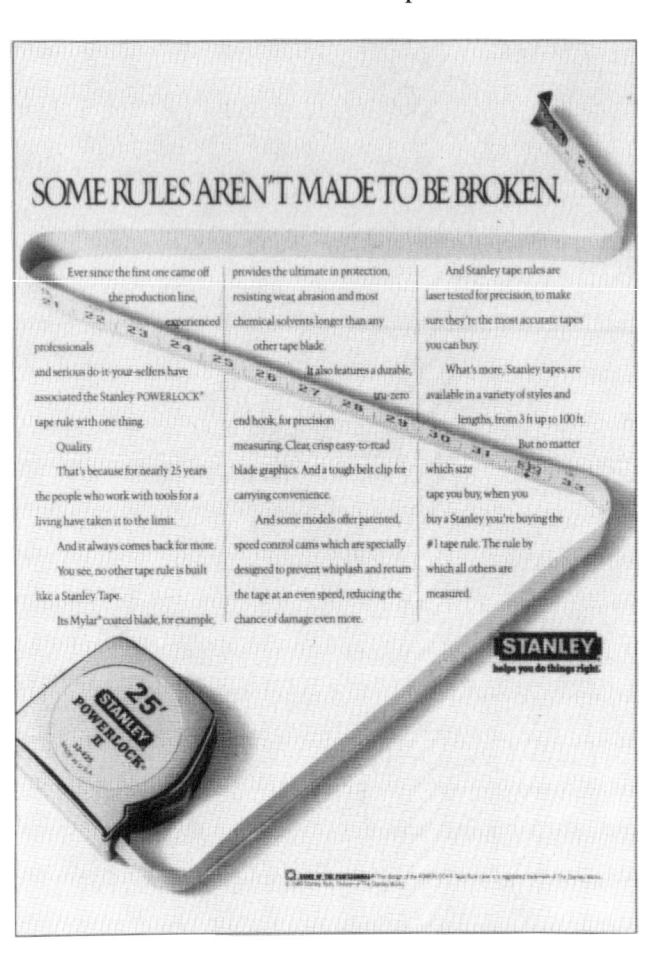

Exhibit 6.2
Directional pattern within a design.
Art Director: Deborah Lucke—
Copywriter: Fred Bertino. Reproduced with permission of The Stanley Works.

instilled habit, a designer can arrange the elements of an ad so that the reader's attention is first drawn to its focal point. The ad should then lead the eye through the other important elements. The Z axis is an obvious way of controlling eye movement, as **Exhibit 6.2** demonstrates. Our attention is grabbed initially by the large visual of the Stanley tape measure and continues as the tape guides us carefully from the top of the page down through to the end of the copy.

The *unifying force* or *unity* of an ad refers to that which holds it together. The elements of the ad work together to offer more than each could offer separately. In a unified design, the design elements work harmoniously. They should also bring the idea behind the ad forward. You should be able to tell by looking at an ad whether it has unity. Look at the typeface chosen, the proportion of type to white space, the use of color or non-color, the proportion of the elements within the ad, and the size of the ad. For an example of how unity can bring impact to an idea, see **Exhibit 4.1**, the ad for Zero Pet Population Growth.

Exhibit 6.3
Unity within a design. Art Director: Bob Brihn—Copywriter: Jarl Olsen. Reproduced with permission of Fallon McElligott.

The following questions should be considered when evaluating an ad for unity. Does it have a border surrounding it, and does it work to contain the elements? Are there several borders within the ad? Do they work together? How is *white space* used? Does it add air and balance to the ad or is it a disharmonious force? Are all points of emphasis equal or is there a *three-point layout*? Three elements are easier to unify with regard to proportion than four. Examine **Exhibit 6.3** and decide how unity is brought to this ad.

Finally, one element should be given *emphasis* over all others in an ad. It should be either the art, the headline, or the copy block. If it's the art, then which one element of the art? Emphasis can be created by singling out the item of reference and moving it away from the other elements. Or the item to be emphasized could be presented in a different shape or made larger, bolder or more colorful than others. Take another look at **Exhibits 6.1, 6.2,** and **6.3** to see how a single item was given emphasis in each ad.

Remember, in **Chapter 4** when ideas and concepts were discussed, we advised you to use only one idea per ad. This same rule applies to emphasis. Only one item receives emphasis per ad. To give emphasis to any more than that means that there is none.

In ad design, then, it is important to consider balance, proportion, sequence, unity, and emphasis. Once you have completed an ad design, check to make sure that all these are present. If any one element of an ad can be removed without disturbing the others, then the integrity of the design is in question.

The Mechanics of Layout

The *layout* is the first form advertising artwork takes, whether it is a print ad to appear in a newspaper, magazine, or on an outdoor or transit board, or whether it is a collateral or direct mail piece.

For print media, layouts serve as guides or blueprints for those who work on the ad. Laying out an ad is the physical act of putting all of the elements of design together. It is an orderly compilation of the parts of the advertisement: the headline, subheads, illustration or photograph, copy, picture captions, slogan, and logotype.

The layout serves to show where the parts of the ads are to be placed, the size and proportion they are to have, and the amount of copy needed. The layout can also serve to help determine the costs of production.

Layouts go through several stages of development, from thumbnail sketches to roughs, from roughs to comprehensives, from comprehensives to mechanicals, ready for printing.

- **Thumbnail sketches.** The *thumbnail* is the first stage in the layout process. This is a miniature ad. Thumbnails can be one-fourth the size of the finished ad or smaller. They are rough sketches used by the art director and copywriter in the very early stage of working out ideas to examine how an idea might look, in print.

- **Roughs.** After the thumbnail stage, ideas that merit further consideration are taken to a more advanced layout, a *rough*. A rough is generally the actual size of the ad to be designed. The headlines and subheads can be hand-lettered or computer generated to give an idea how they will look in relation to the other elements of the ad. Often, the copy —which might not yet be written—is *greeked in* (indicated by squiggly lines or solid gray lines in place of words of copy). An outline of the visual (illustration or photography) is drawn. The rough is meant for presentation and decision making among those working on the advertising. It isn't used for formal presentation.

- **Comprehensives.** Ideas that make it through the rough stage and designated for presentation to the client are then taken to the next layout stage, the *comprehensive*. A comprehensive, or *comp* as it is called, is as complete a representation as possible of an advertisement without finished artwork. This means, the design of the advertisement is complete, the typeface has been chosen and has been either hand-lettered or computer generated to give an approximation of the final product. Everything is as close to the final ad as possible because the comp is what is used to sell the idea to the person making the final decisions. By necessity, the comprehensive must give those who see it a real feeling for the ad. Body copy is written even though it may still may be greeked in. This depends upon how the comp is put together. After the comp is approved, type is ordered from the printer, and photography or illustration is commissioned to complete the final artwork.

- **Mechanical.** The final stage in the layout process is the *mechanical* stage. When the type has been set and the illustration or photography is complete, the elements of the ad will be pasted upon mat board, ready to be filmed prior to printing. This is the end of the layout stage and the first stage for print production.

- **Dummy.** A *dummy* or *mock-up* as it is often called, is a finished comprehensive for a collateral piece, a direct mail piece, or a point-of-purchase display. It is used to present ideas that appear in a three dimensional format. Again, the purpose of a dummy is to give a feeling for the final piece.

Typography

Most consumers who look at a print advertisement do not immediately notice the type font an art director has selected. They read the words, the type is taken for granted. But in advertising, typography is an art unto itself. Effective selection of type to suit the tone, the product, the design, and the copy of the ad can help carry and communicate the message.

Let's look at some examples of different type fonts and notice the effect the choice of type has on conveying a message. Below, the very ordinary message, "You are cordially invited to a party," is printed in six different type fonts. Can you guess from each font what type of party you are being invited to?

You are cordially invited to a party. (Goudy Old-style)

You are cordially invited to a party. (Avant Garde)

You are cordially invited to a party. (Brush Script)

You are cordially invited to a party. (Futura Extended Bold)

You are cordially invited to a party. (Korinna)

You are cordially invited to a party. (Zaph Chancery)

So what kind of party is it? Formal? Informal? Should you wear blue jeans? Evening dress? Shorts? Each font suggests something different about the tone of the invitation, and the formality of the party. In each, your expectations are affected simply by the type font chosen to convey the message.

Classes of Type

There are two broad classifications for type, *display* type and *text* type. Display type is larger and usually heavier than text type and is used in headlines, subheads, logos, and addresses. Text type is smaller and is used for body copy in an advertisement.

Because there are thousands of typefaces available and new ones being developed every day, it is not particularly useful to memorize every typeface you can find. However, it is useful to remember the five major type groups into which every typeface fits.

- **Roman**. Roman is the most popular type group and considered the most readable. Characteristics that most distinguish it are the *serifs*, or small tails, that cross the ends of the main strokes, and the variation in thickness of the strokes.

- **Sans serif.** Sans serif is another popular type group and is sometimes referred to as block, contemporary or gothic. Characteristic of this type group is—as the name implies—the lack of serifs and the uniform thickness of the strokes.

- **Square serif.** Square serif typefaces, sometimes called slab serifs, combine the distinguishing characteristics of roman and sans serif. The letters have serifs but the strokes are uniform in thickness.
- **Cursive or script.** Cursive or script typefaces resemble handwriting. Used mostly in headlines, these typefaces are not always the easiest to read.
- **Ornamental.** Ornamental typefaces provide novelty and are used for special effects. Look at the examples of fonts used to write "You are cordially invited to a party" earlier in this chapter and decide which ones are ornamental. These typefaces are not commonly used because they are difficult to read.

Type Families

Each *typeface*, also known as a *font*, comes in a host of sizes and widths, known as its type family. For example, Goudy, Futura, or News Gothic each have as many alternatives as there are possible variations in proportion, weight, and slant of characters. The variations that make up a type family commonly include light, medium, bold, extra bold, condensed, extended, and italic. Each font, no matter what the size, also comes with a complete set of capitals, small capitals, lowercase letters, numerals, and punctuation marks.

Type Measurement

The height of type is measured in *points* and its width is measured in *picas*. There are 72 points to a vertical inch of type, so one point measures 1/72 of an inch. Points are measured from the bottom of the descenders or the letters that extend below the body of the type to the top of the ascenders, the letters extending above the body of the type. The point sizes for text type are point sizes 6, 8, 10, 12, and 14. The sizes for display type are point sizes 18, 24, 36, 42, 60, 72, 84, 96, and 120.

Picas are the horizontal unit of measurement for type. There are six picas to the inch. Width of a typeface varies according to the style and that must be considered when ordering type from the typesetters. Newspaper column inches are two inches wide and magazine columns are just a little wider. For readability, body copy should not be set in columns wider than three inches.

Legibility

Much care should be taken when choosing a typeface. The first and most important factor in determining which typeface to use is *readability*.

When choosing type, consider what your target audience is used to reading. Remember that the task of advertising is to communicate a sales message quickly. Does it make sense to work diligently on a bold, creative message only to make it hard to decipher by using unreadable or unintelligibly designed type? Of course not. So remember that people are used to: reading text presented in upper and lower case (even headlines set in all-caps are difficult to read); lines of type running horizontally, not diagonally; and words evenly spaced. Because roman typefaces are selected most often, they bring with them a certain familiarity which means the reader doesn't need to be reacquainted with the typeface before receiving the message. When space and time are critical, there is no place for a hard-to-read typeface, no matter what its style.

Another thing to consider for increased legibility is limiting the number of typefaces used within an ad. If several typefaces are used, they are usually closely related or are from the same family. Mixing typefaces leads to clutter and disharmony.

Using Type Only in Ads

Sometimes, an idea can be best emphasized by using type as the major design element. Several print ads used to illustrate other principles in this book also demonstrate this point. If a visual doesn't add anything new to an idea, then the complete story can be told with language. See, for example, **Exhibit 4.1**, the ad for Zero Pet Population Growth, and **Exhibit 5.1**, the ad for Beans and Barley Restaurant. In both, the style and size of typeface are critical. It must harmonize with the message, emphasize it, and carry the appropriate tone.

In **Chapter 11**, this discussion on type selection is continued, emphasizing how your personal computer can help in type selection and specification.

Selecting Illustrations and Photography

Though an art director often is not involved in the actual drawing or sketching of illustrations or in taking photographs, he or she is responsible for the overall visual effect of the ad. The art director is involved in creating the initial concept for the ad and decides how this is to be translated into a visual.

As an art director you will work with illustrators, photographers, and their representatives and will be responsible for choosing the right artist or photographer, and the right illustration or picture for the job. You will be in contact with any number of artist's representatives who can supply you with samples of artistic work. These reps manage a portfolio of various talent. Some handle only photographers, others also work with illustrators. Some specialize in special product categories, others cover a wider range.

Make sure you have a clear idea of the message you wish to convey through illustrations or photographers before you make a choice. Decide on the tone the ad will take and look for an artist who has created similar effects in previous work. Examine style differences among photograhers and illustrators, and pick out those who achieve the effect you are looking for. Find out which photographers specialize, for example, in fashion, and which specialize in automobiles or food. Look for a photographer with experience in the category in which your product falls—he or she will be most familiar with the lighting, sets, and camera techniques needed to make these products look their best. The styles of different illustrators, too, can be seen in samples of their drawings. The work may vary according to the weight of the lines in the drawings, for example, the shading used, or the realism or fantasy used in depictions. Again while some illustrators do a better job with food than with fashion, others may be good with people.

Selecting Visuals

When most people look at an ad, they look first at the visual, then they read the headline, and if still interested, they read the body copy. Visuals serve to attract the attention of the reader just the same as headlines. They also identify the subject of the ad, qualify the prospects by stopping those most interested, create further interest in the headline and copy, present the product in its most favorable light, provide support for claims made in the copy, and bring continuity to a campaign.

Art directors choose visuals on the basis of their ability to represent the idea, their cost, the technical limitations of producing them, the time required to obtain them, the printing process to be used, the paper on which the ad is to be printed and the availability of the artist chosen in the desired medium.

Let's look at the different types of illustration used, and define some of the terminology used when talking about visuals.

Drawings

Sometimes drawn illustrations work better than photographs. For instance, you might want to illustrate an event from the past or from the future for which no photographs are available or can convey the image you wish to create. You may need to exaggerate. You may need to create a precise picture of a product and its many components that would be obscured in a one-dimensional photograph. The media in which you advertise might also lead you to choose a drawing over a photograph. Imagine, for example, you are designing a food advertisement to be placed in newspapers. Because of the reproduction quality, photography may not be effective. But a simple line drawing can make food appear quite appealing.

Line drawings or pen and ink drawings provide clear detail and a visual with no shades of gray. Everything is either black or white. Because of their simplicity, they are less costly than other visuals. Examine the Volkswagen ad in **Exhibit 4.5** to see how powerful a line drawing can be.

Cartoons

Cartoons, like the one in **Exhibit 4.5**, are humorous line drawings. They can be used to exaggerate an idea or to emphasize a familiar experience. The headline takes the place of the traditional cartoon caption or gagline. Cartoons simply drawn can be used successfully in almost all of the print media. More complex drawings should be reserved for media with better than average reproduction quality.

Repros

Art reproduction (repro) can be done in two ways: line reproduction and halftone reproduction. Artwork done in black ink on white paper in lines or solid areas of black uses *line reproduction*. Here, the printer takes a photograph of the art using high-contrast film. The film is then used to expose a sensitized plate. The plate goes through the etching process so that parts of it that are not to print are eaten away and only those to be printed remain.

Halftone reproduction is used when handling photographs or artwork that have a continuous *tone*. Photographs with a wide tonal range give the best reproductions. In order to represent the original as closely as possible, the printer inserts a screen between the lens and the film. This screen is a two-ply piece of glass with lines etched on each piece. The cross hatching effect that results breaks the light into dots of various sizes, depending upon how much light is reflected off the subject. From here, the negative is used the same as for line reproductions.

A halftone is made up of small dots covering the areas to be reproduced, even the white areas. To get tonal variations and shades of gray, printers use black ink, but with varying sizes of dots. Lighter areas are defined by pinpoint dots and the dark areas by larger dots.

Color separations

If you order a black and white ad, you have ordered one color, black. Add a splash of red for accent, and you have two colors. Color photography can be done in two, three, or four color with an occasional fifth color. In magazine advertisements, an occasional fifth color is silver or gold.

Four-color photography requires highly technical processing. The printer (photoengraver or camera operator) separates the primary colors in the original art (color transparency, color print, or painting) and records the separation on film. The primary colors used are magenta, yellow, and cyan blue. Next, the film negatives are rephotographed through a screen to make new negatives. These screened negatives help make plates—one for each primary color and one for black. The combination of these colors provides a full-color effect.

Spot color is color applied to parts of a black and white illustration to add emphasis. With spot color an art director can separate the colors before they go to the printer. The artwork for each color is done on its own sheet. The main part of the drawing, most often the black part, will be done on a piece of illustration board. The rest of the main colors of the drawing will each be done on a sheet of frosted acetate. From these, the printer will make plates and add the correct color inks.

Use of Color

The medium that carries your advertisement often dictates the use of color. In a glossy fashion magazine, for example, your ad will be in full color, whereas an ad designed for a newspaper will usually be in black and white. Your creative concept, too, may direct you in how best to use color: you might decide that using black and white in a full color magazine will help highlight your ad, or that black and white will convey a particular tone, for example, to express realism as in a documentary work. An illustrator's use of color is usually tied in with his or her style, and can also convey a particular tone. Within an illustration, the source of color may be watercolor, tempera, pastels, or felt tip pens—each media is used to create a different effect. In many cases it is the advertising budget that is the deciding factor—on a low budget you might choose black and white or spot color.

A broad body of research shows that color ads draw more attention than do black and white. A survey by Starch INRA Hooper found that a four-color full-page ad attracted 50 percent more readers than the same ad produced in black and white. Another study, examining the use of color in ads across the last five decades, shows the use of four-color in ads increasing from 31 percent in the 1930s to 68 percent in the 1980s.[3] The increase in advertising over the past 50 years is one explanation for this change. But there are other reasons that have to do with the advantages of using color. For one thing, color shows off a product to its fullest advantage. This is true for most products and is particularly important when it comes to the subject of appetite appeal for food products, and attitude or tone for apparel products. Color can indicate quality or mood, and can be used to bring continuity to an advertising campaign. Color not only makes the product or service look more appealing, it gives the viewer more information at a glance. Subtleties lost in black and white are easily noticed when color is used.

The technological requirements of the four-color process make color much more expensive than black and white. For instance, a four-color magazine ad costs nearly one-third more than the same size ad in black and white. Because color reflects the object photographed in more detail, flaws and uneven lighting are picked up quickly. This means considerable preparation involving extra time and expense must be done before a photograph is taken. One question an art director always asks is whether or not full color is worth the time and trouble it takes. In most cases, unless restricted by a very small budget, the decision to use color is a wise one. But another important factor influencing that decision is, of course, the idea or concept being executed. While full color is generally required for fashion advertising, recall the recent Calvin Klein underwear campaign executed in sepiatone. There, the use of one color cut through the clutter and communicated the message even more strongly than four-color could have done.

Two Principles of Great Advertising

In learning about the qualities of creative art direction in this chapter, we have also come across two principles important to the development of great advertising. The first is the gestalt psychology principle that claims that *the whole is greater than the sum of its parts*. By looking in detail at the process of creating advertising art, it is easy to see how well-crafted visuals use and balance different design principles to communicate an idea effectively.

The second principle that applies to great advertising is summed up in an expression that has been floating around advertising circles for several decades, *less is more*. The basics of good design help us see that a good idea or a clear message should not be obscured by elaborate design techniques. Simplicity is important.

As we move in the next chapter into a discussion on creative approaches to broadcast advertising, keep both these principles in mind.

NOTES

[1] Roy Paul Nelson, *The Design of Advertising*, 6th ed., Wm. C. Brown, Dubuque, Iowa, 1989.

[2] *Ibid*.

[3] Florence Feasley and Elnora Stuart, "Magazine Advertising Layout and Design: 1932-1982," *Journal of Advertising,* 16:2, 1987.

Chapter 7

Creating Broadcast Advertising

Unlike print media, advertisements that are aired through broadcast media attract a "passive" audience of listeners or viewers. Whereas we purposely choose to pick up and leaf through newspapers and magazines, radio and television often function in the background of daily life. Broadcast advertisements, therefore, have to work all the harder to communicate a sales message.

In the early 1920s, when radio began, its novelty alone drew the attention of listeners. A straightforward message or a pleasantly sung jingle was enough to entertain audiences and persuade them to buy. Radio didn't come into its own as a medium until the 1930s, ironically during the depression. Programs airing lively dance music and radio hosts like Jack Benny brought both an escape from reality and an opportunity for advertisers.

As with early radio, when television first became widely available in the 1950s, programs were initially sponsored by a single advertiser, and the host of a program would take time between scenes to "talk about our sponsor."

As the medium developed and programming costs began to mount, the 30-second television commercial was introduced. This brought the opportunity for multiple sponsorships meaning each advertiser could bear less of the cost and still enjoy the advantage of television. This was the next best thing to sending a salesperson into millions of homes at once. Product demonstrations and before-and-after-dramatizations became the most frequently used formats for television commercials.

By the 1960s television advertising had become a sophisticated marketing tool that could deliver messages from the most simple to the most complex in ways that were entertaining, dramatic, humorous, and—most importantly—persuasive.

Television Advertising

Everyone agrees that television is a uniquely powerful advertising medium. Its combination of sight, sound, and motion can convey quality images instantly and can activate imagination and interest in ways no other medium can. No matter how complex a product is, or how fantastic the concept chosen to present it, television can make it work. It is by far the best medium to use for new product introductions, and is highly effective for products where image is key to the sale.

Considering that over 86 million homes in American have television sets, the reach of television is almost without limits. Network television can deliver a message to audiences with an enormous range of interests, tastes and needs, and the proliferation of cable and satellite channels brings the opportunity to target specific viewer groups, too. Through television, you can reach millions of

Exhibit 7.1
American Tourister commercial. Reproduced with permission of American Tourister, Inc.

(VO) Dear clumsy bellboys...brutal cab drivers...careless doormen... ruthless porters...and all butter-fingered luggage handlers all over the world...have we got a suitcase for you.

66   Chapter 7

potential new customers, all at the same time. You can talk directly to them in their homes, and the screen brings your products to life right before their eyes.

Yes, through television, you can lead a million customers to your product. The catch is, you can't always make them buy. Unfortunately for advertisers, television does not promise a captive audience. Most people watching television do not use commercial breaks to catch up on new products on the market. They head for the refrigerator, tend to their knitting, flick through the TV guide, or make quick telephone calls while the commercials are playing. Unless you have something extraordinarily newsworthy to say, most people simply won't be curious.

Look at this problem as the challenge of creative advertising. With so many other activities and so many other messages vying for the viewers' attention, the task is to make them interested in yours. Remember, people like television commercials when they are good ones. When done well, they can be tiny jewels of enjoyment and viewers will look forward to watching them again. This is the aim of creative television advertising.

What Makes a Television Advertisement Great?

It's easy to list what a good television commercial should have in it. It should have a beginning, a middle, and an end. The visuals and script should complement and not repeat each other. There should be no more than 90 words in a 30-second spot. The product should be "hero" and client recognition should be instant. And it should have entertainment value.

It's more challenging to remember what a television commercial should *not* have or be. First, the budget should not be too low for the idea. Decide which is more important—quality production or low cost—and choose one or the other. There should not be too much visual stimuli. Make sure your commercial has one, clear visual focus. Neither should there be too much copy. Don't overload your audience with unnecessary detail. And, finally, there should not be "borrowed interest" from anything outside the product. Nothing—no matter how entertaining or how cleverly executed—should distract the viewer from the product.

Let's look at some successful TV commercials and notice how well their creators have followed these ground rules. Look at **Exhibit 7.1**, Doyle Dane Bernbach's classic commercial for American Tourister luggage. There is just one idea and one message in this commercial: American Tourister luggage is strong enough to stand up to anything. This is communicated in only 30 seconds. Notice how few words were used and how well they complement the visuals.

Next, look at the three commercials in **Exhibit 7.2**, a campaign the State of Virginia launched to announce the new drinking age. The commercials play off the images commonly conveyed in advertisements for alcoholic beverages, which are popular with young people. Is this borrowed interest? No, it isn't. The commercials cleverly "borrow" an established image and message and use them to deliver a counter-message. Here, the use is totally appropriate. And there is nothing irrelevant or distracting about it.

Exhibit 7.3 shows a commercial for Hyundai automobiles that uses humor to entertain viewers as well as to interest them in the product's key benefit. Here, Hyundais are presented as very good buys. So good they cost half as much as other, similar cars. This point is humorously conveyed by showing a customer who couldn't pass up such a good deal—he's driving two Hyundais home at the same time.

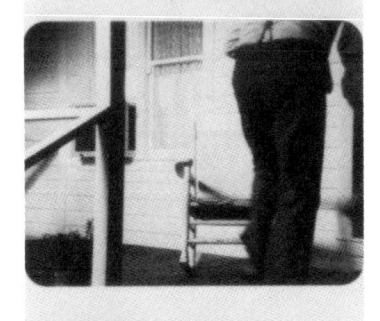

◀ **Exhibit 7.2**
Virginia Drinking Age commercials. Art Director: Walt Taylor—Copywriter: Rebecca Flora. Reproduced with permission of Lawler Ballard Advertising.

(Open on Frank Bartels and Ed Jaymes look-alikes sitting on a familiar porch. They get up, walk inside and pull down the window shade)

Anncr.(VO): *In Virginia, if you're under 21, Frank and Ed don't want your support.*

(Dissolve to art card)

(Open on pastoral setting. Elegant table with grapes, ▶ *bottle of wine, glass and cork in foreground)*

Music: *Vangelis-like theme throughout.*

(Hand removes bottle, than glass and, finally, the cork)

Anncr. (VO): *Here, in the beautiful Commonwealth of Virginia, we will sell no wine before your time.*

68   Chapter 7

(Open on neighborhood tavern interior. Young man steps up to the bar)

Music: Throughout. Young Man: Gimme a light,

(Bartender clicks on flashlight in young man's face)

Bartender: Gimme some I.D.

(Young man shuffles around nervously, then exits)

Anncr. (VO): Just a reminder. Virginia has a new drinking age.

(Dissolve to art card)

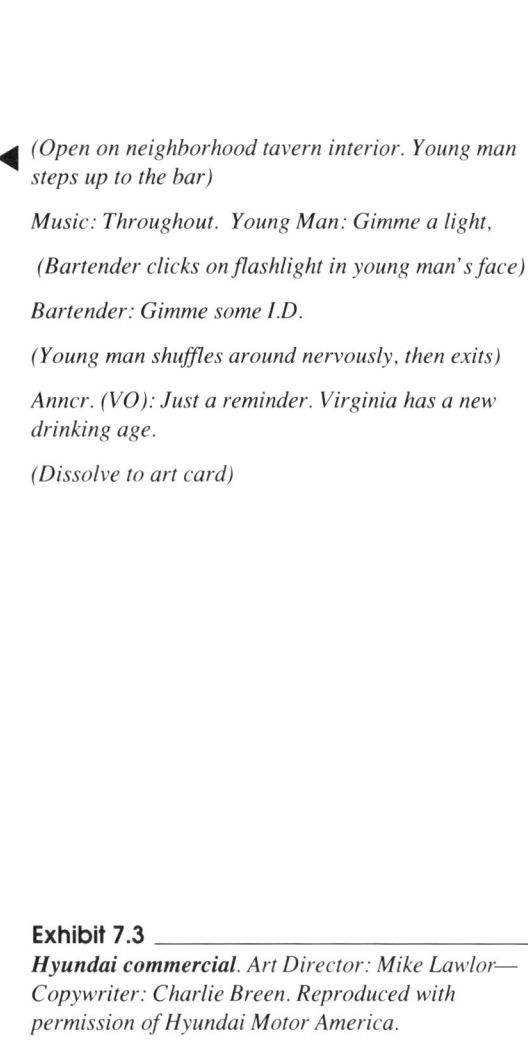

Exhibit 7.3
Hyundai commercial. Art Director: Mike Lawlor—Copywriter: Charlie Breen. Reproduced with permission of Hyundai Motor America.

(SFX: Halting tire screech and running footsteps throughout.)

(VO): For less than the average price of a new car, you can get two new Hyundai Excels.

They're both dependable, have front-wheel drive,

room for five and more standard features than any cars in their class.

The only problem is . . . getting them home.

Hyundai. Cars that make sense.

Broadcast Advertising 69

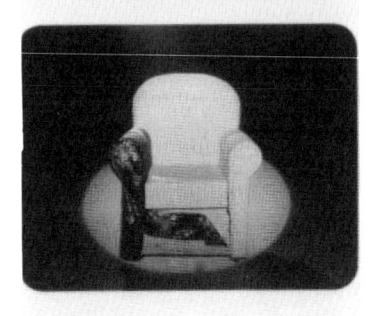

◀ **Exhibit 7.4**

Nynex commercial. Art Director: Marty Weiss—Copywriter: Robin Raj. Reproduced with permission of Nynex Information Resources Co.

(Open on upholstered chair)

SFX: Opening chime. (Lights go down and spot light hits chair)

Music: Stripper music.

SF: Clapping and whistling.

(Upholstery starts to fly off the chair. Foundation materials fly off chair and springs pop off, exposing the bare wood frame)

SFX: Springs popping

(Cut to zooming in on yellow pages)

SFX: Whooshing sound.

Anncr. (VO): If it's out there, it's in here.

(Camera stops on Furniture Stripping heading)

SFX: Man whistling

Anncr. (VO): The NYNEX Yellow Pages.

(Camera pulls back. Phone book closes to show cover)

Anncr. (VO): Why would anyone need another?

Look at the Nynex commercial in **Exhibit 7.4** to see how a single, simple message is given an unusual and highly creative twist. The message is: no matter how esoteric, whatever you need is listed in the Nynex Yellow Pages. The commercial used grabs the viewers' interest immediately, and keeps them guessing to the very last frames what the product behind the advertisement is.

Writing Scripts for Television Broadcast Ads

As we have seen with writing print ads, it is important to understand thoroughly the product concept and decide the message you are going to convey before any writing begins. You will also, by this stage, have worked out in general terms the visuals that will be used.

As you begin writing, the most important consideration is that your copy should complement the visuals. Scripts should emphasize the visuals, not repeat them. In television, you have two means of reaching your audience—sight and sound. Remember that if viewers can see a product, they don't need to hear you describe it, too. The same goes for tone. For example, if your commercial has a visual joke in it, then perhaps the script should be straightforward. If the visuals are straightforward, then the humor or entertainment value has to be in the script. A straightforward script, too, can build up to a verbal punchline, surprise, or joke. Look through the sample commercials in **Exhibits 7.5** and **7.6** and notice how the visuals and script interact to convey the message.

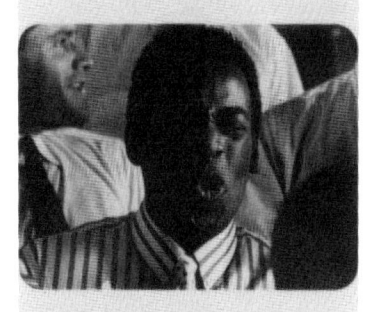

◀ **Exhibit 7.5**
Arrow Shirt commercial—visual humor. Art Director: Michael Smith—Copywriter: Graham Turner. Reproduced with permission of The Arrow Company.

(Open on large hall. Camera zooms to men's chorus)

Music: Chorus singing chords. (Dissolve to pan of close-up)

Chorus: Your love has lifted me higher than I've ever been lifted before. So keep it up...

Soloist 1 (VO): So keep it up. (Camera pans to soloist wearing bright, striped shirt. Cut to other singers looking at soloist with surprise)

Chorus: Quench my desire. (Pan to another soloist wearing a bright shirt)

Soloist 2: Quench my desire. (Cut to other singers looking at second soloist with surprise)

Chorus: And I'll be at your side for ever more. (Cut back to second soloist)

Soloist: Yeaaaaaaaaaaaaaaaaah! (Cut to various shots of singers snapping fingers and dancing to music as more and more of them are wearing brightly colored shirts)

Soloists: You know your love, keeps on liftin'. Higher. Higher and higher. I said your love. Keeps on liftin' me higher...

(Fade to black. Tag fades in)

Anncr. (VO): Arrow shirts. We've loosened our collar.

Exhibit 7.6 ▶
Conran's commercial—visual humor. Art Director: Dean Hanson—Copywriter: Philip Hanft. Reproduced with permission of Fallon McElligott.

(Open on shot of man standing in front of an easy chair. He looks and walks around chair.)

SFX: Footsteps.

Anncr. (VO): At Conran's we don't believe that beautifully designed furniture should be so expensive...

(Man finally tries to sit in chair)

Anncr. (VO): ...You're afraid to even sit in it.

(Man sits in chair and chair swallows man)

SFX: Hollow tumbling sound.

(Super fades in. Chair burps)
SFX: Burp.

Broadcast Advertising 71

Formats for television commercials

Most television commercials will take one of six standard formats. These are:

- *Vignette.* A short sketch, usually telling a story about or showing the lifestyle of people who use the product.

- *Spokesperson.* A person who is identifed with the product or with an activity relevant to the product makes the pitch. You might use a celebrity, a corporate president, or an ordinary person in an easily identifiable "role."

- *Demonstration.* A commercial that uses a real or imagined scenario to show how the product actually works.

- *Comparison.* A commercial that matches one product against another, usually a competing brand.

- *Case history.* A sketch that identifies an unusual use of the product or that focuses on a person, possibly a celebrity or an eccentric, who has adopted the product.

- *Product as hero.* A problem/solution scenario: the consumer problem is presented, and the product solves it. This is also known as *slice-of-life* advertising.

Preparing a script for filming

To make sure that your script is easy to read and to follow during filming and production, you will need to be familiar with some broadcast terminology. Here is a brief list of terms and acronyms most commonly used.

Camera Angles:
CU	Close-up
ECU	Extra close-up
MS	Medium shot
ELS	Extra long shot

Camera Moves:
PAN	Camera turns slowly, either left or right
DOLLY	Camera and cart move in direction indicated: forward, around to the left, around to the right, up or down

Directorial Commands:
ACTION	Signal for cameras to roll film
CUT TO...	This can mean cut to another camera, cut to another scene, or cut to a SUPER (see below)
DISSOLVE	The visual present on the screen can still be seen while the next one is coming up
FADE	The visual present fades into the next one; the difference between this and DISSOLVE is the button used to make this happen technically; a dissolve is controlled by hand, and a fade is electronically timed
FADE OUT	The visual present gradually fades to black
SUPER	A frame with a typed message on it, such as: **Call 1-800-123-4567**

In the next section we will find out more about preparing for the filming session, when we discuss the art director's role in preparing the storyboard, ready for shooting.

Art Direction in Television Broadcast Ads

In television broadcast, the art director takes on a range of new responsibilities and is working with outside suppliers: a director, the film crew, actors, and production personnel. The main task is to communicate successfully to a new team of people the advertising concept, the creative team has worked out and the visuals and dialogue you intend to use to carry it.

Broadcast planning: Preparing the storyboard

During the planning stage, the art director and copywriter work from the creative concept they have developed and decide how this may best translate into a broadcast commercial. Together they visualize how the commercial will run, frame by frame, word by word. The copywriter invents the dialog that will sell the product, and the art director works this dialog into a *storyboard*. The storyboard is the means by which the art director visualizes each scene of a planned advertisement as it will appear on film. It is the main tool used in broadcast planning. **Exhibit 7.7** is an example.

The storyboard is a sheet containing a series of boxes that represent television frames. The art director slots into each frame an illustration that represents the various camera shots that will be used in a television commercial. Each illustration is accompanied by the section of dialog that will be used with it, and by annotations regarding filming and audio requirements. It is the art director who must ensure that the advertising concept is successfully worked into the storyboard, as the director, production people, film crew, and actors will all use this to communicate that concept to viewers.

The storyboard is also used to present the advertising plan to the client. Though you may deviate from it during actual shooting as new and better ideas for visuals or dialog emerge, you should never do so without the full approval of the client.

A word on choosing film or video

Choice of film or video in broadcast advertising depends largely on the client's budget. Most television commercials are expensively produced using 16mm film. Film provides crispness, clarity, and precision—all of which are important in good advertising. With film, however, cost can be prohibitive and the turnaround time in processing and production is considerable. Quality means money and time.

For this reason, some advertisers prefer to shoot commercials using videotape. The quality is not as good but the cost is much lower and production is instant. Remember, too, that if you decide to use videotape you have less control over color and texture—videotape leaves a grainy texture and is imprecise when registering contrasts and color.

Consider the product you are advertising and the camera shots you want before you choose. For example, if you plan to create something with "appetite appeal," don't use videotape—it does nothing to enhance the appearance of food.

Exhibit 7.7

Bayless storyboard. Art Director: Gary Yoshida—Copywriter: Bob Coburn. Reproduced with permission of Rubin Postaer & Associates.

(Open on tight shot of jar of Best Foods Mayonnaise. Hand reaches into frame and begins to play bottle top like a bongo drum.)

Anncr. (VO): Maaaaayo...

(Cut to super showing price)

(Cut back to hands playing bottle top.)

Anncr. (VO): Mayo, mayo, maaaayo... (Cut to super)

Anncr. (VO): The new Bayless. We even carry your bags

Working with an agency producer

If you work at an agency large enough to have a broadcast producer, you have expert help in developing a campaign for television. The producer acts as a business manager and as a creative consultant. A good agency producer knows how to negotiate fees, where to cut costs, and how best to stay on budget. On the creative side, he or she knows where to find the best talent and the most accommodating facilities for every phase of production, from prop-finding to postproduction editing.

Together with the producer, the creative team selects the creative suppliers they want. First, the director, and then—with the director's help—the film editors, the actors and actresses, composers and lyricists. The producer will also help in finding the best studio for the job, and the best suppliers for costumes and props.

Choosing the director

The director you hire takes your storyboards and brings them to life. To some extent, when you pass on your ideas to a director, you are also handing over control of the project. It is therefore essential that you take care to choose the right director for your project.

Before you make a decision, consider the effect you wish to create in the commercial, the image your client has in the marketplace, the degree to which your storyboard is developed, and the budget and deadline for your project. Just like commercial photographers and illustrators, directors specialize. Some work better with people. Some cast for drama and realism, others cast for comedy. Still others have a better eye for landscapes or nature. Some work best with foods, others with cars. Director's imprints can be found in every aspect of film production—the look they bring to the visual part of the communication, the way in which lighting and camera angles are used in cinematography, the choice of the background music, the way in which the lines of dialog are delivered, and in the pacing of the frames, highlighting some while minimizing others.

Preproduction meetings

Preproduction meetings take place after the concept or campaign has been approved by the client, and after the director has been hired, but before another step is taken. It is imperative that these meetings take place early, because you want to make certain that the director and everyone else involved understands your storyboard. There should be no room for misinterpretation. Only through careful and early analysis of the concept, and of the director's plans for conveying that concept can you be sure that the idea you sold to the client does not go off track during filming.

The purpose of preproduction meetings, then, is to iron out any differences in perception as soon as they occur. Work through the entire project with the director, ask for his or her opinion on the script and the storyboard. Make sure you know exactly where the director intends to take them from here. Every frame should be carefully reviewed, as should every line of script. Any changes that you make should be reported immediately to the client before they are finalized.

During filming

At the shoot, your main responsibility as art director is to work alongside the director. You must keep track of all the director does and each decision he or she makes.

You are present at the shoot to make sure that the advertising concept is captured successfully during filming. The director may have suggestions that make aesthetic improvements, but remember, they are *suggestions.* It is up to you and your client to approve or reject them.

Once the director has finalized the film set and the lighting and camera moves, it is the art director's responsibility to look through the camera and make sure that each scene is an accurate representation of the storyboard. Most often, cameras are set up with videocameras attached so that you can receive instant playbacks. By looking through the lens, you can get an actual idea of what you will see in the frame. By looking at the videotape, you'll be able to monitor the scene from a broader perspective.

It is also the art director's responsibility to pay attention to detail. Listen to how each line of dialog is delivered, contrast the colors of the actors' and actresses' clothing with the backdrops, notice whether the food looks fresh and appetizing. Attend to every detail.

Keep the storyboard at hand and make sure that every frame on it is shot. Setting up shoots costs too much money to repeat if even one frame is missing. Not only is there the cost of renting the studio, but the whole production crew and cast—often as many as 50 people—will have to be rehired. If you are shooting outdoors, changes in natural light may mean that each and every frame has to be reshot.

Again, if during shooting you and the director decide to make changes from the original storyboard because new and better ideas for camera shots or dialog have emerged during filming, make sure you inform the client first. If the client is not present, make sure you have captured the storyline as presented on the board as well as with the changes you recommend. Always have on film or tape every scene you sold to the client—it is the client who has the final say.

Television has been identified as the most persuasive of advertising media. Perhaps this is due to the fact that it appeals to more of the senses than any other medium. It also provides a closer simulation of reality, and is therefore more readily believed than other media. It offers the viewer the opportunity to identify with any situation as it is portrayed. Even though a commercial reaches thousands of viewers at once, each person experiences it alone. It is a personalized medium. And the sale is made one-on-one.

Radio Advertising

Almost all products and services can be given a fair chance through radio. For the copywriter, specializing in radio provides endless opportunities to develop writing and creative skills. For the client, radio can be a low cost and effective advertising media. It is much less expensive than television, even when top celebrities or broadcasters are used. Radio time can be bought station by station, and so regional advertising, in particular, can be obtained relatively cheaply. The turnaround time, too, is much faster with radio than with television—you can produce a radio spot today and have it on the air tomorrow.

Most people in advertising agree, however, that radio advertising works better for some products and markets than for others. It is generally considered most effective for local advertising, usually to narrowly defined target audiences. It is used most frequently by local businesses or local branches of larger organizations to reach listeners in specific geographic regions.

The wide variety of radio stations, shows, and formats means that the medium can isolate very specialized audiences. Your advertising budget, therefore, is spent only on those people you want to reach. Not unlike special interest magazines, radio shows draw certain people and exclude others. There are stations that cater to almost every musical taste, for example, from classical and country, to jazz, blues, and rock. There are talk shows aimed at different age groups; there are programs for special interest groups; there are sports and news frequencies. The time of day shows are aired segments each listener group even further. However narrowly defined your target audience is, there will be a radio show that can reach it.

Preparing Advertising for Radio Broadcast

With radio—as with all other advertising media—you must first consider your target audience and completely understand your product in relation to the market in which you are competing. You commonly have up to 60 seconds to get your message across, but radio spots can be as short as 30 seconds. The challenge is to use this time and the client's money wisely. Review your research and make sure this is the best media in which to proceed.

As radio communicates purely through audio, the next step is to work out an advertising idea or concept that will translate well into sound. Radio advertising allows enormous creative scope. Anything is possible. You can have elephants and rhinoceroses march through your spot. You can set scenes in the middle of a desert, or on the high seas. You can select dialects from around the world. You can have Benjamin Franklin or William Shakespeare promote your product for you. All at low cost on a comparatively fast production schedule.

The ideas that work best in radio are those that can be highly dramatized. Typically, creative ads can tell stories to keep listeners spellbound, they can introduce fascinating characters and dialog that can charm or entertain, or they can appeal to the listeners' sense of humor through exaggeration of characters or circumstances. As we have seen with print and television commercials, however, the maxim "one idea per ad" still holds true. Choose your idea or theme and stick to it.

Remember, too, that the average listener has a short attention span. On radio, you have no bright colors or trick visuals to focus interest. Don't overload your listeners. Make sure you highlight one selling point, and offer as little supplementary information as possible. For example, if your goal is to promote your client's image, make sure you feature the client's name center stage. Or, as shown in **Exhibit 7.8**, if you want people to telephone in an order immediately after hearing the commercial, make sure the telephone is a focal point of the ad.

Using celebrities and radio personalities

If you decide to use a celebrity to promote a product, the first step is to be certain that the celebrity you have chosen suits the image you wish to create. Make sure you know how your listeners feel about or will respond to a particular celebrity. Do you want them to respond in the same way to your product? How about the celebrity's style? Does this match the tone of your advertisement? For instance, if you choose the radio personality, Joy Golden, allow her to do what she likes to do, comedy. She is a comedienne and writes hilarious material. The same applies to Dick Orkin from Dick Orkin's Radio Ranch, and others. Each of these personalities is famous for his or her style.

```
Music:  (Under throughout.)
Tom:    Hi. Tom Bodett for Motel 6. A lot of you
        have written in lately and said, Tom, we'd
        sure like to make reservations at Motel 6,
        but you say the phone number so doggone
        fast, we don't have a chance to write it
        down, let alone remember it.

        Well, the folks at Motel 6 thought a jingle
        would help you remember it a little better.
        I told 'em I could just say it slower and
        you'd get it but they said no, they want a
        jingle. I even told 'em I wasn't very good
        at that sort of thing, but they said that's
        OK. So get your pencils ready. Here goes.
        (Sing very off-key) 505-891-6161.

        Ah, I told you I wasn't any good at that
        stuff. I hope it worked. I'm Tom Bodett for
        Motel 6 and, boy, am I embarrassed.

                        #####
```

Exhibit 7.8
A radio script for Motel 6. Prepared by the Richards Group (Dallas). Copywriter: Thomas Hripko. Reproduced with permission of The Richards Group.

If you are unsure about a celebrity's image or style, call the representative agent or office. Ask for a demonstration tape to review.

Hiring voiceover talent

As with choosing celebrities to feature in an advertisement, always consider your concept and the image you wish to create before you choose voiceover talent.

Again, you can contact voiceover agencies and request demonstration tapes. If you are casting for a sea captain character, for example, you can send the talent agency your script and you will be supplied with a reel of samples of the best and most appropriate people reading the part you have written. The agency may also send a general agency reel, a composite recording of all the voiceover talent on file.

Using music

Music can be used two ways in radio advertising. You can choose background music to underscore and accentuate a script and sound effects, or you can work with a composer and create a song—or a jingle—about the product.

Background music can be either prerecorded or original. Prerecorded or "canned" music is available from music libraries which can be found in most cities. Libraries usually stock pieces that belong to the public domain. This means no one holds copyright to the works, so they can be used freely, without permission and at no cost. You may know from the start that you wish to use, for example, Monteverdi's *Vespers* as conducted by Helmuth Rilling. Or you may simply have an idea that you want something classical, or something with a chorus that sounds as though angels are singing. Whatever your needs, music librarians can help. If you telephone in a request, the librarian will have a stack of selections prepared for your listening pleasure when you arrive.

Professional recording studios tailor public domain music into various time slots, usually of 10, 15, or 30 seconds. This is called a prerecorded *needle drop* and is available at low cost from studios.

Prerecorded music may not match your spot exactly, but it is cheap and readily available. A good sound engineer can help you find a selection and splice it in so that only you know it wasn't written especially for your commercial.

Used often enough, background music can persuade consumers to associate subconsciously the music they hear with a particular product or with a particular company. The obvious bonus here is that whenever they hear that score or that refrain, they will be reminded instantly of your advertisement.

Songs and jingles, too, can help reinforce an advertising message in the consumer's mind. In some musical advertisements a complete song is sung that does everything from describing the product and pointing out benefits, to explaining how to respond. In others, the song tells a story, and the chorus alone plugs the product. In still others, blocks of voiceover copy are broken up by short, lively jingles that are easy to remember and that repeat the key message of the ad. Be careful not to overburden the listener—ads that keep to one idea per song, or one idea per jingle work best.

Suppose that you decide your advertising concept requires a completely new song. Some copywriters work with composers and lyricists, others work directly with the composer and write their own lyrics. If you have ever wanted to write a song, here's an opportunity to try your hand at it.

Writing Radio Scripts

Radio is a writer's medium. It's the one advertising medium in which the copywriter has complete control over the creative process. Though a conceptually oriented art director may to some extent be involved in developing the radio concept, the finished product will come from the copywriter.

When writing for radio you are writing for the ear. This means that you must write the way people speak. Your choice of words, your use of grammar and colloquialisms should all reflect the way in which the voiceover of the advertisement will speak. For example, if you are writing a commercial for a western apparel retail outlet that is featuring a sale on silver belt buckles, boot tips, and other accessories, imagine how a cowboy or cowgirl might describe these products. First of all, cowboys don't speak of "silver accessories," they are much more likely to say "silver trimmin's." The phrases as you write them may look clumsy, but imagine how they will sound with a western drawl, or whatever dialect you have chosen. Every word of dialog you write must *sound* natural.

Don't try to say too much. Unlike print and TV, the message you communicate in a radio script is not reinforced by a visual. Those listening may feel overwhelmed if you give them too much detailed information and will tune out rather than concentrate on it.

Don't write wall-to-wall copy. Think of "air" in radio in the same way you think of white space in print design.[1] Used well, it can develop contrast and drama.

Even though you don't have the advantage of hearing your commercial as you write, try to place yourself in the position of your listeners. Read it aloud to yourself. Try recording it on cassette tape to hear how it will come across—choose words and images with which everyone can identify. Here's an example.

> It's the middle of the night and you've been standing in the rain for hours. Layers of wet clothing hold the night's 32 degree chill close to your shivering skin....

Who can't recall being so uncomfortably cold at one time or another? This radio commercial for the homeless brings an experience we have all shared home once again. Reading the words on a page reminds us. Imagine how powerful the message will be with a recorded human voice and sound effects added.

The scripts you write should be prepared with care so that they can be read easily at recording sessions. Double-space your radio scripts. This makes them much easier to read and leaves room for the voiceover talent to pencil in instructions or changes. Make sure you spell out colloquialisms or inflexions in dialog the way they should be pronounced, for example, leave *g*s off *-ing* endings when appropriate. Write out all figures or abbreviations the way they are to be spoken—write "five dollars" instead of $5.00. By paying attention to such minor details as these you will be doing all you can to make the most of the studio time available to you.

Radio Production

Copywriters often have a direct hand in the production of radio spots. As its creator, the copywriter can best decide how an advertisement should sound and how the copy should be interpreted. You should, therefore, be present during the recording session to make sure the talent reads the script just as you intended. You should be there in case the script needs to be cut or changed.

One well-known creative director suggests that every time you go to the studio to produce a radio spot, you should have three—not one—spots approved by the client and ready to go. His rationale: you never know which spot is going to work until you hear it, complete with all recording tracks in place.

Here are a few rules that will make your studio session go smoothly.

- Show up early for every recording session.

- Make sure beforehand that your script—or scripts—is complete and has been approved by the client.

- Bring copies of the script for everyone who will need one. That means one for each voiceover, cast member or singer, for the composer, the lyricist, the engineer, the account executive, the producer, the client, and yourself. Bring some spare copies, too.

- Give the script to the voiceover and cast as soon as you can so that rehearsal can begin.

- Treat the voiceover talent with tact. Give the voiceover time to become familiar with a script and to try out different readings before you make criticisms. If you think the pace or intonation is wrong, speak to the producer before you ask the voiceover to try it your way.

The ideas described here, along with hard work and inspiration, will help you create dynamic radio commercials that sell. Radio is verbal, but it isn't read. Although it doesn't require visuals, it is a very visual medium. As we have discussed, the listener's mind's eye is ready to fill in the details.

The broadcast media offer unique opportunities to create advertising that engages the senses and plays off emotions of prospective buyers. Each message can stimulate action through stimulating feelings. You can make audiences identify with your product and you can build a long-term image for your client. Broadcast advertising is a path that leads you right into the homes of buyers and their families. This is where most buying decisions are made.

NOTES

[1] Roy Paul Nelson, *The Design of Advertising*, 6th ed. Wm. C. Brown, Dubuque, Iowa, 1989.

Chapter 8

How to Sell Your Ideas

Almost everything you do in advertising has to do with selling. Albert Lasker and John E. Power termed advertising "salesmanship-on-paper" and later "salesmanship-in-print." Others have called it "the high-end of sales," meaning that advertising is simply selling at a distance. As much as any salesperson, the advertising specialist needs to understand exactly what it is that makes people buy. Because it is so closely akin to selling, he or she has to become an expert on sales, too.

So far in this book, we have concentrated on advertising as a means of selling directly to the consumer. But before a consumer will ever see your advertisements, you have several other sales to make. You must sell your ideas to a whole hierarchy of people who will later be involved in putting them into action. First—and often the most difficult sale to make—you have to sell your ideas to your creative partner. Next, you have to persuade the decision makers within your agency—a group supervisor, a creative director, or an account executive. And then you will have to help the account executive make the most important sale of all—the sale of ideas to the client.

Selling an idea can be a far more complex process than selling a product. For a start, there is usually no single, visible, or tangible feature to which you can point. When you are selling an idea, you are selling a strategy, and all of the reasoning behind it. You need to analyze and be absolutely clear of the reasons why you think the idea will work and why you think it is a good one. Then you must explain your reasoning in terms everyone will understand. This requires a thorough and objective thinking process, that will take you from justifying your own ideas to yourself to giving a full presentation to the client.

Sell to Yourself Before You Sell to Anyone Else

Creative people are often their own worst critics. In advertising you need to be a perfectionist—you must convince yourself that your ideas are perfect before you pass them on. Be as objective as you can about your work. Find any flaws yourself and correct them before anyone else has a chance to criticize. Learn to predict how others are likely to react to your ideas and decide in advance how to counteract anticipated criticism.

Alastair Crompton[1] outlines "seven silver rules" for checking the merits of new ideas, and making sure they are on the right track. Use this list during the idea-generating stage to justify any decision or choices you make.

- Is your idea on strategy? Are you claiming the most important benefit and speaking to your audience in language they can understand?
- Is it clear to whom you are talking?
- Is your idea interesting? Is it fresh, provocative? Will it inspire people to find out more?
- Is the message instant? Do the headline and visual communicate immediately everything you intend the customer to know?
- Is your idea believable? Is it honest, and does it make promises it can keep? Or is the promise *irrelevant* to the product, and therefore unreal?
- Is your idea unique or unexpected? Or have you compromised by making it too similar to other advertising for products in the same category as your client's? That may make your client feel safe, but it won't necessarily bring in new customers.
- Has your idea proved its case? If you are making a claim, do you have support for it? Have you presented a logical argument or chosen a credible spokesperson?

Answer each of these questions before you finalize any new idea, any new headline or visual, or any line of copy or script. Cover all of the bases yourself before you take your ideas to others.

Selling to Others

You may think that a good idea will be easily recognized by everyone and will sell itself. This is not the case. In fact, it is usually true that the more original the advertising idea, the more difficult it will be to sell.

If a new idea breaks from a client's or an agency's usual themes or techniques, it may sometimes be too risky to try. For example, let's look at a Nike advertisement that broke the corporation's usual advertising style.

Look first at **Exhibit 8.1**, which is typical of Nike's pre-1984 print ads. It's a fairly straightforward "product as hero" ad, with a striking visual, a headline that carries the concept further, and lots of body copy that outlines features and benefits. Now look at **Exhibit 8.2**, an ad that breaks from Nike's previous campaign. Imagine selling as drastic a change as this to your colleagues and then to the people at Nike. It took strategic thinking and considerable preparation to sell Nike on an ad that was 99 percent visual and one percent corporate signature.

Exhibit 8.1

Early Nike advertisement. Art Director: Dave Kennedy—Copywriter: Dan Wieden. Reproduced with permission of Nike, Inc.

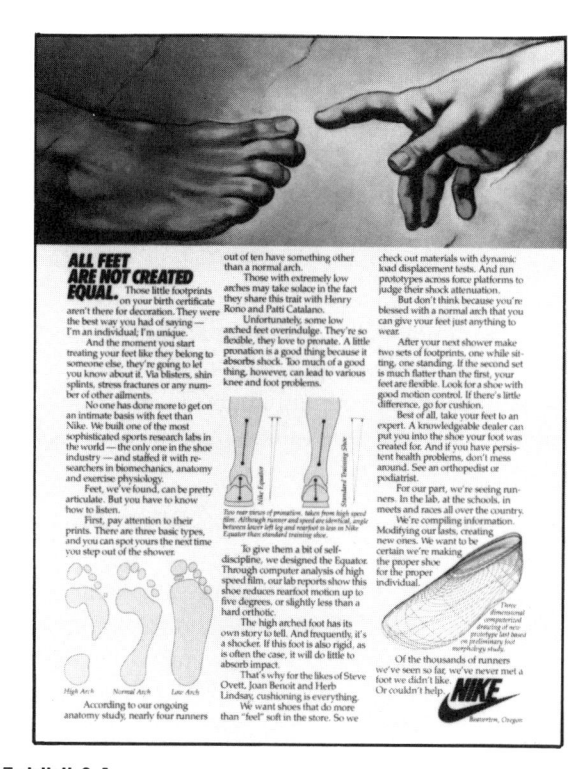

Exhibit 8.2

New look for Nike advertisements. Art Director: Dave Kennedy—Copywriter: Dan Wieden. Photographer: John Terence Turner. Reproduced with permission of Nike, Inc.

Any time you attempt to persuade someone to do something new, it helps if you can show them *why*. Selling creative work is no exception. There is nothing more persuasive than a logical argument, developed and supported by all of the research and thinking that you have done.

Some people think it helps to show two or three directions the campaign could have taken before you show the one you're recommending. Of course, your group head or creative director is most interested in the solution you are going to recommend. But to help this person see it as you have, it is wise to take him or her through the process just as you went through it. Review the strategy, getting agreement as you go. Avoid making this presentation tedious; streamline the process, sharing only the highlights—the crucial points where decisions were made. Include the choices you had at each point, then demonstrate why you made the decision you did.

Prepare well for this meeting. Sit down and make notes and organize the material to make your presentation go as smoothly as possible. Remember, your success in advertising is partially determined by your ability to present ideas persuasively. For reasons that have nothing to do with your ability, every campaign you present won't sell, so, it is wise to approach even the smallest project as though it were the one ad or campaign that will make your career a success. You can never tell when that may be the case.

Making a Presentation to Colleagues

Whether you are going to make the presentation to your group head, creative director, or, finally, the client, keep in mind that a presentation is different than a speech. When you give a speech, you are addressing an audience whose members often have different levels of expertise and interest in the subject. You have to pitch a speech to appeal to all of them. An audience sits and listens. It does not interupt, and it does not ask questions while you are speaking. In an advertising presentation, however, you may be talking formally or informally to one to fifteen people, all of whom have expertise in different areas, and all of whom will have opinions, suggestions, and criticisms of each aspect of your presentation.

The way in which you conduct a presentation and the initial impressions you make are all important to getting a project approved. There are a number of easy techniques you can learn to help you present your arguments clearly, improve effectiveness, and make the right impression. Look through each of the points listed below before you make a presentation.

- Make eye contact with everyone, one person at a time. When speaking, don't move your eyes from one person to the next until you have completed a thought. This is suggested for two reasons. By placing your attention on one person at a time, you make each person feel important. And by purposefully moving your gaze more slowly, you will cut down on distracting visual stimuli that could cause you to lose your train of thought.

- Even though it is human nature to give more attention to the decision makers and more powerful people in your audience, don't ignore anyone. It is not safe or courteous to assume that someone at your meeting isn't important enough to warrant your attention.

- Speak loud enough for the person furthest away from you to hear clearly.

- Watch how you use your arms and hands. Don't clasp your hands in front of you or behind your back. Don't fold your arms across your chest. Don't play around with your papers. These are all tell-tale signs that you are nervous or lack confidence. Allow your arms to hang comfortably at your sides, in a position that shows openness and confidence.

- Use one hand at a time to emphasize some point you are making, unless using both arms or hands serves to dramatize the point.

- Don't be afraid to use your whole body to demonstrate some action you took, or something that happened to you. This will help you create interest and empathy.

- Whether you're presenting only one ad or a complete campaign, there can be key thoughts or ideas that crystallized long before your ad or campaign existed. Showing how these developed can help sell your work.

- No matter how informal the presentation, if you are attempting to persuade someone to buy an idea, it will help to have visual aids. Make as many as you need. If you are using a "chart pack" (a large pad of paper hanging from an easel), prepare an outline beforehand that tells you the order of the visuals you intend to write on it during your meeting. Or write them on the chart beforehand.

- If you are using charts, storyboards, or comps, remember to stand close to them and face the people to whom you will be speaking.

- If you are using an overhead, prepare the acetates ahead of time so that you can practice revealing one line or one idea at a time. Revealing too much at once distracts from your speech.

- Comprehensives can be larger than they will appear in the media. They should be large enough for everyone in the room to see them easily.

- Storyboards can be presented, matted, with all of the frames on one large board, or they can be presented one frame at a time. The creative concept determines which method works best. For example, imagine that your commercial begins with a saying shown in reverse-type on the screen: "In 1920, women were given a voice." Following that, there is a cut to a close-up of a woman talking to the camera about a woman's right to an abortion. Then there is a cut to black and the words: "Now isn't the time to remain speechless." This concept could be demonstrated by showing three key frames, two with type and one a visual of the woman.

- Audio can enliven any meeting—when it's well done. If you record something amateurishly, it will only serve to make people nervous. If you're recommending music and don't have the budget for a professional *demo tape*, you're better off singing the words you would suggest or the jingle, as well as suggesting the tone for the music you have in mind.

- If you have a demonstration tape of actors reading for your proposed radio or TV spot, or if you have a sample of the music you wish to use, play it during the presentation. It can add drama and stir excitement over your work. Give it an appropriate build up and play it loud enough to get everyone's attention.

- As you summarize your presentation, tell your audience what you want them to do next. Be as direct as possible: Buy this campaign. Approve this budget.

- Once your audience agrees to your request, pick up your belongings and leave the room. Don't give them time to rethink, or to raise any new suggestions or criticisms.

Selling to a Client: Sales Presentations

By the time you're likely to be involved in sales presentations where you'll speak to large groups of people, you should have had several years' experience selling ideas. These presentations will call for more theatrics than your usual presentations. Most likely you will work with several other people, including a company whose business it is to develop multimedia slide presentations for sales meetings.
   Use the same basic rules to inspire and motivate your audience.

- Think about who you are addressing and speak to them in language that is meaningful.
- Make as few points as possible while getting your message across.
- Be brief.
- Use humor.

- Be interesting.
- Leave your audience with a clear idea about what you expect them to do. For example, "Choose this campaign." Or, "Participate in the franchisee advertising program."

Advertising is part show business. Not only should your work entertain as well as inform, your presentations should entertain, too.

Learn How to Take Criticism

There's nothing more disappointing than having work rejected. But remember that handling disappointment in a professional manner is part of the learning process.

Be open to criticism. Don't take it personally. It's rarely intended that way. Your critic is only exercising judgment, formed from experience. Learn from it how well your work on a project stands up to the challenge you were given, and use it to avoid making the same mistakes in the future.

A quality most admired and rarely found in the creative personality is the ability to be completely objective regarding criticism of creative work. Nurture this quality, and you will be better able to evaluate the judgments of others and incorporate those with merit into your work.

Learning to present your ideas persuasively is as important as learning to create ideas worth selling. Persuading others to your point-of-view may be natural for you or it may not. If it is not something that comes easy to you, don't give up, just practice. As you can tell so far, there are many skills that have to be developed for a person to succeed as an advertising creative. Selling your ideas to others is just one more.

Putting together a persuasive portfolio is the next step, and the step to take in order to get your foot in the door of an advertising agency's creative department. This is the subject of the next chapter.

NOTES

[1] Alastair Crompton, *The Craft of Copywriting*, Hutchinson Business, London, 1987.

Chapter 9

Putting Together and Using a Portfolio

An advertising copywriter or art director's portfolio or "book" is the calling card used to get each new job or advertising assignment. Your portfolio should always be a complete and honest representation of your skills and should contain your best work. Those who examine it should be able to judge your ability to think through and solve advertising problems, to visualize and to write copy or format designs. As often as not, your portfolio is going to be seen before you are, so put it together with care.

What Should Be Represented in a Junior Portfolio?

If you are developing your portfolio to land your first job, it stands to reason that you will not have finished or produced pieces to show. Your portfolio will be made up of *speculative work*. That's fine. It may be comforting to know that even senior people show speculative work when it happens to be their best.

Opinions vary as to the number of pieces needed to fill a junior portfolio. Some experienced professionals claim that 15 to 20 pieces are necessary. Others say that 10 of a junior's best work are sufficient. The number of pieces will be determined by the range of products or services you choose to work on and the number and type of campaigns selected. So that you have something to aim for, plan on including somewhere between 10 and 20 pieces.

Campaigns

Opinions vary, too, on the number of campaign ideas that should be developed in a junior portfolio, but if you have at least three, you're safe.

The number of pieces in a campaign can also vary. A campaign can be either single- or multi-media. One campaign may include three print ads, two television commercials, three radio spots, and one outdoor board. Another campaign may be comprised of print ads only. Yet another may have two television commercials backed by one outdoor billboard.

Showing at least three differently compiled campaigns will demonstrate your ability to come up with solutions that can be translated into several executions and across two or more media.

Print or broadcast?

Junior copywriters and art directors need to master print concepts before tackling broadcast commercials. Because it is unlikely that you will be working on television or radio commercials in your first job, your highest priority in preparing a portfolio is to prove that you can create powerful and memorable print samples.

For each campaign, concentrate on developing two or three print pieces. For at least two of the campaigns, you can also include from one to three television commercials. If you are a writer, create at least one additional radio spot. If you are an art director, include a sample of outdoor advertising.

How to Choose Products to Advertise in Speculative Work

Here are some dos and don'ts for choosing exactly what to advertise in your portfolio.

- *Do* find products or services that inspire you.

- *Do* choose one or two products that have difficult or unusual problems to solve. Choose, for example, a parity product like a soft drink, a product in a declining market, like a portable black and white television, or an underappreciated product, such as parsley.

- *Do* consider everyday products or services that fall into the following categories: packaged goods; parity products; hard goods (automobile or lawn mowers, for instance); consumer electronics; fashion or cosmetics; public service; retail goods; or new products.

- *Don't* work on a product that is represented by the agency at which you are applying for a job. This invites the agency to compare its finished ad with your speculative work. The agency has the advantage of having access to much more information than you, and is likely to be critical of your efforts.

- *Don't* take a bad ad and redo it. Work from original ideas.

- *Don't* take an existing campaign and extend it. This does not show strong powers of creativity.

- Ignore these rules if you come up with a great idea that breaks them.

Compiling a Portfolio

In any portfolio you put together there will be some pieces you prefer to others or that you judge to be better than others. Look through each of your pieces and decide which you think are the most creative and which best represent your abilities and style.

Here are a few guidelines on how to order and compile your portfolio to make it as professional, as interesting, and as easy to use as possible.

- Place the very best ad first. If that is part of a campaign, begin with the very best ad in the campaign.

- Place your next best ad last. This will create a good final impression.

- Place the rest of your work in an order that reflects variety and flexibility.

- Keep all pieces of a campaign together. (If your storyboards are oversize, however, keep these at the back so that your portfolio is easier to study.)

- If you choose a portfolio with sleeves, place any comprehensives of print ads on the right-hand side of the page, and the body copy on the facing left-hand page. That way, everything can be seen at a glance.

- Give each idea the spotlight by presenting one idea on each page, or on each set of facing pages.

- Don't make interviewers search for pieces that go together. Keep copy and concepts together, and, as we have seen, keep elements of the same campaign together.

- When everything is in place, go through your portfolio again and make sure it is interesting. As David Ogilvy said, "Nobody ever bored anybody into buying anything."

Some job-hunters prepare two complete portfolios of their work. This is a good idea if you are looking for jobs in more than one city, or if you are called to interview by one agency while your portfolio is being screened by another. A second portfolio is a good backup in case of loss or damage. If you can afford the time and money to put it together, by all means create a second portfolio. At the very least, make sure you keep copies of all your work in case of emergency.

Portfolio Cases, Lamination, and Paper Quality

Most people in advertising carry a standard black portfolio case. Most are of vinyl, made to look like leather. As for size, the smallest case is 8 1/2" x 11". The largest case a junior would need is 17" x 21". A more experienced copywriter or art director who has posters to show may need a larger one.

Some portfolios are simply zippered cases. Others come with a ring binder in the center. This is used for attaching plastic sleeves which protect comprehensives. The ring binder also allows you to insert your work on pages that can be turned rather than leaving pieces loose in the portfolio case.

Lamination is a process of applying a low cost plastic coating that protects paper. Your copy should be glued or pasted to the back of the appropriate ad (if you have not had it typeset and placed on the front) before the lamination is done. Since your copy will be there permanently, make sure you've written it the way you want it.

If you choose to laminate your work, note that this will dictate the way it will be presented—it is more cumbersome to lift laminated pieces than it is to simply turn pages. Make sure, too, that your laminated pieces are in the correct order before you present your portfolio—you will not have a ring binder to hold them in place.

Before laminating, check the paper and marker quality of your comprehensives. Sometimes artwork is ruined during the lamination process when markers or ink run and fade.

Showing Your Portfolio

Many advertising agencies have a "drop-off policy" which means that, prior to interview, employers will ask you to send in your portfolio so that they can see samples of your work. Your portfolio, then, truly is your calling card and should be assembled with care.

On other occasions, you will be asked to bring your portfolio with you when you attend an interview. Here are a few suggestions on how you may best present yourself and your work.

First, rehearse your full presentation at home until you can present each piece clearly and without skipping any important points. You should also practice introducing yourself and describing your work in general terms. Just in case the interviewer does not ask you to open your portfolio during the interview, practice ways in which you can make this suggestion yourself.

Some interviewers will let you take control of your presentation and will listen as you talk through each piece. Before you pull any pieces from your portfolio or turn its pages, begin by defining briefly the advertising problem which each ad solves. Next, explain your strategy and then show your solution. This presentation style is particularly effective because you are showing your audience that you understand the problem and that you have thought it through completely. You are also engaging the interviewer in the problem-solving process. Producing a solution that is both well-reasoned and highly creative enhances the good impressions you make.

However, some interviewers will not let you present your work in this way. They prefer to look through the portfolio by themselves, undisturbed. Answer questions when asked, but don't interrupt or otherwise distract them while they are concentrating on your work. Prepare your portfolio as well as you can in advance and then let it speak for itself.

The Job Search

Cover Letters, Resumes, and Self Promotion Pieces

Foote, Cone & Belding's San Francisco office rates each applicant using three criteria: education, experience, and the cover letter. This is because the cover letter can often tell more about you than the details of your background can.

Remember, advertising is a creative and energetic industry. A boring cover letter or one that has been carelessly prepared tells a prospective agency that you lack imagination or confidence, or that you are not highly motivated. It tells the agency that you do not belong in advertising.

Think of your cover letter—and all correspondence you have with prospective employers—as a means of selling yourself. It is your opportunity to tell the agency exactly why they should hire you. Prepare it with as much care and energy as you would prepare any other sales advertisement.

Practice your concept skills here. Find a personal feature or quality and turn it into a benefit. Sell that benefit as creatively and uniquely as possible. The benefit in hiring you could be that you are willing to work for peanuts to get a start with a good agency. It could be that you have experience—or a special interest in—preparing ads for the product line they specialize in. It could even be your throwing arm for the softball league. Whatever it is, highlight your unique skill just as you would in a product ad. Tell employers how you will benefit the agency. Tell them what you will bring that no one else has. Sell yourself.

Many creatives dispense with the cover letter and create instead a finished self-promotion piece. This can be anything from a postcard to elicit initial interest, to a detailed, three-fold brochure. Again, treat this as though it were an ad. Find something new and interesting to say about yourself. If you lack confidence, ask your friends what they think is the most remarkable thing about you. Think about your lifestyle, your interests, and your experiences. If you are, for example, an active, outdoor person, sell this. Tell employers that participation in outdoor sports and group activities shows an adventurous nature, a willingness to accept responsibility and to take risks. A self-promotion piece emphasizing these qualities might, for instance, begin: "I risk my life for my employer every day."

A cover letter or self promotion piece can be as clever and as creative as you are. One copywriter, Sharon Rich, used her name to its best advantage. She sent out postcards with this line written in reversed type on one side: "How to get Rich quick." She used a cliche in a fresh and humorous way to set herself apart from others—employers didn't expect to flip the card over and see this line used in reference to hiring a copywriter. Later in her career she sent out a card with the line, "You can't get Rich like you used to," informing agencies of a change of address and telephone number.

Exhibit 9.1
Sample self-promotion piece.
Reproduced with permission of Keith Wymetalek.

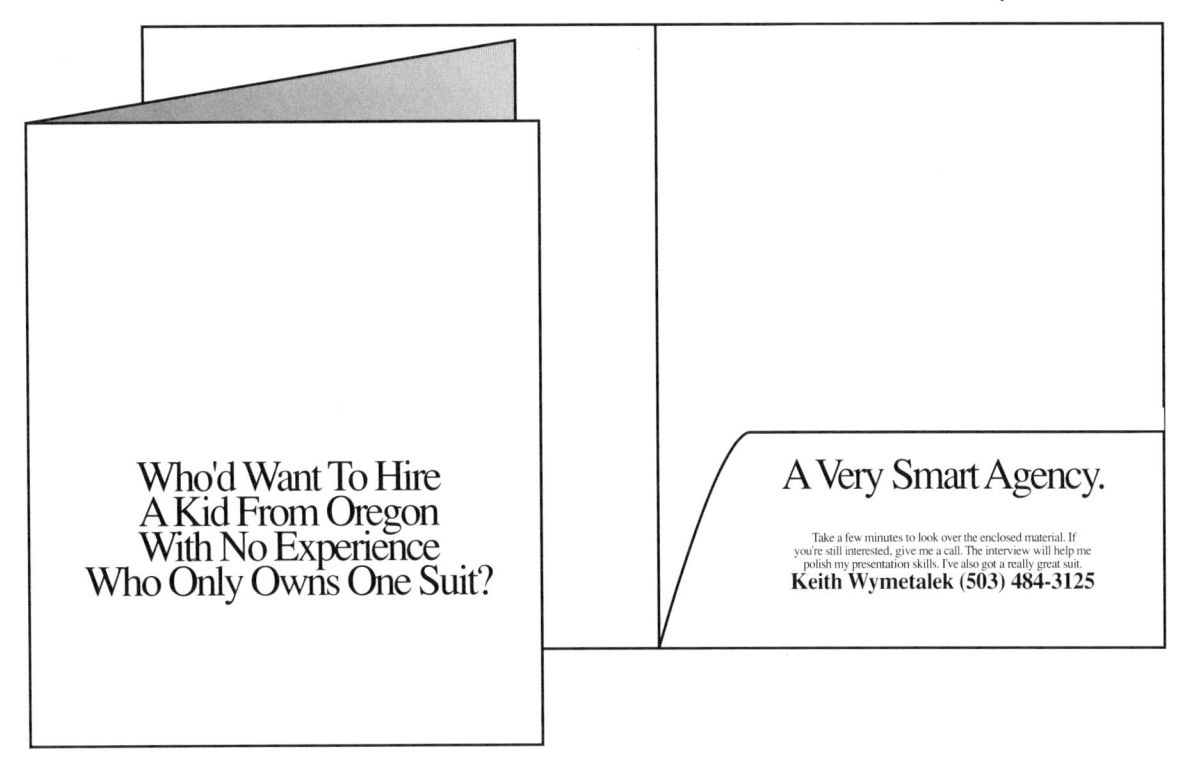

Portfolios 91

Keith Wymetalek, a recent graduate from the University of Oregon's School of Journalism sent this creative piece (see **Exhibit 9.1**) along with a resume and cover letter maintaining the same theme. Within a month of mailing this piece to a number of agencies, he was called in for interviews and offered a job.

For another example, consider **Exhibit 9.2**, a self promotion piece for a confident art director.

If you choose to send out a resume, here are a few points to consider.

- A resume should be no more than one page long. It is a summary, not a detailed report.

- Though you may be creative in terms of the layout, design, and copy of a resume, make sure your name, address, and telephone number are easy to find so that you can be reached right away.

- Clearly and precisely state your career objective. For example, don't write, "I desire a position in advertising." Be specific. Do you see yourself as a copywriter, an art director, an account executive, or a broadcast producer?

- Organize the sections on education and experience to your own best advantage, placing the strongest and most relevant points first.

- Include extracurricular activities, hobbies, interests, awards, and other tidbits that indicate more about who you are and how you can benefit the employer.

- Make sure your cover letter reflects or complements the style and tone of your resume. If you make your resume dramatic or humorous, for example, your cover letter should stick to the same concept.

Should You Use an Advertising Recruiter?

It never hurts to let as many people as possible know that you're looking for a job. Some recruitment firms specialize in placing senior advertising personnel. This is because they are paid on the basis of commission, assessed from the recruit's starting salary. They can make higher commissions through placing highly paid professionals.

As a junior, your best route may be to contact employers directly —if your portfolio is outstanding, you will not need a recruitment bureau to speak for you. However, if you do decide to enlist professional help, there are some rules of etiquette.

Only work with one recruiter at a time. Tell the recruiter where you intend to inquire about jobs on your own. It could be awkward if you call Saatchi & Saatchi, and the recruiter calls there on your behalf, too.

Are the Help Wanted Ads in the Trade Magazines Sincere?

Yes. These are advertising people using advertising to reach their target audience directly. Make it a practice to answer as many relevant ads as you see. At the very least, the more ads you answer, the better you become at letter-writing. Real jobs can come from these ads, so take them seriously. One word of advice: read each ad carefully and follow the instructions given to you. If the ad requests no more than five samples, send only five samples. If it requests written responses only, don't telephone.

How Often Should You Contact an Agency That Shows Interest?

If you genuinely believe that an agency is interested in hiring you, keep contacting the decision makers. Make sure they remember you by writing and telephoning them occasionally. Keep them up to date on any changes to your resume or personal details. Read the trade press to keep in touch with changes at the agency, and inquire about progress with your application if anything happens that might affect this. After all, by applying the same persistence needed to develop great advertising ideas to your job search, you will demonstrate that you are enthusiastic and interested.

How often you contact an agency is determined by common sense and common courtesy. Learn the difference between being persistent and becoming a pest.

If you are told when you telephone that your contact is not available, politely ask when would be a good time to call back. If you are told that your contact will be away for a lengthy period, ask if there is anyone else available who could look at your portfolio. If you are told the agency is not hiring juniors at the moment, ask if you can show your portfolio to the relevant people, just in case an opening should come up in the near future.

Your goal is to land a job. Each of these telephone calls extends your network and increases your chances of reaching your goal. You need to take care of your contacts and treat them with respect. But don't be afraid to ask for what you want.

Exhibit 9.2
Sample self-promotion piece. Art Director: Lloyd Wolfe—Copywriter: Marc Deschenes. Reproduced with permission of Lloyd Wolfe.

Should You Begin in New York, Chicago, Minneapolis, or Closer to Home?

This is a difficult question to answer. If you're bound for the fast lane, you may arrive there sooner by going to New York. It is still the most active advertising center, offering more jobs and more opportunities than other cities. Some say this is the real world of advertising. If you can make it in New York, you can make it anywhere. Because many major agencies are located in New York, there are opportunities to work on almost any product or service, in every media, and with sizable budgets.

New York is not the only center, however. Chicago, Atlanta, Los Angeles, and San Francisco are all advertising centers in their own right. There may be fewer jobs, and because of this, competition can be even more intense and standards can be higher. Other cities, like Minneapolis, Portland, Dallas, and Charlotte have agencies that produce some of the most creative work found. However, these agencies are usually smaller than those in larger cities and "run lean," meaning they don't have a large staff of creatives so there isn't room for many new juniors.

Starting off at a small agency in your hometown will help you build confidence in your ability. It will also help you build a portfolio of finished work. However, you may find that because the competition is less intense, standards are not as high. Learning to create great ads requires that you work with people who are good at what they do. You must learn from the best and compete with talented beginners. These opportunities usually do not exist in local agencies.

If you want to make the most of your career, you should be willing to go wherever you have the opportunity to do your best work. Your location should become secondary to the opportunity to develop your skills.

Good luck putting your portfolio together and progressing in your career in advertising. Of course, it takes more than luck to become a successful advertising copywriter or art director. It requires a commitment to do the best work of which you are capable—all of the time. It requires that you master skills in every area of advertising problem solving, from initial research and concept development, to transferring ideas through unique executions in both print and broadcast media. Most of all, it requires that you bring creative thinking to everything you do. The reward is inspiration.

Part Two

Computers:
The Added Ingregient

Word Processing

Typography

Photography

Illustration

Layout

Printing

Chapter 10

Word Processing

If desktop publishing was a revolution, word processing was its harbinger. For years, secretaries, clerks and writers of all kinds struggled with traditional "word processing" tools. From the simple pen or pencil to the clumsy but memory-capable "mag-card" typewriter, the tools of the writer have become increasingly sophisticated. The problem, of course, was that many writers balked at the new technology. Mark Twain was one of the first American writers to buy and use the typewriter, but he rejected it in favor of the pen, finding the machine too clumsy for his tastes.

In the same way, modern writers were slow to adopt the computer as a method of composing and setting down their words. And no wonder. The earliest computers were linked to huge main frames and weren't designed for anything as mundane as text typing. Then came the revolution. Now, we'd be hard put to find an office *without* a computer. Secretaries can't find jobs without computer knowledge these days, and it is the unwise college student who doesn't gain this vital skill prior to graduation.

Since word processing burst upon the scene, software programs have abounded—ranging from the sublime to the ridiculous. The earliest programs were cumbersome and quirky. Now they run the gamut from highly sophisticated to dirt-simple. And with all this sophistication available, how do *we* choose a word-processing program? Most of us just use the one that came with our computer. In fact, we become almost religiously devoted to the first program we learned. The reason, of course, is that it is time-consuming and often frustrating to have to learn a new program; and old habits, formed when we learned to use our first program, are hard to break. At the rate software is being updated these days, it's enough just to keep up with the changes in the program we are using.

How to Choose a Word-Processing Program

For ad copywriters, word-processing programs are invaluable; however, their needs differ substantially from those of a publications' editor or magazine article writer. Where these people deal in long, often complex written pieces, the typical ad copywriter works in short, uncomplicated "spurts." Where editors and free-lance writers may need the intricacies of a full-blown software program, ad copywriters may get by with a much simpler program. Regardless of whether you typically write long or short, here are a few tips for deciding on just the right word-processing program to fit your needs, now and in the future.

- Pick a program that meets *all* of your needs, not just some of them. This is not an impossibility. First, decide if ease of use is more important than certain special features. Typically, the more features incorporated into the program the more difficult it will be to learn and use. For example, do you need a program that indexes to write ad copy?

  A word of caution. If you are switching to a Macintosh-compatible word-processing program from a PC-based program, or vice-versa, be prepared for some changes in the way you're used to doing things.

  Not every program that worked well on one system is going to work as well on another. If you are choosing word-processing software for your Macintosh based on how wonderful the PC version was when you used it, think again.

- Pick a program that is compatible with your page-layout program. This is especially important if you are planning to use your word-processing program as a textual base for desktop publishing. Incompatibility can cause some real problems, and the fact that there are levels of incompatibility makes it even more difficult to match up your software.

  For example, some word-processing files may not transfer to your page-layout program at all. Others will transfer, but only as "text" files. That means your original formatting is lost. Some display other quirks when transferred, such as losing everything bold or italicized. Read the documentation that comes with your page-layout program to check compatibility. It will tell you not only which word-processing programs work well with it, but also which versions.

  Remember, software manufacturers update their programs frequently, both to add new features and to eliminate "bugs." These manufacturers don't ask each other's permission before updating. This means that the newest version of a word-processing program may not match the parameters of the page-layout program you have been using.

  One means of ensuring compatibility is to use software manufactured by the same company for each need. Remember, though, that any given software company usually excels only in one or two areas. For instance, Aldus was the first into the market with a page-layout program, *PageMaker*, which became the industry standard for Apple computer systems. However, if you work on PCs, you may find other programs such as *Ventura Publisher* from Xerox, or Quark *Xpress* more responsive. And, although you might find some auxiliary programs by the same company for use with your page-layout program (Aldus also makes *FreeHand*, for instance) you won't find them all. Some computer hardware comes with "bundled" software—packages containing "everything you'll need" for your new toy. Don't be fooled. To our knowledge, there is no *one* company with a corner on the market for any given type of software.

- Pick a program that is compatible with the programs of the other people who will be working with you. Nothing is more frustrating than knocking off a terrific piece of copy only to discover your layout artist uses a page-layout program that won't accept your word-processing program's format. Many word-processing programs have built-in "converters" or "translators" that allow files written in one program format to be transferred to another. However, formats don't usually convert *in toto* and leave many problems, such as no paragraph indents or missing type style commands in the newly converted version of the file.

Of course, compatibility across hardware systems is an ongoing problem. If you are working on a mixed system, with some people using IBMs and others Macintoshes, you're in for some problems. If you are all linked through a local area network (LAN), sharing a system should cut down on transfer problems. Most networks support convert programs that allow you to use Macintosh-generated files on PCs and vice-versa. In addition, there are hardware converters available that can transfer data among disparate system types or even disk sizes and formats, and the newest Macintosh comes with a built-in convert program allowing it to read directly from PC disk formats.

• Read software reviews and speak to other users for straightforward information on the strengths and weaknesses of potential software purchases. A number of reputable magazines, including *PC World, BYTE, MacUser, Macworld, Publish,* and many others, provide monthly reviews of both software and hardware. And, don't just take the word of reviewers and friends. Obtain a test version and try it out. Many software companies will gladly send you a sample of their program to "play with." They are usually fairly complete as to the various functions but may not allow you to save your work.

Remember, selecting the right word-processing program is one of the most important decisions you'll make as a desktop publisher and as a copywriter. It pays to take your time. If you try to project your needs are far ahead as possible now, you will save yourself a lot of heartburn later on.

Chapter 11 — Typography

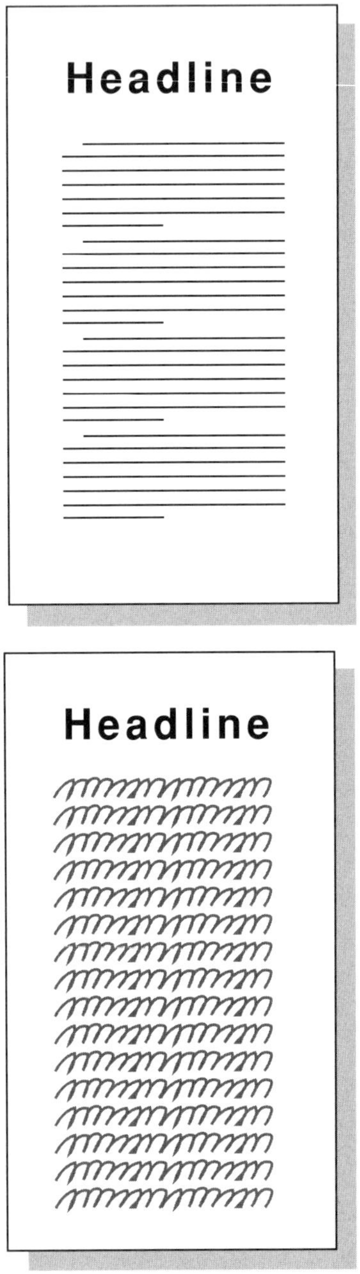

Probably the single most revolutionary breakthrough in computer technology has been the ability to set type. The advent of desktop publishing has been a blessing for some and a curse for others. It all depends on who you are. For years, art directors and layout artists struggled with "conventional" means for mocking up type. One tedious and time-consuming method was to sketch in type blocks and hand-letter display type (see **Exhibit 11.1**). Another method, press-down lettering, required the purchase of sheets of transfer lettering which was painstakingly placed on the mechanical, carefully spaced, and rubbed down and burnished.

With a little practice, *almost* anyone can set their own type for publication. While you can imagine the relief among designers and artists when computer-set type became available to everyone, computer-set type has not exactly pleased the typesetting industry.

Millions of dollars a year are spent setting copy in type. In fact, quite a large percentage of any print production budget goes into typesetting. Computer typesetting has cut down on cost and time. Before, you had to type your copy, spec it for copy fitting, mark it, take it to the typesetter, wait until it was typeset, proof the type, have the typesetter make any necessary corrections, and then paste it up. Now, typesetting, corrections and additions, and pasteup can all be done by one person at the same time. And costs can often be cut by a third or more.

Exhibit 11.1
Traditional type layout techniques. Indicating type on a mockup the "old-fashioned" way meant developing a technique for "graying out" the areas designated as type blocks. This gave an illusion of type without actually having to set it just for the mockup or comp. Two of the most common techniques were lining in copy blocks or rendering them as rows of "squiggles." The headlines were usually set in press-down lettering.

Smart typesetters and printers have been quick to keep themselves in the production chain by offering valuable services such as Linotronic output or some other computer-assisted production function. Many printers and typesetters now accept computer disks or direct feeds from your computer.

Desktop publishing has probably been of the most benefit to the smaller or single-person office. What once took a number of intermediaries to accomplish can now be done by one person. Of course, you have to know something about writing, design, and editing to have your ads look professional. Before, sending your copy out to a typesetter meant that a professional would be setting your type—someone with expertise and knowledge in type and typesetting. If you are going to take on this job yourself, you'd best become something of an expert in your own right. Fortunately, the basics of type apply to computer-set type as well as traditionally set type.

Digital Fonts

Digital fonts are computer-designed and -generated typefaces, and although type generated on the computer should be identical to type set the conventional way, it's not. First of all, computer-set type is standardized. That is, the eccentricities and flourishes of hand-designed typefaces are often sacrificed when the type is digitized. What this means to the true type afficionado is that many of the built-in irregularities that give typefaces their distinctive charm are missing.

For example, some of the older typefaces had different length descenders for different letter or word combinations or leading. For example, a *y* on a line above a word with an ascender such as a *d* might need to have a version with a shortened ascender, but if set above an *o* it might use a longer descender. This slight irregularity from letter to letter within the same face is what adds the charm to traditional type.

Bit-mapped and Outline Fonts

Your computer's printer also affects your finished product. Let's assume that for most publications daisy-wheel and dot-matrix printers are ruled out. If you are outputting directly to a printer for final copy, you'll want to use a laser printer. And, you will most likely use one of two technologies—a printer based on Apple's LaserWriter or one based on Hewlett-Packard's LaserJet. Both will give you quick, clean copy, but each handles type differently.

The LaserJet-type printer stores type in its memory as bit maps (dot patterns) that restrict the printer to specific sizes. If the printer has information on 12-point Helvetica then it will only print 12-point Helvetica. It won't print 24-point Helvetica. If you want other sizes or other fonts, you have to provide them either through cartridges or software that is downloadable (can be loaded from your computer into your printer). The only problem with downloadable fonts—and it affects both types of printers— is that the more information you download to your printer, the less memory it has. A standard laser printer with 1 megabyte or less of RAM (Random Access Memory, which is what your printer or computer uses *while* you're working) will quickly run out of memory.

Apple LaserWriter-type printers use an outline method of storing type shapes. That allows you to scale your type to any size, rotate it, distort it, print

Exhibit 11.2
Outline vs bit-mapped fonts.
Outline fonts (far left) are stored as mathematical values allowing the printer to perform adjustments of almost any sort on the type. The fonts print out "object oriented," that is, they appear as unbroken curved and straight lines instead of the ragged bit-mapped fonts (right). Although on some laser printers, bit-mapped fonts show up as near letter perfect, under a magnifying glass you will see the ragged edges. When used as display type, the raggedness is even more apparent.

it backwards, or anything else you want. This is important to desktop publishers who need to have the flexibility to work with type in all its forms. But, recent advances in hardware and software have allowed the LaserJet-type printers to approximate or equal the capabilities of the LaserWriter-type printers.

WYSIWYG

Another problem peculiar to desktop publishing is WYSIWYG (pronounced wizzy-wig), or "what you see is what you get." Many computers and computer monitors promise WYSIWYG, but when it comes to type, few deliver. The problem is that most monitors build images out of tiny squares called pixels. Computer type fonts appear on the screen as composites of these pixels regardless of whether you are using a LaserJet-type printer or a LaserWriter-type printer. The result is that you can't often tell from your screen what your type is going to look like or, especially, how it's going to fit until you print it out. This is mostly, though not exclusively, true of display type. The larger the point size, the more distorted it will tend to be on your screen.

One method of cutting down on distortion at larger point sizes is to load screen font versions of your typefaces in the largest available sizes.

Screen and Printer Fonts

Type fonts for the Macintosh computer, for instance, come in both printer and screen versions. You have to have both to operate efficiently. Basically, the printer font version is loaded into (or is already resident in) your printer and becomes available when you use it. Depending on your system, fonts can be loaded in a number of ways. Placing them into the system file allows some programs to load them as needed (which frees up printer memory after each font is used). Manually downloading them as you need them ties up quite a bit of printer memory which then can only be cleared by reinitializing the printer. Placing them in separate files for downloading later, storing them on a separate hard disk, or using printer cartridges are other options.

The screen font version has to be loaded into your computer system or program so that you can get a representation of that font on your screen. To save memory space, most people load a minimum of point sizes—usually 10, 12, and 14 points in each font. As long as some point size is loaded, you can scale up or

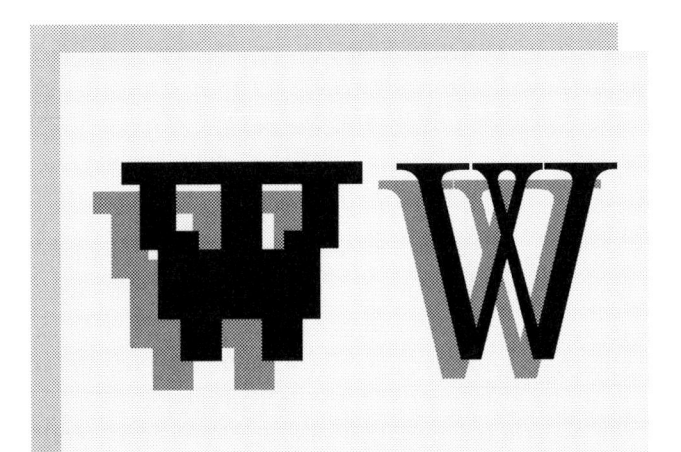

Exhibit 11.3
Screen vs printer fonts. The W *on the left is a 72-point screen font much as it might appear on a Macintosh screen. As you can see, the bit-mapping at this size can cause you trouble if you are trying to align characters or kern. The printer-produced version on the right (from an outline-font printer) is proof that what you see on your screen isn't always what you get.*

down to any point size you need. However, unless you've loaded a screen font in the exact (or near exact) point size you ultimately scale to, your screen type is going to look extremely ragged.

The problem, of course, is WYSIWYG. It is impossible to kern, for example, with large point sizes on the screen. All you can do is do it, print it, look at it printed out, and do it again. But, help is on the horizon. Already there are several programs (including Adobe *Type Manager*) available that help reduce the disparity between the type you see on the screen and the type that comes out of your printer.

Using Computer Type

Once you have decided on how your ad is to look you can decide on the typefaces, styles, and sizes you want to use. The precautions and guidelines that apply to traditional type also apply to selecting computer type. Some faces and styles go with certain types of messages and others don't. Let's look at the type faces commonly available as resident fonts in many printers.

Times	New Century Schoolbook
Helvetica	Palatino
Bookman	

In addition to these, there are several other faces appearing as "most used" on laser printers.

Avant Garde	*Zaph Chancery*
Garamond	Souvenir
Goudy	

Typography   103

The computer typographer can choose from among hundreds of faces available through dozens of software manufacturers in a range of prices. One word of warning. It is usually best to stick to the traditional faces manufactured (or digitized) under auspices of the original designers or their agents. For instance, of the hundreds of faces available from International Typeface Corporation (ITC), dozens of these have been packaged by Adobe Systems. As you become more familiar with type and aware of the vast array of faces available for the computer, you will undoubtedly be tempted to purchase some of the many cloned faces. These are basically altered copies of already existing faces. Since most typefaces are copyrighted, all you have to do is alter one letter slightly in order to market a clone.

The difference between an original type face and its clone isn't readily apparent to everyone; however, such things as line thickness, legibility at smaller point sizes, and clarity of individual characters can be important to your final product. We're not saying to avoid everything but brand-name type, but at least consider the best for your publications. After all, a lot of design skill went into the original type face. Use that to your advantage.

Copyfitting on the Computer

Copyfitting used to require patience, a ruler, patience, a calculator (or knowledge of math), patience, knowledge of type-fitting formulas and measurements, patience, and more patience. With a computer, all you need is a little know-how. Under the traditional (read "old-fashioned") method, you decided on column width and type size and the typesetter gave it back to you set that way. Unless you had a lot of money to waste, your copy might as well have been carved in stone. If you suddenly decided you needed 18 pica-wide columns instead of 24 pica-wide columns, you paid to typeset the whole thing over again.

Now, all you do is pick a point size and column width and *voila!*—it's done. And, if you don't like it, you can do it again. It only takes seconds. Naturally, some planning is necessary up front. It might be fun to sit in front of your computer for hours playing with column width and point size, but you're probably on a deadline. Once you have a basic design in mind, copyfitting becomes a breeze.

Although ad layout artists work with far less copy than other types of publications, for most page-layout programs, copy is imported directly from a word-processing program and then positioned on your page. That's why it's important to choose a compatible word-processing program and to follow a few, basic guidelines when writing your document.

- Use a program from the same system type. That is, don't write your story on a PC system and try to transfer it to a Macintosh system. It's usually too much trouble. If you're using *PageMaker* for the Macintosh, write your copy on a Macintosh-based word-processing program such as *Macwrite* or Microsoft *Word* for the Macintosh.

- Keep formatting within your word-processed document to a minimum. It is usually easier to write in word processing and format in your page-layout program. Some minimal formatting can be done, but most of it will be lost when you import it into your page-layout program.

- Don't justify your copy in your word-processing program. It will seldom match your final column width and will probably only confuse you when

Exhibit 11.4

Placing type in a page-makeup program. All of the modifications below were accomplished in under a minute. (Clockwise from the top): 12-point Times justified with auto leading; the same with 11.5 leading; auto leading flush right; in Helvetica 12-point; at 18 points; and auto leaded flush left.

I was a fresh, new journalist, and needed a *nom de guerre*; so I confiscated the ancient mariner's discarded one, and have done my best to make it remain what it was in his hands—a sign and symbol and warrant that whatever is found in its company may be gambled on as being the petrified truth.

Mark Twain

I was a fresh, new journalist, and needed a *nom de guerre*; so I confiscated the ancient mariner's discarded one, and have done my best to make it remain what it was in his hands—a sign and symbol and warrant that whatever is found in its company may be gambled on as being the petrified truth.

Mark Twain

I was a fresh, new journalist, and needed a *nom de guerre*; so I confiscated the ancient mariner's discarded one, and have done my best to make it remain what it was in his hands—a sign and symbol and warrant that whatever is found in its company may be gambled on as being the petrified truth.

Mark Twain

I was a fresh, new journalist, and needed a *nom de guerre*; so I confiscated the ancient mariner's discarded one, and have done my best to make it remain what it was in his hands—a sign and symbol and warrant that whatever is found in its company may be gambled on as being the petrified truth.

Mark Twain

I was a fresh, new journalist, and needed a *nom de guerre*; so I confiscated the ancient mariner's discarded one, and have done my best to make it remain

---

I was a fresh, new journalist, and needed a *nom de guerre*; so I confiscated the ancient mariner's discarded one, and have done my best to make it remain what it was in his hands—a sign and symbol and warrant that whatever is found in its company may be gambled on as being the petrified truth.

Mark Twain

Typography 105

you go to place it on the page. Usually, there is no need to hyphenate, either. Remember, your final formatting will be done in your page-layout program.

- Don't worry about faces, styles, sizes, and so on. You can assign them in your page-layout program. If you do use a specific style, bold subheads for instance, you might lose it anyway when you import the copy, or if you designate the entire copy block with a style from your page-layout program (see below).

- Set headlines and subheads right in with your word-processed copy. Even if their style is lost during the transfer process, they will serve as designators as you begin to format. You can always re-bold as you go along. Another option, is to set display type separately in your page-layout program. It is then more easily manipulated since it is a separate element.

Once you've imported the copy, you can place it, fit it, and change face, style, leading, spacing, and size till your heart's content. **Exhibit 11.4** illustrates just some of the adjustments you can make on your own, and as many times as you want.

A Word About Style Sheets

Although style sheets are mainly of use to those working in extended formats, such as magazine or newsletter editors, they can be helpful for longer ad copy assignments as well. In a nutshell, style sheets are electronic menus in which you designate how you want your copy to appear in its various incarnations. It remembers each description and on command will change designated text to the selected style. For example, *PageMaker* includes a style sheet on which you can pre-set type face, size, style, leading, tab sets, indents, alignment, and a number of other designations for any of several categories such as *body text*, *headlines*, *captions,* and *subheads*. You can also add categories, such as *kickers*, to suit your particular needs.

To use a style sheet, you simply select the portion of text you want to set a certain style and then choose that style from the **style menu.** In an instant, the original text conforms to your pre-set style.

Display Type

Display type is handled pretty much the same way as body copy. You can manipulate each of these elements to suit your needs. There are some special considerations you should be aware of, however.

- Don't always assume that the typeface you use for body copy will be just fine at 24 or 36 points. Some faces are better suited to headlines than others. The key to the proper display type is clarity. If it's clear, *then* check out the aesthetics.

- Be aware that the larger the point size, the more obvious the leading will be if set at *auto.* For example, a stacked, 36-point headline with auto leading is going to look very "loose" to the trained eye. The trick is to reduce the leading until the stack tightens up somewhat. Be careful not to let descenders bump the tops of ascenders in the lines below.

TIP: Altering the leading on display type on a Macintosh or compatible screen will often result in letters that seem to have been chopped off at the top. This is simply a screen aberration. If it bothers you, just switch to a different page view ("fit in window" to "full page view," for instance) and back. The image will clear up. You can also try moving the headline and then replacing it.

- Don't justify headlines. In longer headlines, this will create unsightly spaces between words. To center them, use the alignment command for centering rather than manually placing a flush-left headline in the center of a column. Aligning each headline will insure consistency.

- Designate in advance exactly where you want your headline to appear. In *PageMaker*, for example, if you want to extend it beyond your column width, simply place the text tool at the starting point, depress the mouse button, and drag a dotted square to the farthest right-hand point you want your headline to extend to. When you type, your headline will ignore column designations and continue to the designated point. Or, you can drag the handle out to the needed width (see **Exhibit 11.5**).

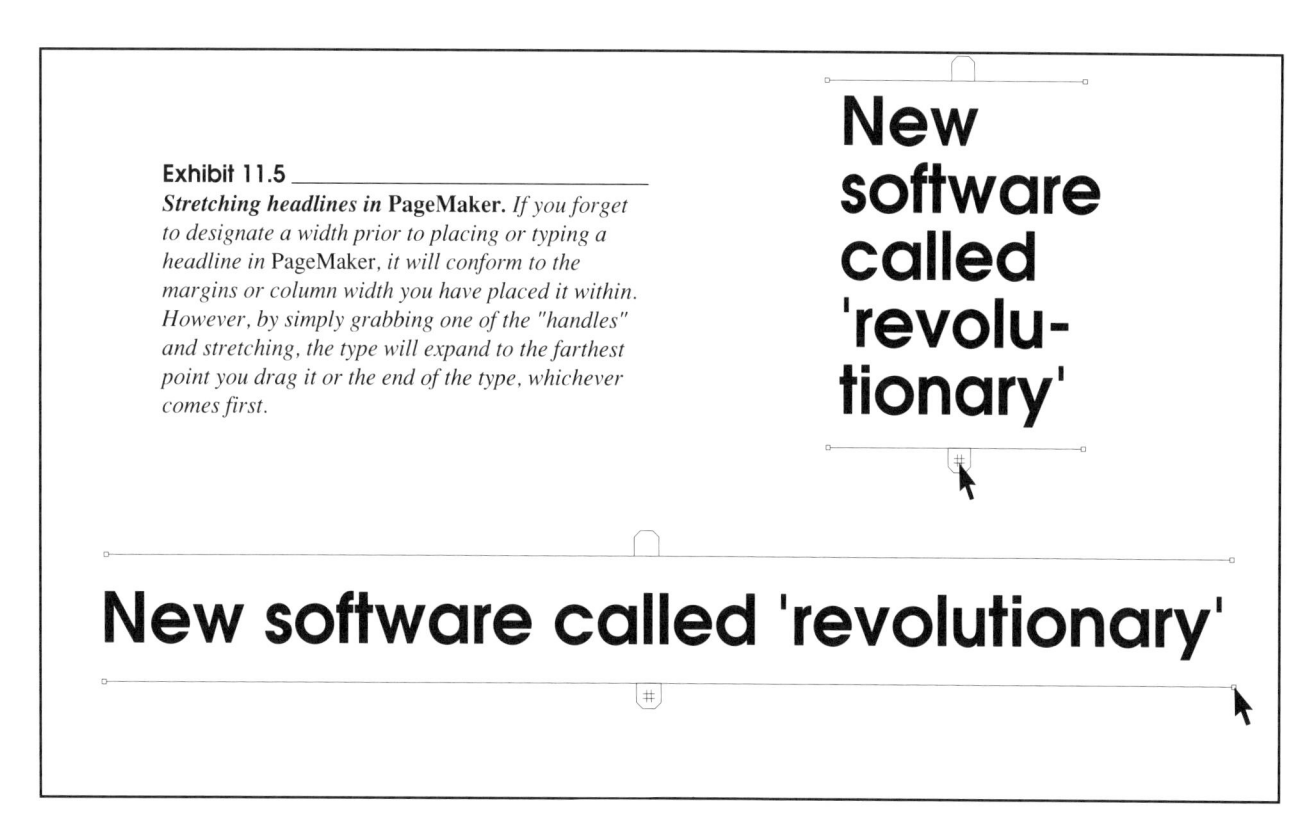

Exhibit 11.5
***Stretching headlines in* PageMaker.** *If you forget to designate a width prior to placing or typing a headline in* PageMaker, *it will conform to the margins or column width you have placed it within. However, by simply grabbing one of the "handles" and stretching, the type will expand to the farthest point you drag it or the end of the type, whichever comes first.*

Kerning

Kerning, of particular concern when dealing with display type, refers to the amount of space between letters (or sometimes words). Layout programs usually account for a certain amount of automatic kerning between pairs of letters in any given typeface. For example, in some faces *o* and *e* will fit differently when paired than *t* and *e* . But, discrepancies in letterspacing at larger sizes are more apparent.

Toy
Toy
Toy

Exhibit 11.6
Kerning. At 72 points, the word Toy *(top) has an unsightly spread between the* T *and the* o. *By manually kerning in* PageMaker, *we can tighten both the* o *and the* y *slightly (center). If we are not careful, however, or if we rely on the screen for accuracy, we might over kern (bottom).*

This was a problem with earlier versions of most page-layout programs. Headlines often looked awkwardly spaced. For instance, an upper case *T* might aesthetically fit closer to a lower case *o* in a headline than the automatic-kerned setting allowed. The newer versions have compensated for this by adding manual kerning, which lets you tighten that space to your specifications. See **Exhibit 11.6** for an example of how kerning works.

Using initial caps

In most page-layout programs, initial caps can present some problems. In *Ventura Publisher* dropped caps are created and aligned automatically with a few key strokes. In other programs, such as *PageMaker*, using them is more difficult. You can either designate the actual first letter of your body copy by bolding it and raising the point size (which requires manually adjusting the leading between the line in which the cap appears and the line below it), or creating the cap as a separate piece of copy and placing it in the body copy (which requires moving the body copy to compensate for the space). See **Exhibit 11.7.**

All in the merry month of May, the green buds they were swellin'. Young William on his deathbed lay, for love of Barbara Allen. He sent his servant into town to call at Barbara's dwellin'. He said,"My master sends for you, if you be Barbara Allen."

I was a fresh, new journalist, and needed a *nom de guerre*; so I confiscated the ancient mariner's discarded one, and have done my best to make it remain what it was in his hands – a sign and symbol and warrant that whatever is found in its company may be gambled on as being the petrified truth.

I was a fresh, new journalist, and needed a *nom de guerre*; so I confiscated the ancient mariner's discarded one, and have done my best to make it remain what it was in his hands – a sign and symbol and warrant that whatever is found in its company may be gambled on as being the petrified truth.

Exhibit 11.7
Initial caps. Although programs such as Ventura Publisher *allow you to set guidelines for raised initial caps,* PageMaker *requires that you manually set the leading between lines. The procedure, which is simple, eliminates the problem seen in the top example. Raising the point size of a single letter set into a body of text increases the leading between the line it is on and the following line based on the point size of the raised letter, not the body copy. To avoid the gap, simply set the leading for the block manually.* PageMaker *calculates its auto leading at 120 percent of point size, regardless of the face. So 12-point Times will be auto-leaded at 14.4 points. Since* PageMaker *doesn't allow for increments of leading less than .5, you must set your manual leading at 14.5. This allows the lines to remain leaded properly despite the raised initial cap. Make sure that your leading is set to "proportional" not "top of caps" in the type menu under "spacing." An alternative method on the Macintosh is to type in the letter you want in* PageMaker, *bold and size it, copy it to the scrapbook file, then place it by accessing the system folder and scrapbook file. The resulting placement icon will have a number on it representing the number of items in the scrapbook. Place only the last item (the first number showing on the icon), then "unload" the icon by clicking on the arrow in the toolbox.*

Chapter 12

Photography

The standard way to deal with black and white photos for publication is to have them halftoned. Printing presses cannot replicate shades of gray. They only print in *solid tones*. This means re-photographing them through a screen that breaks the *continuous tones* of the photograph into dots of various sizes. The larger the dot, the darker the area it covers (makes sense so far). Although the dots come in a virtually unlimited number of sizes, the frequency at which they appear is controlled by the number of lines in the screen used to produce the halftone. A 130-line screen will produce 130 lines of dots for every inch. A 60-line screen will produce 60 lines of dots for every inch. These dots literally trick the human eye into seeing various shades of gray (see **Exhibit 12.1**).

Until recently, even if you created your entire publication on computer, you still had to convert your photographs to halftones before they could be printed. Then along came **scanning**. Scanning is a term loosely used to describe a process whereby a continuous-tone photograph (or any artwork for that matter) is "scanned" electronically and is transferred into information that is readable by various computer software programs.

There are basically two types of scanners: **bi-level** and **gray-scale**. Bi-level scanners save information as bit maps like a computer "paint" program produces and works fine if you just want a bit-mapped reproduction of line art. But, if you want to produce a photograph with a simulation of grays, you're going to have to use a gray-scale scanner. Gray-scale scanners run the gamut from expensive to cheap, from "this is okay for layout" to "this is almost magazine-quality."

If you're serious about getting some functional mileage out of a scanner, buy one that will give you at least 64 levels of gray. You can get by on 16 levels of gray, but only if you're producing a comp or if you're just using your scanned

A Brief Glossary of Terms

Bi-level scan—A bi-level scan produces bit maps at roughly 300 dpi. Although bi-level scanned images look okay at greatly reduced sizes, they plainly show the bits when enlarged. They don't print well on a Linotronic since the 300 dpi is "locked in" during scanning and will print at that figure regardless of output device.

Cell/dot—The "dot" produced by a computer output device that replicates a halftone dot. This cell is itself composed of smaller **printer dots**. These smaller dots determine the number of grays in an image by their configuration and by how many are turned on or off. When you send your image to a printer, it determines how many gray levels will be produced by dividing the number of dots per inch (dpi) the printer can print by the number of lines per inch (lpi) in the image (as defined by your software or the printer's default setting).

DPI—Dots per inch. This figure represents **resolution**. The greater the dpi, the higher the resolution. Some typesetters, such as the Linotronic 300, are capable of producing up to 2500 dpi while the most the LaserWriter can produce is 300 dpi. Since resolution decreases as the number of gray levels increases, an output device with an ability to produce 2500 dpi is about the only way you're going to get anything approximating 256 levels of gray.

Dpi can be set on most scanners as **sampling rate**. For magazine-quality images, scanning at 150 dpi seems to be adequate. For images that will be enlarged later, scanning at a higher rate is recommended.

EPS—*Encapsulated PostScript*. The format in which graphics created in illustration programs such as *Freehand* are transported into page-layout programs such as *PageMaker*. EPS creates large and unwieldy files when used to save photographs. It is best to avoid this format for anything but illustration.

Gray-scale scan—Depending on the scanner, a gray-scale scan can produce up to 256 levels of gray. Although many scanners allow you to set resolution as you scan, gray-scale scanned images depend on the output device for their final resolution. A LaserWriter, for example, can only produce images with a maximum of 48 levels of gray; while a Linotronic 300 can give you in excess of 256 levels of gray in addition to excellent resolution.

Halftone—The traditional method of rendering a continuous tone photograph into a series of dots of varying sizes that can then be printed. This process is replicated on a scanner by the creation of **cell/dots**.

Line screen—The frequency at which dots (or cell/dots) appear in a printed image. This figure is controlled by the number of lines in the screen used to produce a traditional halftone or the setting of the output device in a scanned photograph. Most output devices have a default setting: LaserWriters default to a 53 lpi screen at a 45-degree angle. The Linotronic 100 defaults to a 1250 dpi screen at a 45-degree angle. A typical newspaper photo uses about an 85 or 90 lpi screen while a typical magazine photo is run at 133 lpi.

LPI—Lines per inch. This is normally representative of the screen you use in the halftone process; however, lpi is a determining factor in scanned image quality as well. See **line screen**.

Moire effect—A shimmering effect resulting from scanning an image previously halftoned, such as an image from a magazine. You can reduce this effect by scanning in the negative mode (if your scanner allows) and returning the image to a positive in a photo manipulation program such as *Image Studio*.

Output device—The device by which you print your document. It can be any type of printer (e.g., LaserWriter) or typesetter (e.g., Linotronic) or any number of graphic plotters or other such instruments.

PICT—A picture-type, object-oriented format common to many draw programs. It uses *PostScript* to print out on most output devices.

Resolution—Resolution is determined by **dpi** or dots per inch and can be set as you scan (see **sampling rate**), reduced during importation into a photo manipulation program, or enhanced or limited by your output device.

RIFF—*Raster Image File Format*. The working format in Image Studio, it takes up less room than a standard TIFF file and can be converted to TIFF, or other formats, if need be. At this writing, it can't be used as-is in many other programs.

Sampling rate—The number of dots per inch scanned into your image file (sampled) as a result of your scanner's setting. Many allow up to 300 dpi while newer models are offering 400 dpi. Theoretically, the higher the sampling rate, the better the resolution (see **dpi**). Lower settings (such as 72 dpi) are sufficient for locator graphics used only for placement in your layout. Most high-quality publications can use 150 dpi images quite well. Line art and images that will be enlarged later should be scanned at 300 dpi or higher.

TIFF—*Tagged Image File Format*. One of the most common file formats for saving scanned images. It is usable in almost all page-layout programs, photo manipulation, and illustration programs. Its major drawback is the amount of file space it takes up. An image scanned in TIFF can be reduced by lowering the resolution as you scan or as you import it into a photo manipulation program.

images as "locators" for final artwork in your mechanical. If you ever plan to use your scanned photos for a higher-quality comp or for a final ad, you might as well start with a higher-quality scanner. Don't assume that higher quality means higher price. You'll be surprised at what you can get for under $2000.

Even if you pay a fortune for your scanner, you're still only going to get a maximum of 256 levels of gray out of it. The only real difference between full gray-scale scanners is in the way they compute the levels of gray—a subject we don't need to get into here. However, you do need to understand something of how a scanner, computer, and printer produce those "miracle" halftones.

The Method

Photographic halftones are made up of actual dots. The *levels* of gray derive from dot size. Laser printers and other computer output devices can't reproduce dots of varying sizes. They only print "dots" of one size. In fact, these "dots" aren't really dots at all but individual, rectangular cells composed of even smaller cells which, depending on whether they are turned on or off, simulate dot size. (Most of us can't tell, even with a magnifying glass, that these are cells instead of dots.) This is known as **dithering**. To keep confusion to a minimum, we'll call the larger cell the **cell/dot** and the smaller cells that compose the larger cell **printer dots**.

The size of the cell that replicates a halftone dot is important. Cell size depends on how many printer dots are in that cell. A 4x4 cell has 16 individual printer dots. A cell this size will yield 17 possible shades of gray ranging from all 16 printer dots turned on (black) all the way down to all the printer dots turned off (white).

The basic difference between a bi-level-scanned image and a gray-scale-scanned image is the ability of the individual cells to vary their sizes. In a bi-level scan, all the printer dots in any given cell are either on or off. That is, the cell is either all black or all white. This arrangement is determined at the time of the scan and can't be altered no matter what type of printer you use.

Exhibit 12.1
Cell/dot. *The cell/dot (left) is itself composed of smaller "printer dots" unlike a typical halftone dot which is both the largest and smallest unit. Seen here (right) are dots and corresponding cells at 100%, 50%, and 25%.*

Photography   111

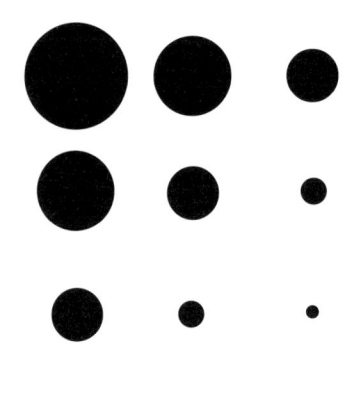

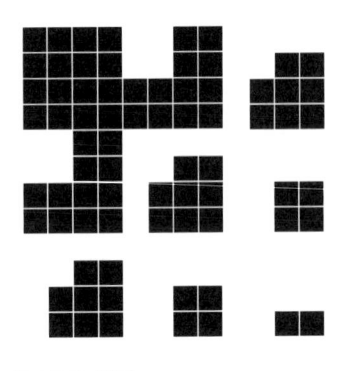

In a gray-scale image, the individual cells simulate varying degrees of gray depending on how many printer dots are in the cell and how many are turned on. This number, in turn, depends on the ability of the output device (printer or typesetter). The output device's interpreter calculates how many printer dots will be turned off or on. The printer interpreter divides the number of *dots per inch the printer can print* by the number of *lines per inch in the halftone*. The resulting number defines the size of the cell/dot.

For example, if you print out a photograph on a LaserWriter, the number of grays you will be able to simulate will be decided by the size of the cells the LaserWriter can physically produce. There is a relatively easy formula for determining how many gray levels you will get from a given output device.

$$(\text{dpi} \div \text{lpi})^2 + 1 = \text{number of usable gray levels}$$

dpi = dots-per-inch your printer produces
lpi = lines-per-inch screen you are using. Either you designate this before you print by using your software program or it defaults to the printer. In the case of a LaserWriter, the default line screen is 53 lpi (regardless of the fact that other sources including Apple place it at 60).

Exhibit 12.2
Dots or cells? The pattern above shows halftone dots ranging in size from 100% to 10% and corresponding cell/dots.

Let's assume that you set your line screen in *PageMaker* to 75 lpi before you print. So, knowing that a LaserWriter produces 300 dpi, your formula would look like this:

$$(300 \div 75)^2 = 16 + 1 = 17 \text{ levels of gray}$$

This means that your printer will produce a 16-dot cell (4x4). Adding one to that number represents the cell with no printer dots turned on—or white—giving you 17 possible gray levels.

If you let the printer default to 53 lpi, you get more levels of gray. Thus:

$$(300 \div 53)^2 = 32 + 1 = 33 \text{ levels of gray}$$

This brings up an interesting point. You would think that by increasing the resolution (number of lines per inch) you would automatically get a better looking photo. Not so. As you can see from the results of the above examples, the finer the screen (the more lines per inch), the fewer the gray levels. The reason is not so complex as it might seem.

The size of the cell determines not only the possible number of grays that will result, but also the resolution of your image. A 4x4 cell composed of 16 printer dots yields 17 levels (including white). An 8x8 cell composed of 64 printer dots yields 65 levels of gray (including white). However, *resolution decreases as number of gray levels increases.* Why? Because the size of the individual cells increases as the number of printer dots in them increases. The result is that the cells take up more room. A larger cell/dot means a larger screen size because certain size cells will only accommodate certain screen settings (lines per inch). When a finer screen is applied, the larger cell/dots are broken up thus reducing again the number of possible grays.

One way around this problem of increased resolution versus decreased gray levels is to use an output device that produces smaller cell/dots that can contain a more complete gray-scale. Although the number of printer dots within the cells depends on the above formula, the actual physical size of the final cell/dot can change depending on the printer you are using. A Linotronic 300, for example, produces a much smaller cell/dot than a LaserWriter, thus allowing for more dots per inch. In fact, the Linotronic 100 can produce up to 1270 dpi (the Linotronic 300, twice that many). That means that a cell/dot printed on the Linotronic 100 at 150 lpi (the Linotronic can actually print much higher in lpi than that) only takes up 1/150 of an inch. If you remember, the LaserWriter default screen is only 53 lpi, so each cell/dot will take up a whopping 1/50 of an inch. You can see what this means for resolution. Obviously, printing to an output device that allows for higher lpi will give your scanned photograph a much higher resolution and take advantage of as many gray levels as possible.

Again, don't expect that even with line screens of magazine quality (133 lpi) you're going to get 256 or even 64 shades of gray just because that's what you scanned your photo at. For example, supposing you run a photo on the Linotronic 100, screened at 133 lpi. Then:

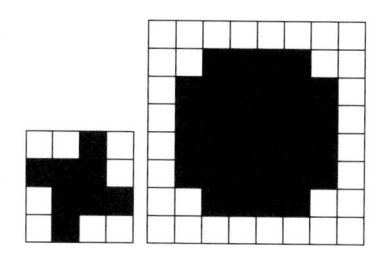

Exhibit 12.3

Cell/dot size. The 4x4 printer cells in the cell/dot on the left will produce up to 17 different combinations representing 17 different levels of gray. When cell/dot size is raised to 8x8, the number of potential gray levels goes up to 65 (64 with varying degrees of black and one solid white).

$$(1270 \text{ dpi} \div 133 \text{ lpi})^2 = 91 + 1 = 92 \text{ levels of gray}$$

As you can see, you only (*only?*) get 92 levels of gray. For most of us, that's plenty; but to the trained or discerning eye, there will be noticeable problems. The most common problem is "banding"—an unsightly demarcation between gray levels in which not enough differentiation has been made. The obvious solution is to either increase the dpi (go to a Linotronic 300, for instance) or decrease the lpi.

The Process

Let's suppose you have a scanner, or access to one. Here's how the process works, in a nutshell.

1. Place your original photograph on the scanner. You should start with a good original. Here's why:

    - When you scan photos that have already been published or printed, you are laying one dot pattern over another. There is literally no way you can align your scanner so that your scanning pattern will match

Exhibit 12.4
MacPaint *dithered photo. Cell size is unalterable in this bi-level-scanned photo. The cell/dots are either 100% on or 100% off. The result is a very rough simulation of gray areas based on size and arrangement of cell/dots.*

the original halftone screen. You'll often get a disturbing *moire* effect—the result of superimposing two incompatible patterns on each other—usually most noticeable in backgrounds and solid gray areas where it will give your image a sort of mottled look.

- Since a typical halftone darkens with each generation it goes through in the publication process, it is best to start with a low-contrast (flat) photo. Printers and lithographers will tell you that the best results are obtained from a scanned photo in which the lightest areas are at least 10 percent gray and the darkest areas are no more than 90 percent.

    Few scanners allow you to set this kind of detailed assignment of light versus dark areas. However, photo retouching and manipulation programs such as *Digital Darkroom* and *Image Studio* now include techniques for making these adjustments once you import the scanned image. See below for more on these programs.

2. Set the **sampling rate** for your scan. Most of the better scanners let you indicate how many dots per inch you want to store from your photograph as information in your computer. Current wisdom recommends scanning at a rate roughly analogous to the line-screen density or lpi you plan to use when you print. Both *PageMaker* and *Image Studio* recommend scanning

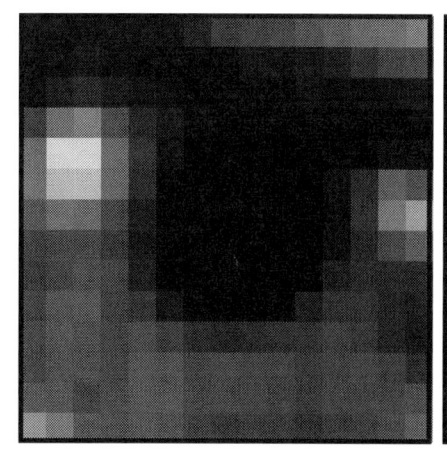

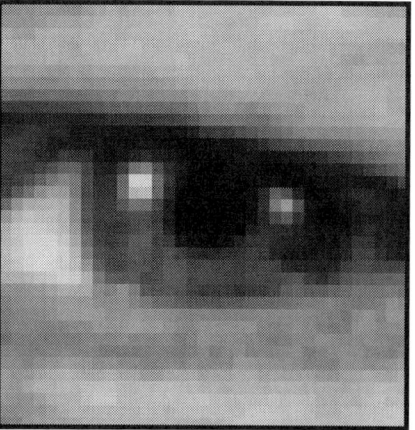

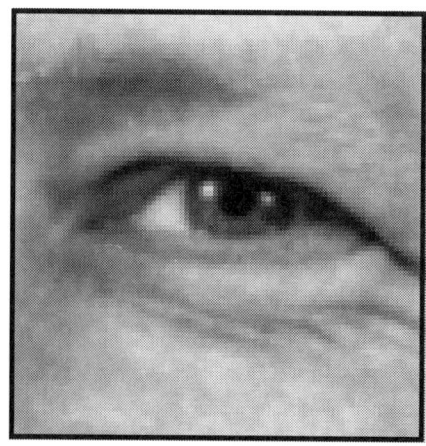

Exhibit 12.5
Gray-scale scanning. This photo, scanned at 150 dpi at 256 levels of gray, shows the individual pixels when blown up. Even then, it maintains a much closer simulation of the various gray levels.

at 150 dpi. When you scan at 150 to 300 dpi, you're really covering your bases pretty well. If you're using a scanner capable of recording 256 levels of gray to scan a photo at 150 dpi, you're creating an image that will give you at least 72 gray levels on a Linotronic 100 and more than 256 levels on a Linotronic 300. If you print to a LaserWriter, use the default setting. You're not going to get any better image than that produced with a 53-line screen at 300 dpi. Keep the following guidelines in mind when determining sampling rate.

- *PageMaker* recommends scanning any images for use in its program at 150 dpi, regardless of the output device. This is good advice. This dpi is high enough to give you excellent resolution off both the Linotronic 100 and 300 and won't hurt your output to the LaserWriter if you use its default screen.

- In some cases—photos with sharp diagonal angles, for instance—scanning at a higher dpi can *help* final resolution since at a lower dpi these edges appear jagged. Don't scan any higher than twice the final screen lpi, however. You're wasting disk space after that. But remember, if you designate a lower screen value in your output program, you void the higher sampling rate. That is, if you print to a Linotronic with a designated screen of 150 lpi and you scanned at

Exhibit 12.6
LaserWriter vs Linotronic. The LaserWriter *printout on the left is usable in some newsletters and for proofs. It contains 33 shades of gray because that is all the* LaserWriter *can produce at the default setting of 53 lpi and a 45 degree angle. Although other combinations are possible, this setting is the optimum. The photo on the right is run on a* Linotronic *set at a 133-line screen with a 45 degree angle at 1250 dpi.*

300 dpi, you're only going to get one dot every 1/150 inch—no matter what. This means that you effectively lose 150 dots, or half your stored information.

- Use a higher resolution sampling rate such as 300 dpi to scan black-and-white line art. It will take up more space, but it will give you much cleaner images.

- If you plan to enlarge your scanned image after you place it in your page-layout program, use a higher sampling rate. For instance, if you scan at 100 dpi and enlarge 200 percent, your dpi drops to half the original or 50 dpi. The reverse is also true. If you plan to reduce, you can scan at a much lower dpi. A 100 dpi scan reduced 50 percent will give you a 200 dpi image.

- Some photo software programs like *Image Studio* will allow you to scale your image by lowering the resolution as you load it into the program for touch up or manipulation. For example, if you are importing an image scanned at 300 dpi, you can lower the resolution to 150 (50 percent) as you load it into *Image Studio*. This also shrinks the size of the image file.

3. Choose the proper format for saving your image. Most scanner software allows you to save into the most common photo formats: TIFF (*Tagged*

150 dpi 256 gray scale   *150 dpi 16 gray scale*    *72 dpi 256 gray scale*

Line art    *Dithered MacPaint*

Exhibit 12.7
Sampling rates and formats. *With 256 gray-scale images, scanning at above 150 dpi is usually a waste unless you plan to enlarge the image later. (Clockwise from the top) scanned at 150 dpi at 256 gray scale setting; 150 dpi at 16 gray scale setting; 72 dpi at 256 gray scale setting; scanned as a dithered* MacPaint *image; scanned as*

Image File Format), EPS (*Encapsulated Postscript*), and *MacPaint*. Both TIFF and EPS files take up a lot of space. In fact, a complex, 8.5" x 11" photo scanned at 300 dpi could take up over 1 megabyte of space! Unless you've got a lot of memory, you're going to be concerned about file size. Here are some ways to save space.

- Saving to RIFF (*Raster Image File Format*) can cut your file size by 30 or 40 percent. Programs such as *Image Studio* use RIFF as an operating format (even though you can still save in TIFF, EPS, and *MacPaint*), but unless your layout software accepts RIFF, you're not going to be able to use it.

- As mentioned above, you can open your file into *Image Studio* at a reduced resolution, say 150 dpi instead of 300 dpi. This will seriously cut down the amount of file space your photo will take up. We've found, for instance, that TIFF files created at even 150 dpi can be formidable in size. But, when opened at a reduced resolution of as much as 50 percent the original loses very little when run on a Linotronic 300. Most photos will be reduced or cropped when placed in the final publication layout. An 8"x10" photo scanned at 150 dpi, reduced 50 percent, to 75 dpi, then reduced in physical size to 2.4"x3" (70 percent reduction), will still give you a 127 dpi image and a potential Linotronic output of up to 250 lpi screen.

- Scale your image as you scan it. If you know that you're not going to use an 8"x10" full size but rather at 50 percent, scan it at 50 percent and save half the disk space.

- Reduce the sampling rate. Remember, you rarely have to sample any higher than 150 dpi for any gray-scale image.

- If your scanned images will only be used for placement or rough layout, scan them at a very low resolution such as a 72 dpi *MacPaint* file. This saves you space and makes manipulating the images in your page-layout program faster.

4. Use a photo software program such as *Image Studio* or *Digital Darkroom* to edit, crop, touch up, and do virtually anything to a photo that a trained darkroom specialist can to.

5. Use a page-layout software that allows you to manipulate your scanned images further. *PageMaker*, for instance, has an image control menu that allows you to set line screen and angle (best stick with 45 degrees) brightness and contrast. In fact, if you don't set your line screen in your page-layout program, it will default to the printer settings automatically. Be aware, however, that in order to save file space, *PageMaker* only stores a screen image of your photograph. It won't look very good, but it will give

Exhibit 12.8

Cropping and Scaling. The advantage of sizing your images to your exact needs without going through the painful steps of figuring sizes mathematically can't be overstated. As quickly as you can think of a size, you can scale to it in PageMaker *and many other programs. Scaling won't solve all of your problems, however. If you have to fit a specific sized area, you may have to crop, or scale and crop both. As you can see, scaling alone won't make the original conform to a horizontal space when it is vertical. Of course, you could distort the image, but that won't make the subject of your photo very happy. The best answer is often to crop to the space you have to fill.*

you a good idea of how to place it, adjust it, and crop it. When printing, you'll have to "link" the photos to the file in which the original resides. *PageMaker* documents will ask you for this information each time you open them. Once you've linked the photos, however, *PageMaker* will remember where they are unless you move them to another folder or disk.

6. Once you've placed your image into your page-layout program, you can make a number of adjustments. Some programs allow gray-scale image adjustments to brightness or contrast. Most programs allow for cropping and scaling. The adjustments you make depend on whether you're going to be using your placed image as final art or just for placement. Here are some things to keep in mind.

- Cropping can be done in any one of the several stages prior to placement in your page-layout program. Some scanners allow for cropping before you scan; however, cropping as you scan prevents you from changing your mind later on. Although you can further crop the photo, what you crop out as you scan is gone until you scan it again. Photo software programs such as *Image Studio* allow cropping as well as many other subtle adjustments. Using this type of program also finalizes your cropping once your image is placed in your page-layout program. You should always save your original photo as well as your adjusted version just in case.

    The beauty of cropping in your page-layout program is that you can crop your whole photo to your heart's content. If you don't like it, just uncrop it. The adjustment isn't cut in stone. The only problem is that the original size of your image is always resident in the page-layout program file, whereas a precropped image only uses the memory it needs to represent that size.

- Scaling is the single most attractive feature of using a computer to generate photos for your layouts. In the traditional layout approach you had to measure the exact amount of space you allowed for your photo, measure your photo, scale it using a proportional wheel or calculator, indicate cropping to your printer or lithographer, and have your photo shot and screened in the appropriate size.

    Now, all you do is place it, and scale it until you get it the way you want it. If it won't fit proportionally, crop it to the proper proportions and then scale it again.

    Remember, if you know in advance that you are going to scale a photo down, say 50 percent, either scan it at 50 percent at the resolution (sampling rate) you intend to use for your final printout, or scan it at a lower sampling rate since resolution will double when you scale the photo in your page-layout program.

- Take advantage of any fancy layout techniques your software allows. for example, *PageMaker* has a text wrap function that allows you to literally wrap your text around your photos or other scanned images. This is very helpful if you are using silhouette photos that you have cropped in a photo manipulation program.

    One reminder, however: don't get carried away. Just because your program allows you to wrap text (or something else) doesn't mean your message supports that sort of look. Be sure of your intended message and its "look" before you experiment too much.

One of the great benefits of computer layout is the ability to make changes, change the changes, change them back again, and make some more. If you're careful and systematic, you won't lose any of your best ideas.

- Save frequently! Although some programs save automatically, don't rely on them too much. After each major change or addition, save your file. And, if you aren't sure of which page arrangement you like, save each version under a slightly different name using a "save as" function.

7. Don't take what you see on the screen at face value. Most Macintosh screens only show a 75 dpi dithered image. This means that you're not going to see a real gray-scale image until you print it out. And, if you're viewing a 300 dpi image on a 75 dpi screen, it's going to look much larger than it actually is. Both of these conditions will lead you to make a number of sample copies of scanned photos before you get them just right.

And, even if you do get them to your satisfaction off the laser printer, they won't come close to what they'll look like off the Linotronic. Using a high-resolution monitor will help. The Mac II monitor or one of the larger layout monitors such as *Radius* will give you a complete range of grays. In fact, the monitor image will often be better than even Linotronic output. Here are some things to consider when preparing for your final output:

- If you're using your scanned photos for a simple, not too flashy newsletter, scan at 150 dpi or lower and use laser printer output as your final image. You'll be surprised at how clear it really is.

- If you're looking for a more sophisticated, near-magazine quality look, scan at 150 dpi or greater (depending on whether you plan to enlarge or reduce the final image) and run it on a Linotronic with a 100- to 133-line screen.

- Bottom-of-the-line 256-level gray-scale scanners will produce a very good image, but it will darken considerably when it's run on a phototypesetter like the Linotronic.

  The solution is to learn to manipulate your images with the software so that your final product will match your desired product. This may require setting density ranges at 10 and 90 as mentioned above, altering brightness and contrast, or changing screen resolution. The trick is to experiment. Some scanners, such as the *Apple Scanner*, produce test strips using various settings. You can produce a test strip of your own by varying the settings on a page full of the same photo (or section of a photo with the most representative contrast) and having it run on the Linotronic. Be sure to indicate the exact settings above each photo.

- Don't fall for what you read about it taking 30 minutes or an hour to run one scanned photograph on a Linotronic. Sure it will if you run a 8x10 photo scanned at 300 dpi unaltered. If it takes up 2 MGB of disk space, it's going to take forever to print out. But, if you reduce the file size by one of the methods cited above, you won't lose any noticeable resolution and it won't take much time at all to run a photo.

TIP: In PageMaker, *"saving as" will compress your file and clear up a lot of disk space.* PageMaker *files with a lot of graphic elements take up a lot of space. Each move, crop, scale, delete, place, and wrap stores in your file, whether you need them or not. "Saving as" will save only the final version of each of these, not every little indecisive move.*

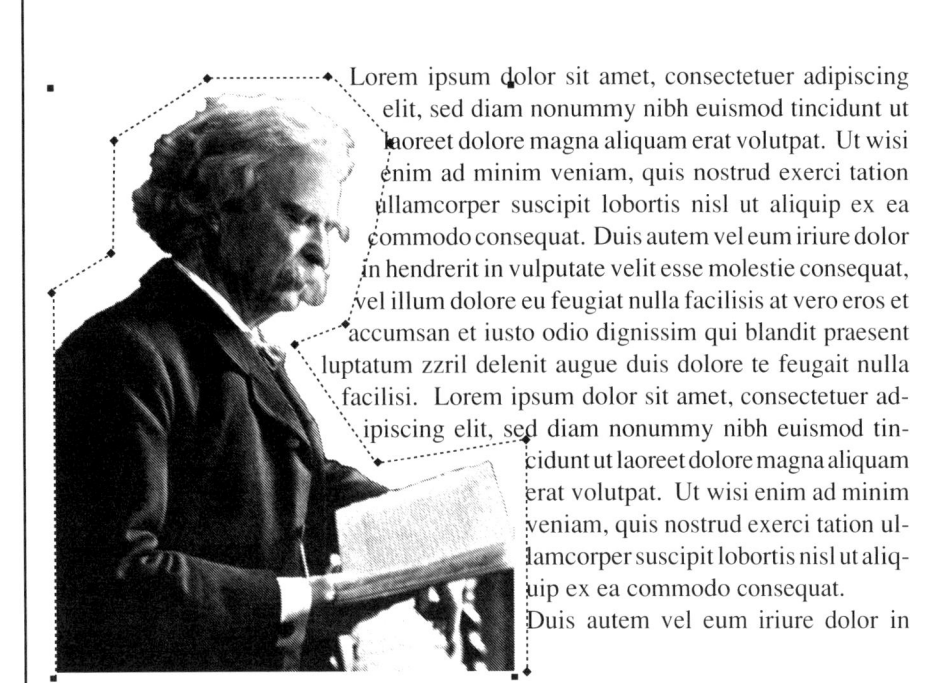

Exhibit 12.9
Text wrapping. One of the more creative aspects of newer page-layout programs is the text wrap function. *In* PageMaker, *it is accomplished by moving individual "handles" which then inscribe an outline about your image. Text flows automatically around this outline instead of over your image. At the bottom, the image showing how it would look printed. Above, with the text wrap function selected.*

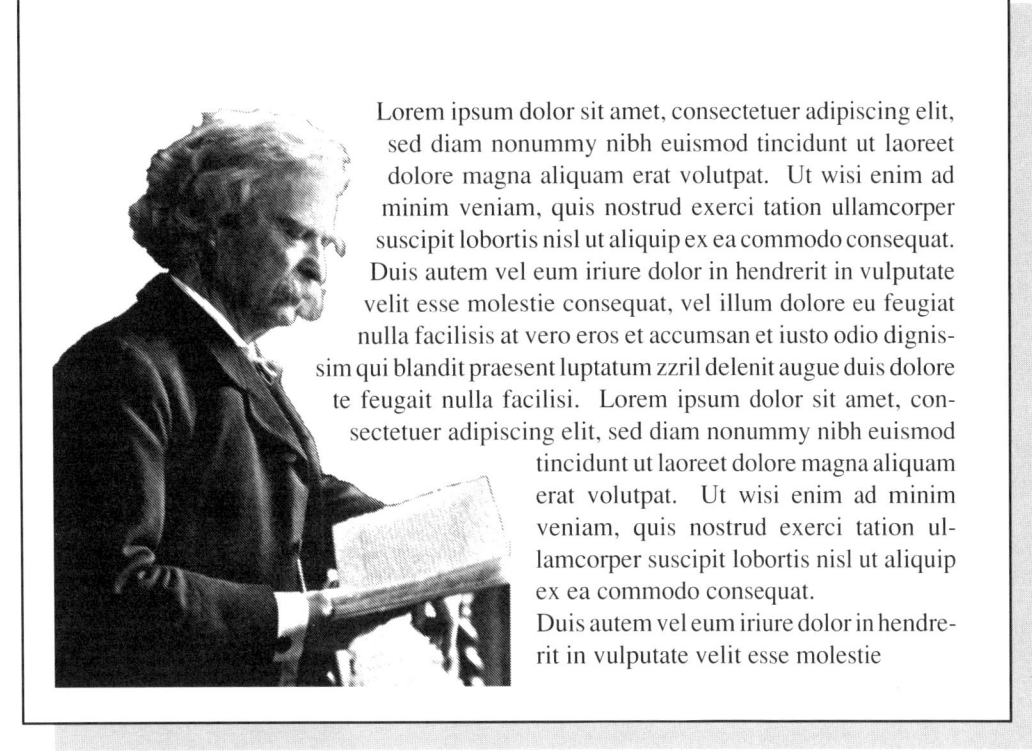

Our experience has been that a photo scanned at 150 dpi, manipulated in *Image Studio* to reduce file size, physically reduced to the final placement size, and printed on a Linotronic 300 along with a complete 8.5"x11" page of copy only takes from 4 to 6 minutes. In fact, we've run tabloid-sized pages with as many as five photos in 6 to 7 minutes per page. Remember, the size of the image file affects how long it will take to run the scanned image. And, unless you are certain your final product will come out right the first time, keep experimentation to a minimum. Experimenting on the Linotronic can be expensive, and every test photo you run will decrease the cost effectiveness of the process.

- If your final product will be offset printed, consider running your pages directly off a Linotronic as negatives. Although most of us are familiar with Linotronic paper positives (very much like PMTs), it also produces negatives that can then be used to make the printing plates.

    If your Linotronic service doesn't charge any more for negatives than positives, this alone can save you money by eliminating a step in the printing process—shooting the negatives from your camera-ready mechanicals.

    Another reason for going with negatives is that the photos produced on a Linotronic positive at anything over 100 lpi screen will be too fine a halftone to be reshot as a negative. The result will be a "muddy" image. Printing directly to negative film will save this step and maintain clarity.

Chapter 13

Illustration

Illustration is one of the hardest publication elements to accomplish on the computer. But the beauty of computer-generated illustration is that it can be manipulated at will and used over and over again. In essence, you create your own clip art each time you commit an illustration to computer.

Computer illustration can be broken into four categories:

- Art created from scratch by an artist using computer software, or scanned art or photos manipulated in some way after scanning
- Scanned art used as is after scanning
- Clip art (created in either of the above two ways)
- Technical illustration.

Let's look at these one at a time.

Illustration Programs

For artists or illustrators, the computer is just one more tool at their disposal. Earlier illustration programs were fun and easy to learn and use, took up very little file space, and looked just like computer-generated art when printed. For the non-artist, they were little more than toys; however, for the artist or illustrator, they opened new doors into the world of computers—a world heretofore left primarily to the number-crunchers and newly initiated word processors.

Programs like *MacPaint* and *MacDraw* (once put out by Apple and now by Claris) were pioneers in the field of computer illustration. *MacPaint*, a bit-mapped, freehand art program, allowed even the novice to play artist on the computer screen. The only problem with these programs was the final product. Unless severely reduced when printed, the bit maps showed the end product to be typical computer art.

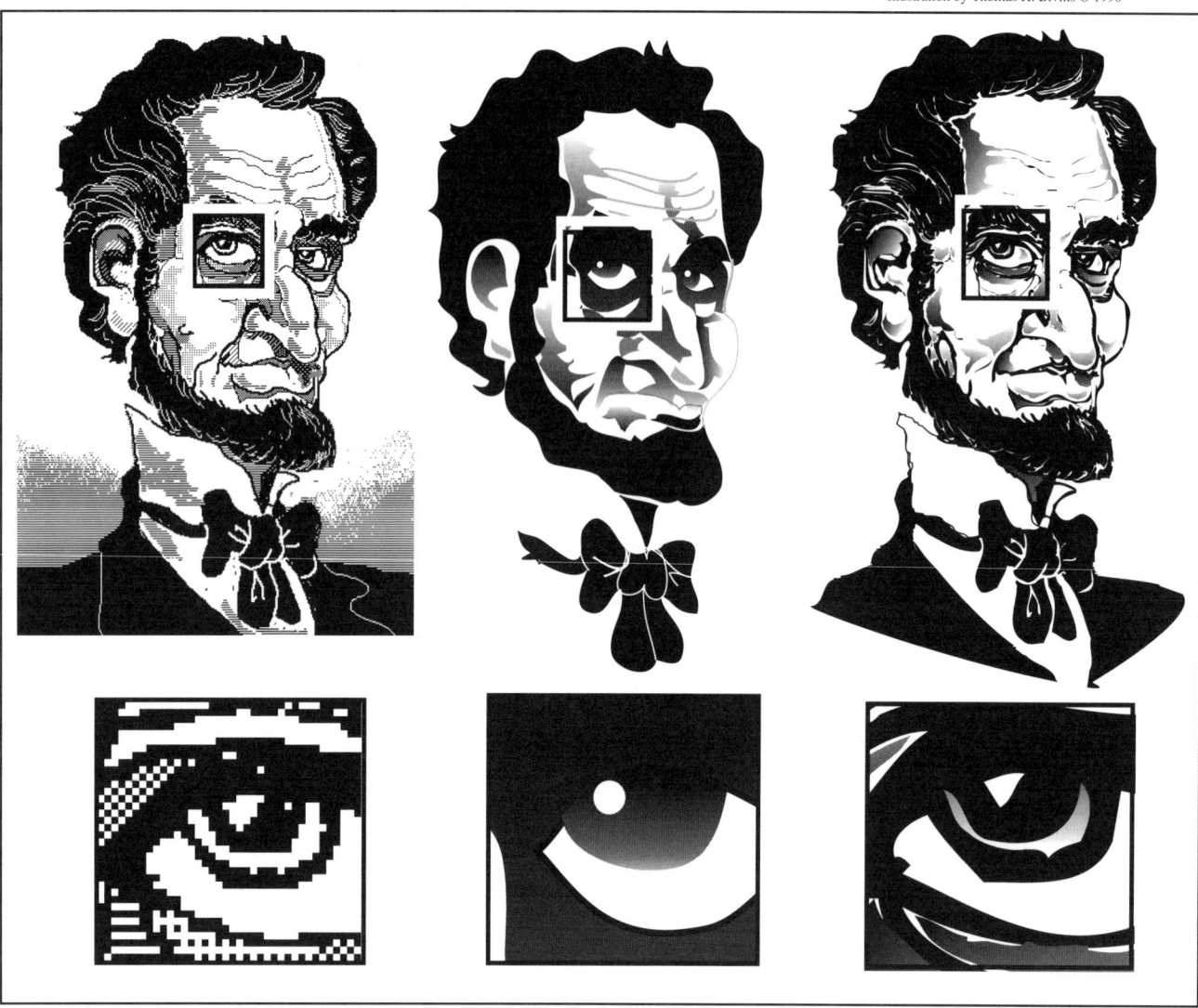

Illustration by Thomas H. Bivins © 1990

Exhibit 13.1
Bit-mapped vs PostScript.
Although in trained hands paint-type programs provided a creative outlet on the computer, the resolution of the final printed product suffered from bit-mapping. Unless severely reduced, the bits clearly showed, even on a laser printer. Once PostScript illustration programs became available, clean lines and multiple gradations of shadings could be reproduced with excellent resolution. Above, Lincoln drawn from scratch in Macpaint, *drawn from scratch in* FreeHand, *traced from the* Macpaint *original in Adobe* Streamline, *transferred to* FreeHand *and shaded.*

Object-oriented illustration programs such as *MacDraw* were next on the scene. Object-oriented art used *PostScript* to create precise angles and straight lines for the printer. The result was illustration that had a pen-drawn rather than a computer-drawn appearance—sort of. Although newspaper illustrators took programs like *MacDraw* to their artistic limits, the flexibility wasn't there for the dyed-in-the-wool perfectionist or the technical illustrator.

Then, along came Adobe *Illustrator* from the people who had invented *PostScript*, the language that allowed object-oriented art and computer typesetting to enter a new age. Adobe *Illustrator* literally rocked the illustration and computer world. It could create lines, Bezier curves, geometric forms; and scale, distort, rotate, and reflect any shape you created. *Illustrator* was to the graphic artist what *PageMaker* had been to the layout artist. It was based on a whole new technology and wasn't for the faint-hearted. Even those with previous computer-art experience were at first uncomfortable with *Illustrator*; however, once mastered, it became *the* computer tool for artists.

Illustrator, and later its competitor Aldus *FreeHand*, are still the preferred methods for creating computer-generated art that doesn't look like computer-generated art. The two basic methods for doing so are to scan an original and manipulate it in the illustration program, or draw it from scratch.

For the novice or non-artist, scanning and manipulating art may be the best approach, although learning a program as complex as *Illustrator* or *FreeHand* just to use scanned art is a bit like learning to fly a 747 just to use your family car on the weekends. In any event, the method is simple enough.

- Scan the art you wish to use as **line art**. If you are going to trace it in your illustration program (a function now offered by both *Illustrator* and *FreeHand*), it's best to scan it as a TIFF file rather than a paint file. The jagged, bit-mapped lines of a paint file will trace out as jagged, bit-mapped lines as well. In addition, don't try to trace gray-scale scans. Neither illustration program distinguishes between the gray levels well. If you absolutely have to trace a gray-scale photo, make it as high contrast as possible by using a photo software program such as *Image Studio* or *FreeHand* itself, since it allows for image control much the same way *PageMaker* does.

- Once the image is scanned, you can work with it to make it look less like

Exhibit 13.2

Draw-type programs produced object-oriented, geometric patterns excellent for design and certain types of newspaper graphics (especially charts and graphs). They were, however, difficult to work with and provided no true freehand drawing tool. The only rough equivalent produced a sort of polygon which could then be "smoothed." Below are some technical drawings produced using McDraw.

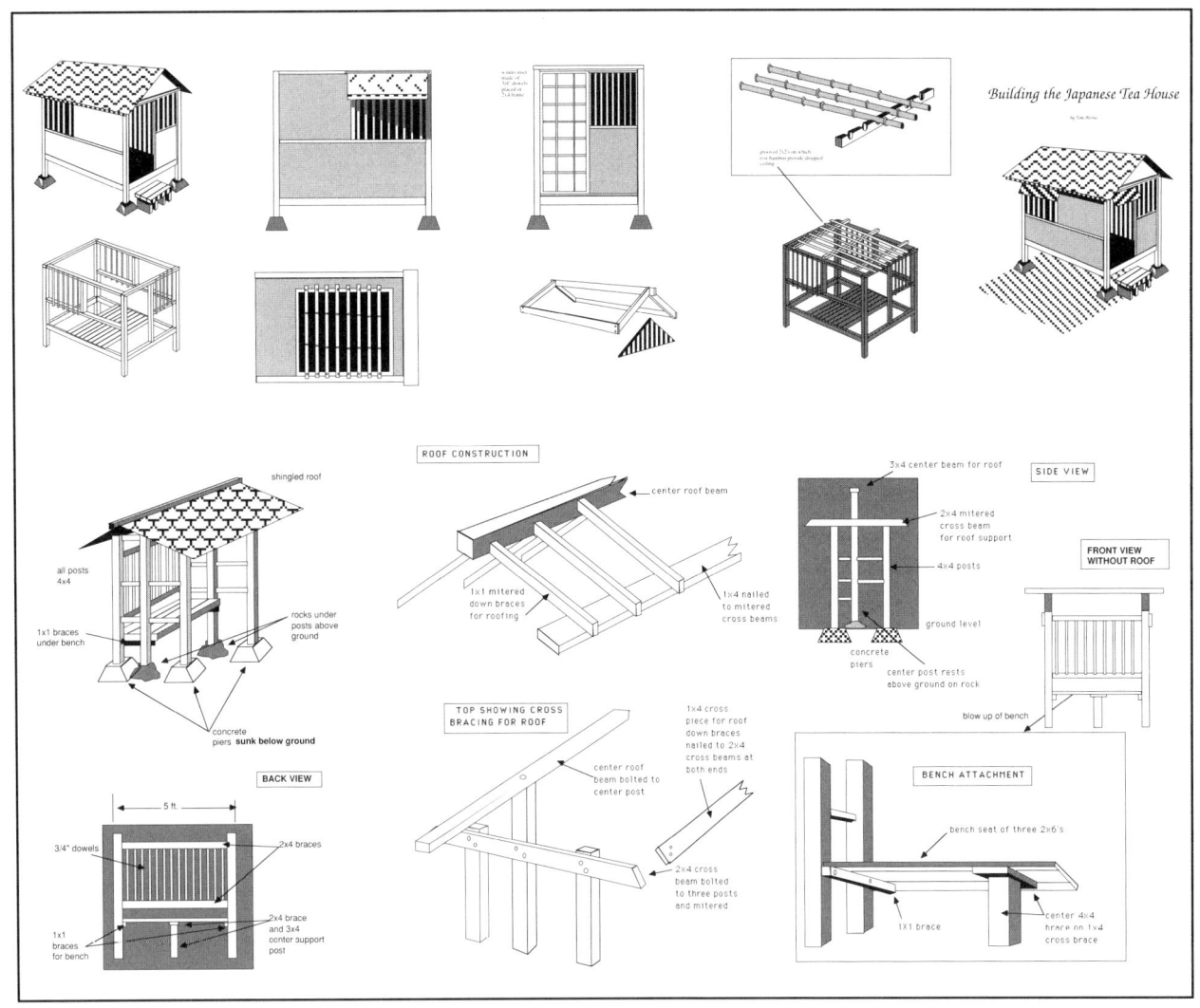

Illustration by Thomas H. Bivins © 1990

a computer-generated drawing. Unless you have one of the new trace programs designed for use in conjunction with an illustration program, doctoring your traced image will be somewhat frustrating and time consuming.

For the experienced graphic artist, drawing from scratch is always rewarding and instructional. The best way to learn an illustration program inside out is to experiment; and nothing tests your skills better than creating from scratch. Both *Illustrator* and *FreeHand* provide a great deal of guidance by way of manuals and tutorials.

Exhibit 13.4

Scanned and traced photos. In order to utilize the trace function in Illustrator *or* FreeHand *(these were done in* FreeHand*)* you must start with a high contrast photo or extremely clean line art. Once the tracing is complete, you still have to do a great deal of touch-up to remove the innumerable points created by trace function as it attempts to pick up shading and cross-hatching. The best method is to simply eliminate roughly every other point.

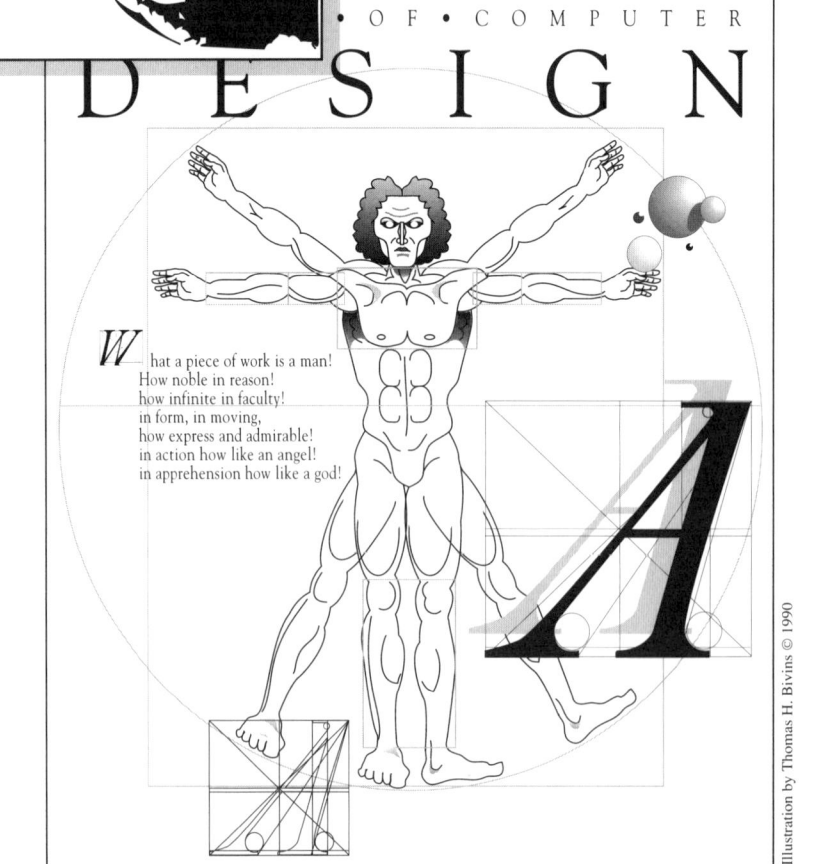

Exhibit 13.5

Drawing from scratch. This illustration, created from scratch, is an example of the complexity of Aldus FreeHand. *All of the text, display type, and illustration are created in* FreeHand, *as are the various shading patterns. One advantage* FreeHand *has over* Illustrator *is the ability to work with graduated fills and to see them on-screen as you work.* Illustrator *only allows you to work in a "preview mode" in which only the outline of your drawing is visible.*

126   Chapter 13

Scanned Art

Reworking scanned art is one way of using an illustration program. However, you can also use scanned art as is by scanning a piece of art directly into your page makeup program for use as a **locator** for finished art or as finished art itself.

When using scanned art, keep a few guidelines in mind.

- When scanning anything other than pure line art, use as many gray scales as your scanner will produce and a 300 dpi resolution. This will allow you to reproduce any art with gradations of coloring or gray areas including pencil drawings, pastels, and paintings.

- For the best reproduction of lines, even in line art, scan to a TIFF or other photo format at a 300 dpi resolution. To eliminate any graying of background areas or lines, adjust your scanner (if it's adjustable) to a higher contrast or use your page-layout program to do it.

- Watch out for file size. A complex piece of line art (say, one with a lot of cross-hatching) can easily take up as much disk space as a large gray-scale photograph. Scaling during scanning, or reducing resolution at scanning or in a photo manipulation program can help.

- If disk space allows, scan at a larger size than your final artwork will be. Reducing scanned line art greatly enhances its crispness although reducing fine lines will tend to muddy the image.

- Using scanned art and photos as place holders or locators for finished art lets the layout person fit copy and graphic elements exactly, leaving spaces for stripping in finished art. If you're using scanned art for this purpose, there is no need to take up valuable disk space with high-resolution gray-scale images. Unless you're fitting copy around art, scan at a low resolution (72 dpi *MacPaint* format is just fine) and import it into your page-makeup program for placement.

Clip Art

Dozens of manufacturers now offer computer-generated clip art services. Originally, these were based on the bit-mapped technology of the early paint programs or the clumsy but clean draw programs. Today you can purchase clip art in either bit-mapped format or object-oriented format (usually referred to as *PostScript* art) that can be placed directly into your page makeup program or loaded and manipulated in either *Illustrator* or *FreeHand*. Clip art usually

Exhibit 13.6
The dinosaur above was rendered by hand first, scanned as line art, traced in Adobe Streamline *(an amazingly fast tracing program for converting line art to computer art), then shaded in Aldus* FreeHand. *The process is much less time consuming than cutting in a rub-down shading pattern by hand. The duck on the left is simply scanned at 300 dpi and full 256 gray-scale from a pencil drawing and placed directly in* PageMaker.

Exhibit 13.7

TIP: Don't blow up bit-mapped clip art. Enlarging the individual pixels (cells) makes them truly look "computerized." Avoid clip art of any kind that comes with several illustrations to a page or file. Instead, purchase bit-mapped clip art in large originals that you then scale down. The larger the original, the cleaner the art.

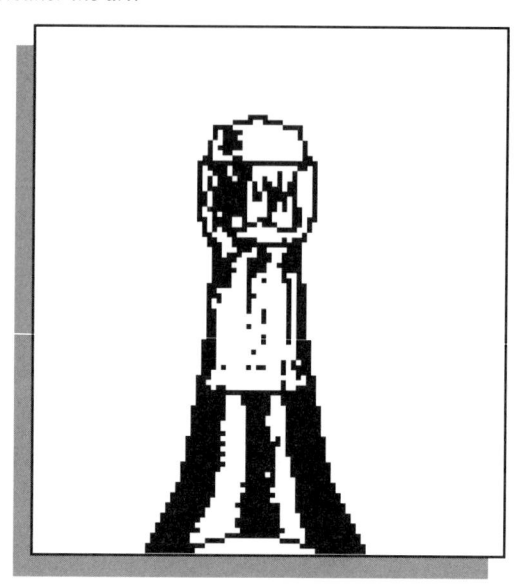

Exhibit 13.8

One of the real beauties of using computer graphics is the ability to place, size, and basically use them at any time—without having to redraw them. Encapsulated PostScript art can also be enlarged many times its original size without any loss of definition. Unlike bit-mapped graphics (above).

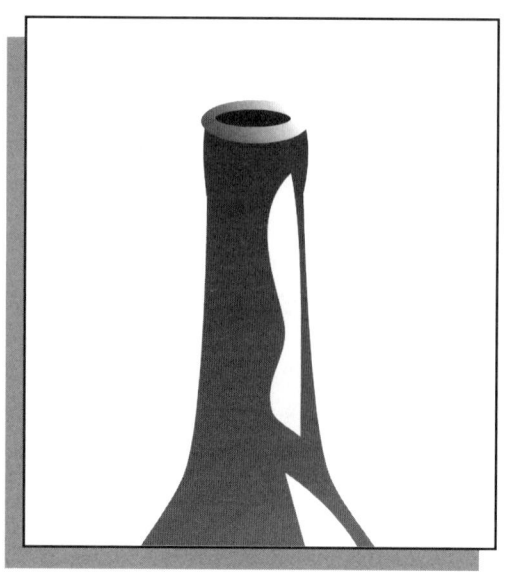

128   Chapter 13

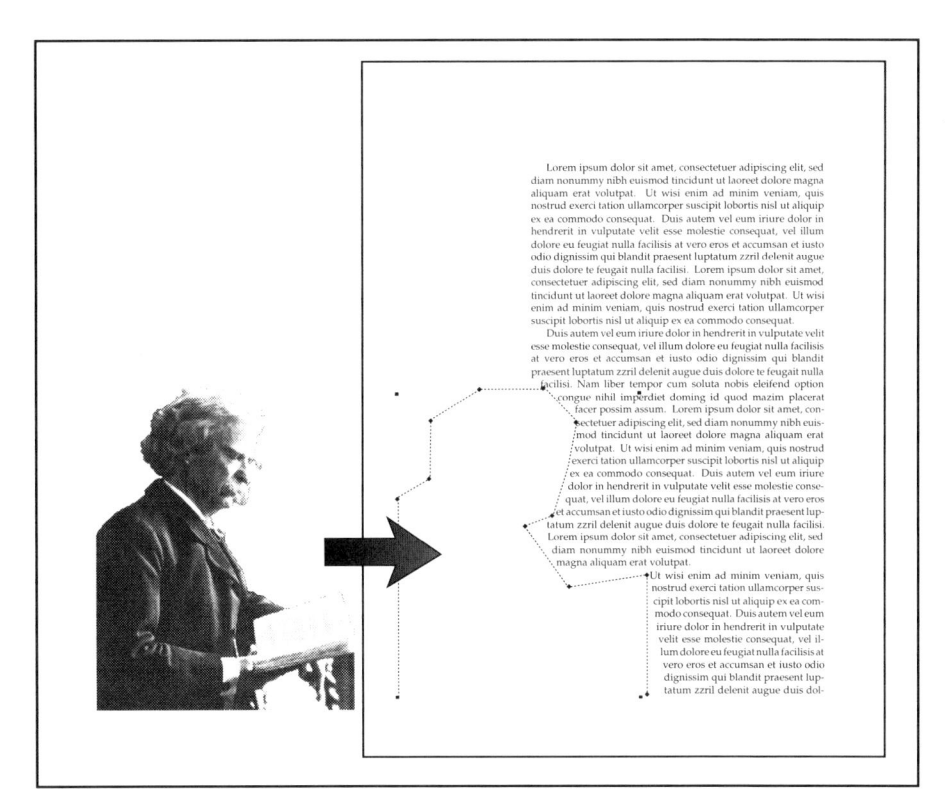

Exhibit 13.9

TIP: If you're using the text wrap function in PageMaker, *you'll run into a small problem when you remove the locator art for placement of finished art—the words that wrapped so neatly around your locator image rush back in like the Red Sea over the Egyptians once you remove it. By scanning your locator art as a gray-scale image at a low resolution, you can use* PageMaker's *image control function to turn the brightness all the way up until the image disappears. Now you can run off your final proof with a dropout ready for your final art.*

comes on disk or CD ROM (Compact Disk Read Only Memory), a compact disk that is accessed by your computer in order to retrieve information only. Because it can store millions of kilobytes of information, clip art that might fill twenty or thirty double-sided, double-density disks to house can be placed on one compact disk.

Much of what passes for clip art now, however, is a mixed blessing. In any given collection, you will find both superb and amateurish examples. The individual pieces may have been created by dozens of artists using any number of methods ranging from scanning original clip art with little or no modification to art created from scratch on the computer. The latter is usually the preferred format for serious clip art users since it is usually divisible (ungrouped) into its various original components and thus highly manipulatable using an illustration program. Scanned images don't ungroup because they were scanned as whole images instead of drawn from scratch.

When using clip art, consider the following rules of thumb.

- Decide in advance on the format you want to use. If your layout requires excellent and sharp reproduction, choose *PostScript* clip art. If you are publishing a daily or weekly newsletter that won't suffer from less than magazine-quality artwork, use bit-mapped clip art. It can be cheaper and often is available in greater variety than *PostScript* art because of the disk space requirements. Some very excellent bit-mapped clip art is available.

- Don't use it in its original size. Clip art isn't usually intended for use as a 3"x4" or 1"x2" piece of illustration. Nothing offends the artistic sensibilities more than a layout peppered with tiny illustrations. Experiment with sizes and different croppings. Make a number of thumbnails or quick layouts until you're satisfied with your illustrations.

Chapter 14

Layout

One of the key changes desktop publishing has brought about is the speed with which any ad can be laid out. That's because in computer layout, all your layout tools are in your computer and your drafting or layout table and pasteup board are on your computer screen.

This section will discuss computer layout techniques for **thumbnails, roughs, comprehensives,** and **mechanicals.**

- **Thumbnails** are miniature representations of the full-sized ad. They are done rapidly and in as great a number as the designer has patience and imagination to accomplish. The objective of thumbnails is to help the designer, and anyone else in on the process, to quickly sort through the array of options for any given ad without going to the trouble of making full-sized layouts for each possibility. Even though the thumbnail is small, all the elements of the finished ad have to be indicated: headlines, copy, visuals, logos, kicker, etc.

- **Rough layouts or roughs** are full-size versions of thumbnails. They are no more finished than a thumbnail, but they are the actual size the finished ad will appear. Some designers prefer to work at this size, and, as you will see later, a computer makes this technique especially appealing and easy. Whatever the technique, the rough can range from very rough to a more finished layout complete with lettered headlines; however, for a more finished (sometimes almost complete) look, the designer moves on to the comprehensive or **comp**.

- **Comprehensives** sometimes are mistaken by clients as the finished ad. Comps are supposed to look like the real thing complete with headlines, copy, and visuals (often in color). The trick is to let the client see *exactly* what the finished ad will look like without having to go through the actual printing process. This is another area in which computers can be of enormous advantage.

- A **mechanical** is the finished, camera-ready copy. About the only thing missing from a mechanical would be photos that you are having halftoned or art that needs to be reduced or color separated. These will be shot and stripped in later. As you will see below, this is the step that has really saved money and time by employing the computer.

The techniques discussed here are based primarily on Apple *Macintosh* hardware and Aldus *PageMaker* page composition program, but may be roughly transferrable to other systems and software. However, our point is not to detail the use of one system over another, but to demonstrate the versatility of the computer in ad layout.

The Advantages of Computer Layout

There are a number of basic advantages to computer page layout that you need to be aware of before you plunge into designing and formatting ads on your computer.

Placing Text and Graphics

The primary advantage of computer page layout is the ability to place text and graphics right on the page from word processing or illustration programs. Although other page-layout programs require you to create a frame in which you then place text or graphics, *PageMaker* allows you to place these items directly on the page, anywhere you want them. Once there, they can be manipulated in a number of ways. You can also place text one column at a time or in *PageMaker's* textflow mode which allows it to flow uninterrupted from page to page (for longer layouts such as newsletters) until it is completely placed. Text can be confined to any size column or stretched across columns by a simple movement of the mouse. Once on the page, text can be made longer or wider by manipulating the *handles* that are part of each *PageMaker* element.

Graphics, such as those imported from Aldus *FreeHand*, are placed in roughly the same way. By moving the mouse pointer to the position on the page where you want the graphic to appear and holding down the mouse button while dragging diagonally, you may designate the size you want the graphic to be when it is placed. This will then constrain the placed element to that area (in the case of text) or size (in the case of a graphic).

Exhibit 14.1
Stretching text. PageMaker *allows you to place, and then configure, text to any column width you desire by simply grabbing a "handle" and stretching.*

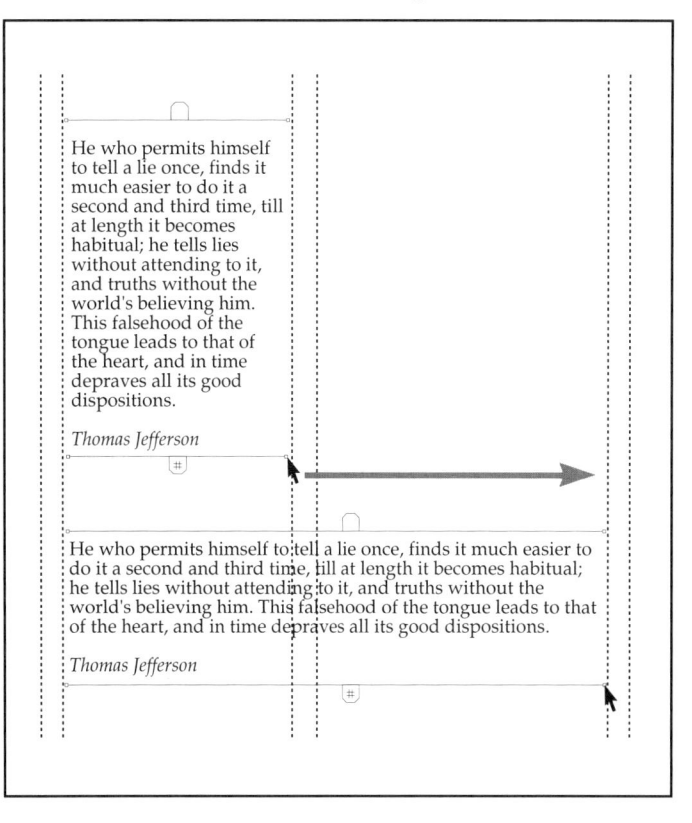

Once placed, the graphic may be sized, cropped, or otherwise adjusted depending on the software used to produce it. Graphics placed from PICT or EPS formats can be sized proportionally in *PageMaker* by simply holding down the *shift* key while dragging a corner handle. Paint-type graphics can also be sized without loss or compression of shading patterns if you hold down both the *command* and *shift* keys as you drag. If you don't hold down the *shift* key or *command* and *shift* keys while executing these maneuvers, the images will distort. Many programs also now include a text-wrap function that allows you to literally wrap text around a placed graphic.

Using Lines and Boxes

Today, even word processing programs allow you to create boxes and lines, but not all that long ago this was one of the primary selling points of a page-layout program.

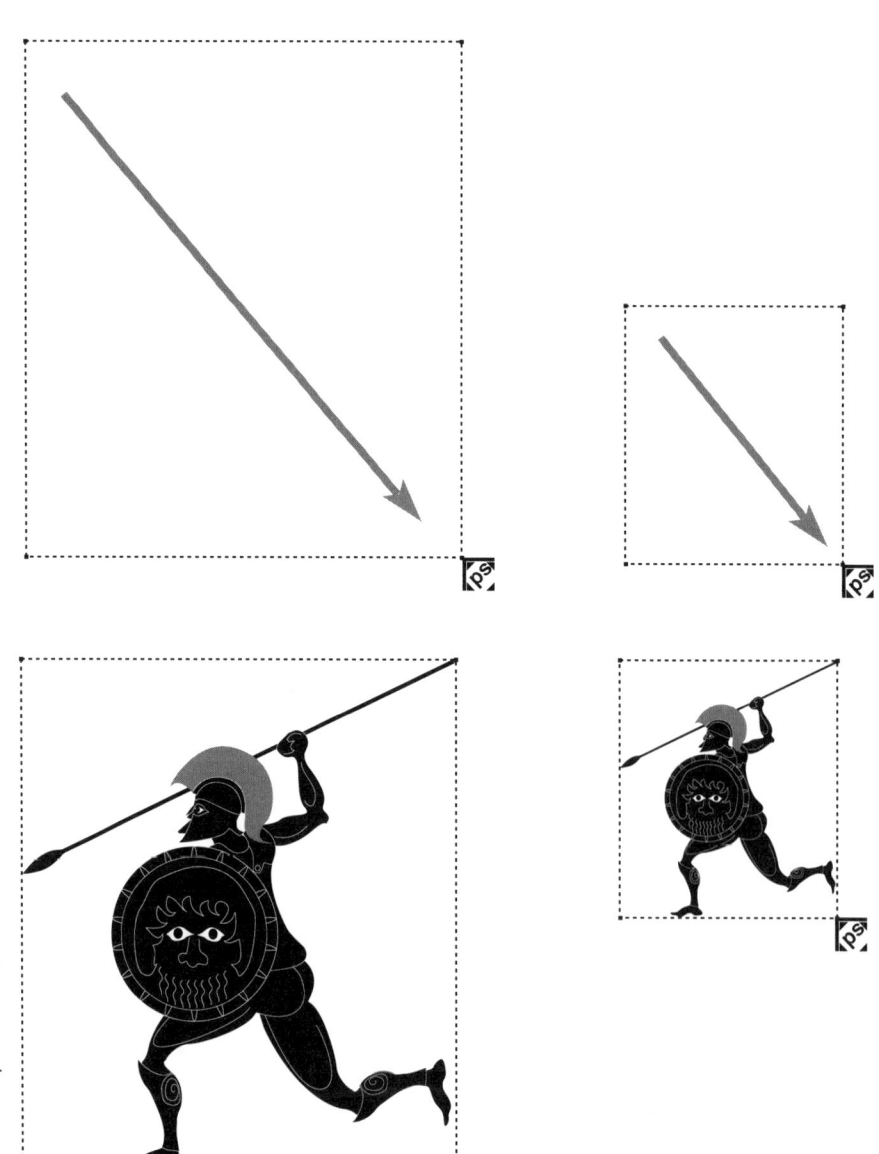

Exhibit 14.2

Stretching graphics. *When placing and stretching graphics in* Pagemaker, *make sure you hold down the shift key or the image will distort. Of course, you can also create some interesting images through distortion.*

Boxes

Although it is possible to import or place boxes and other such simple patterns from other programs, it is easier to create them in the page-layout program. Boxes do have to be moved each time you make an adjustment to type or format, but it's easier to move them in a computer program than on a pasted-up piece of paper.

Drop shadows are easy to create and can be effective if they are not overused. In *PageMaker*, drop shadows are produced by adding a darker shaded box slightly diagonally and to the rear of your original box. Be sure your top box is not transparent, and delete the line around the shadow. Experiment with different shades and don't assume that black is the best for a drop shadow.

Tint blocks, boxes that are filled or shaded, should also be used with care. Very small type or type with thin serifs won't print well over a tint block, especially on a laser printer. Use a light shade (no more than 20 or 30 percent) and a type size of at least 12 point. If your final product will run on a Linotronic, be aware that fills or shades will appear darker than on a laser-printed copy. A 40 percent fill that looks fine on a LaserWriter will be too dark for a copy block on a Linotronic.

Exhibit 14.3

Drop shadows. *Create a shaded box over your existing box (left), move it to the rear (center) and delete the line (right).*

Lines

Like type size, line thickness is usually given in points. This is convenient since line width is much narrower than you would want to measure in inches. The standard seems to be 1 point; however, experiment with line thickness and use what seems most appropriate to your purpose. For example, some programs designate "hairline" as well as .05- and 1-point line thicknesses at the narrower end of the range. Hairlines are excellent for the lines used in coupons or fill-in-the-blanks forms. You'd be surprised how thick a 1-point line looks in these forms. On the other hand, a 2-, 4-, or 6-point line is quite a bit thicker-*looking* than a 1-point line. Use the thicker settings sparingly.

Master Pages

Master pages are useful in the early layout stages (thumbnails and roughs) for producing basic, repeating elements without having to execute them page by

As you can see, as the copy moves from 10% gray at the top down to 40% gray at the very bottom, it gets much harder to read, especially if you are using a serifed type face in a 10- or 12- point size.

Hairline ─────────────

.5 pt. ─────────────

1pt. ─────────────

2pt. ─────────────

4pt. ▬▬▬▬▬▬▬▬▬▬▬▬▬

6pt. ▬▬▬▬▬▬▬▬▬▬▬▬▬

8pt. ▬▬▬▬▬▬▬▬▬▬▬▬▬

12pt. ▬▬▬▬▬▬▬▬▬▬▬▬▬

TIP: On most screens, lines below 1 point don't show any smaller than the 1-point line. Sometimes, blowing the page up to 200 or 400 percent shows the difference. The best way to judge the differences, however, is to print out a proof sheet and look for yourself.

page. Master pages are created (on *PageMaker*) at the beginning of your layout process and consist of any elements you want to repeat from page to page. Every page is then overlaid by the master page elements unless otherwise overridden on a page-by-page basis. For example, if you are roughing out an ad series with the same, repeating kicker and logo placement, you simply create these elements on your master page and they will appear on every page thereafter.

Formats

Before we discuss exactly how computers can help in the layout process, let's look at some basic design formats for print ads. While not all ads, especially the wildly inventive ones, will fall into one of the following eight design formats, most will; and the beginning designer should probably stick to the simpler formats before attempting the more complex designs.

***Picture Window** is probably one of the most popular styles for print ads. The visual dominates this format and usually takes up two-thirds of the page. Note that picture window can also be inverted with the visual on the bottom two-thirds of the page and the headline at the top. Normally, the headline is a single line followed by body copy in two or three columns.*

***Copy Heavy** reverses the emphasis on the visual and places it on the copy. For messages that are complex in nature and require detailed explanation, this is one of the best formats to use. In areas like institutional advertising (mostly public relations), copy heavy ads are very common.*

134   Chapter 14

Silhouette or ***Copy Fit*** usually has the copy "wrap around" an open (as opposed to framed) piece of art. Copy fit takes an expert in typesetting. This isn't something a beginner will normally feel comfortable with, but a good copy fit ad can exude an air of unity that may not be found in other layouts.

Mondrian is named after the artist who developed the style (no, he wasn't an art director). This style is, again, not for the beginner. Mondrian divides the page into rectangles of various sizes into which headlines, copy, and visuals are placed. Balance is the key here.

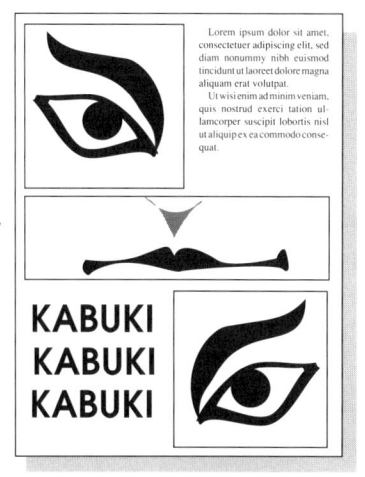

Frame or ***Donut*** refers either to copy framing a visual or vice versa. If the perimeter is open at either the top or bottom, the layout is sometimes called a ***horseshoe***.

Circus is definitely the domain of graphic designers. It takes an expert in layout to balance the eclecticism of Circus. This format often utilizes both framed and silhouetted visuals along with copy fit body copy and numerous subheads.

Multipanel or ***Cartoon*** is exactly what it says. In this format, the panels are usually of equal size. Sometimes the panels tell a sequential story. Multipanel does not always have to frame each picture in the sequence. Some multi-panel layouts use a series of open, or silhouetted visuals — often a repeated image which changes gradually as it progresses.

Type Specimen relies on the effect of a special or enlarged typeface in place of or as the primary visual element. Again, it takes an expert designer or typographer to handle a type specimen design. See the section on typography for more on this

Layout 135

Creating Thumbnails on the Computer

Thumbnails are usually accomplished by hand. Since they are very rough and very small, most artists and designers can quickly sketch five or six in just minutes. A computer can't match a good sketch artist's ability, but it can greatly aid the not-so-adept or beginning designer, *and* the finished product is much easier to judge for design potential than a hand-sketched thumbnail. A number of computer-assisted shortcuts can add consistency to the process and open up some clogged creative arteries.

Size

The first step is to create the master page you will reduce for your thumbnails. You will need to create it in the exact size you want your thumbnail to appear. A number of software programs create thumbnails; *PageMaker* can produce good thumbnails complete with reduced copy (normally greeking) that can be set in any way normal copy can be set. Whatever the size, be sure to work in dimensions you feel comfortable with. You can work full size if you wish, but a smaller dimension lets you place many more thumbnails on a single page and make comparisons on the screen instead of printing them out as you go.

Scaling

Depending on the size and page orientation (*landscape* [horizontal or *wide*] or *portrait* [vertical or *tall*]) of your finished ad, you will need to scale down proportionally to the thumbnail size. To make sure your reduced page is scaled properly, you can use a couple of different methods, depending on the computer hardware and software you are using.

First, decide on the size of the final ad. Suppose, for instance, that you will be producing a standard magazine ad. Your finished product will be 8.5" x 11" laid out vertically. When you open your file for the first time, simply select *letter* from the page setup menu and *tall* for the orientation.

After your file opens, access the master page or pages and set up your templates there. That way, each succeeding page will have your template guidelines already on it. Choose the diagonal tool from your screen tool box and draw a diagonal line (a hairline will do) from the top right corner to the bottom left corner of your page. Now, choose the tool for making boxes and draw another box so that the upper right and lower left corners both touch the diagonal line. No matter what size you make your box, the box will be some incremental reduction of your original folder size if these two corners intersect the diagonal line (see **Exhibit 14.4**). The easiest size to work in is roughly 4.5" x 5.75" placed one above the other on a vertically oriented page.

Now you have a reduced version of the ad in which to place your elements. You can copy just the box portion of your ad at any time and paste it for another thumbnail. In fact, you might want to do that right away and arrange the full page of thumbnail templates in rows before you begin to add the various elements of your folder.

One final note. You will probably want to leave your template unshaded (not white) so as to cut down on having to move items to the front and to the back constantly. Of course, if you want to experiment with different backgrounds, you can add shading as you go along.

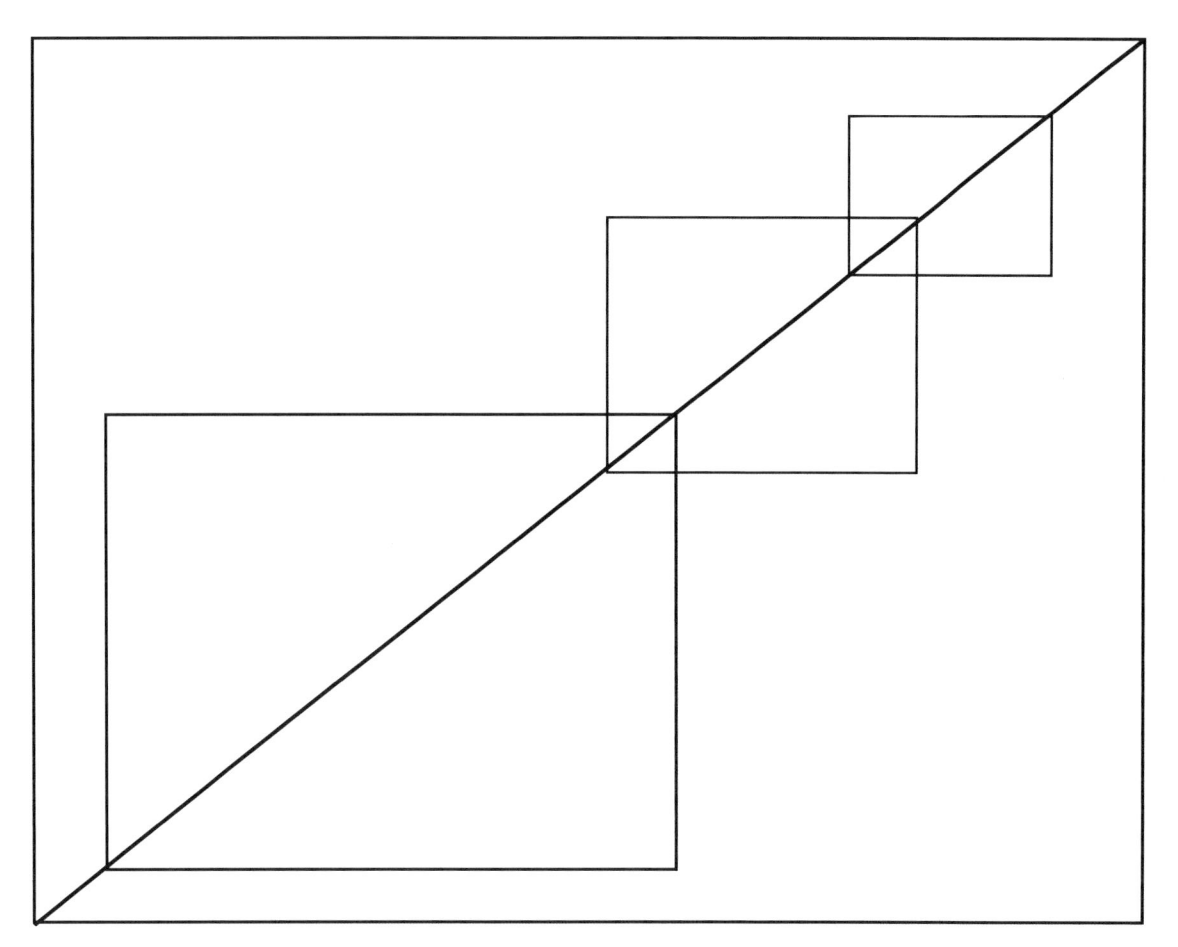

Exhibit 14.4
Scaling. *This may seem old-fashioned, but it's often the easiest way to work in a layout program.*

Visuals

Visuals for thumbnails are a matter of taste. Some designers don't care to mess with detail on a thumbnail, but a computer lets you use a reducible visual again and again with no extra trouble. For instance, the thumbnails on these pages use illustrations created on Aldus *FreeHand* and exported to *PageMaker* in *Encapsulated PostScript*. They can now be placed, sized, cropped, and stretched to suit the designer's needs.

If you don't have pre-made visuals on the computer, you can easily substitute geometric patterns or lines to approximate the shape of the intended visuals.

Headline

Even in small sizes, thumbnails can look quite polished if they use legible, reduced lettering. For example, if you are working with the sizes shown on these pages, your headline can vary from 14 points to 24 points and still replicate fairly accurately what the finished product will look like. Remember, all a thumbnail has to be is close. Exactness comes later.

Body Copy

In a traditional thumbnail sketch (and even in rough full-size layouts), body copy is typically **greeked**—that is, indicated by ruled lines or lines of squiggles made to look like columns of copy. Greeking also refers to copy that is nonsense or unintelligible. With *PageMaker*, you can represent greeked copy with actual lettering. If you have the actual copy written—great. If not, use the greeking that comes with *PageMaker*. Aldus refers to it as *Lorem ipsum* after the first two words of the greeked copy. For years, the only way to get this type of greeked body copy was to buy it as rub-down lettering in the size and font that represented what your real copy would look like or cut it out of magazines and glue it in place. Now, with a computer, you can make your own, or, if you use *PageMaker*, use *Lorem ipsum*.

Exhibit 14.5

Visuals and headlines on thumbnails. At this size (4.5 x 5.75 inches) you can plainly read both display type and body copy. Even if you need to work smaller, greeked copy can still be seen quite well. The smaller ad (top right) shows how you can work with geometric patterns (in this case, rectangles) effectively enough for a thumbnail.

You can place your greeked copy directly onto the thumbnail and size it as small as you need. You can also approximate columns (justified or unjustified, flush right or left, or centered). In fact, you can replicate any style or experiment with any alignment you would use in the finished product—only in thumbnail size! This is the reason for carefully placing column guides on your thumbnails. Greeked copy won't fit properly without them.

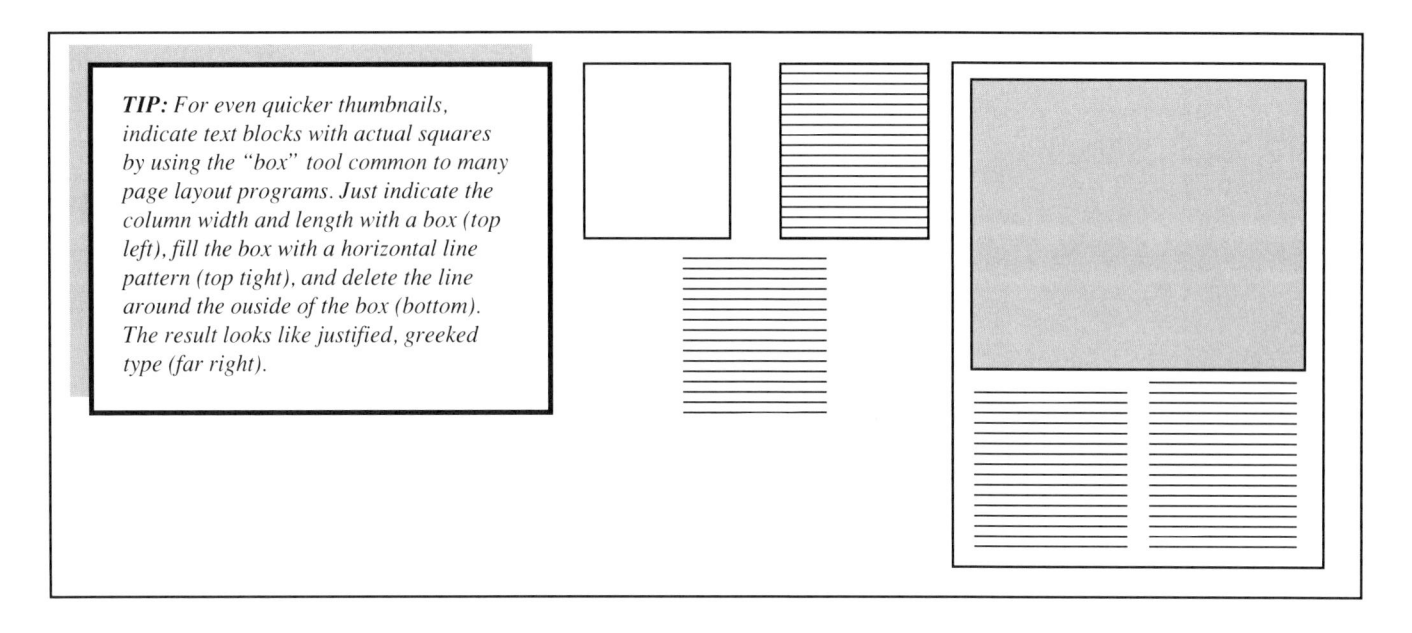

TIP: For even quicker thumbnails, indicate text blocks with actual squares by using the "box" tool common to many page layout programs. Just indicate the column width and length with a box (top left), fill the box with a horizontal line pattern (top tight), and delete the line around the ouside of the box (bottom). The result looks like justified, greeked type (far right).

Creating Roughs on the Computer

The next stage is the rough. Many designers simply skip the thumbnail stage and go right to the rough which gives them a feel for the full-size ad and lets them work in broad strokes without having to render details. Some designers create as many roughs as they normally would thumbnails. The only difference is size. If you like to look at a number of sketches simultaneously, thumbnails offer the most flexibility; however, you can lay out as many roughs side by side as you have room for.

The rough is simply a full-sized version of the thumbnail with copy indicated (usually by horizontal lines or squiggles) and artwork roughed in. Like the thumbnail, it is only used to give the designer several creative approaches to the layout. Time is usually the limiting factor here. A rough can be accomplished much faster than a comprehensive.

The computer can be enormously helpful in letting you place all the elements of the folder just as you would for the final product. While most roughs only indicate copy, a computer-generated rough can use either the actual copy or greeked copy instead of lines and squiggles; and, if the visual has been duplicated or created originally on a computer, it can be used as well. If not, rely on shapes and patterns just as you did in the thumbnails.

Creating Comprehensives on the Computer

The next stage in the evolution from thumbnail to finished ad is the comprehensive or comp, the stage you will ultimately show to the client for approval. With computer-generated artwork, headlines, and body copy, you can come very close to a finished product with none of the costs normally associated with a complete comprehensive.

The comps on these pages were designed after existing ads for real products or services. Artwork was accomplished on Aldus *FreeHand* and layout was done using *PageMaker*. The technique involves creating the artwork (line work and shading) in *FreeHand*; exporting the finished artwork in *Encapsulated PostScript* for placement in *PageMaker*; placing the artwork and sizing it in *PageMaker* (it can be reduced, enlarged or cropped to suit your needs, but it pays to work in *FreeHand* in some increment of your final product); and adding the copy elements in *PageMaker*, which manipulates text more flexibly than *FreeHand*. As you can see, the final product is very polished.

Creating display type in other programs, such as Adobe *Illustrator* and *FreeHand*, does have its advantages. The latest version of *FreeHand* provides for automatic kerning of all the letters in a single word or text block by simply grabbing a handle and stretching the block. In addition, headlines exported to page-layout programs such as *PageMaker* can be stretched, sized, or distorted—something you can't do with display type created in *PageMaker* itself.

Color Comps

Most clients expect color comps, and the newer software programs (*FreeHand* and *PageMaker* especially) take advantage of this. Color separations as well as spot color can both be programmed into your layout, and separations can be

Exhibit 14.6

Comprehensive*. The artwork for this comp was developed in Aldus* FreeHand. *A photo of Mark Twain was scanned and placed in* Freehand, *traced, and filled with black and white. The copy was added in* PageMaker.

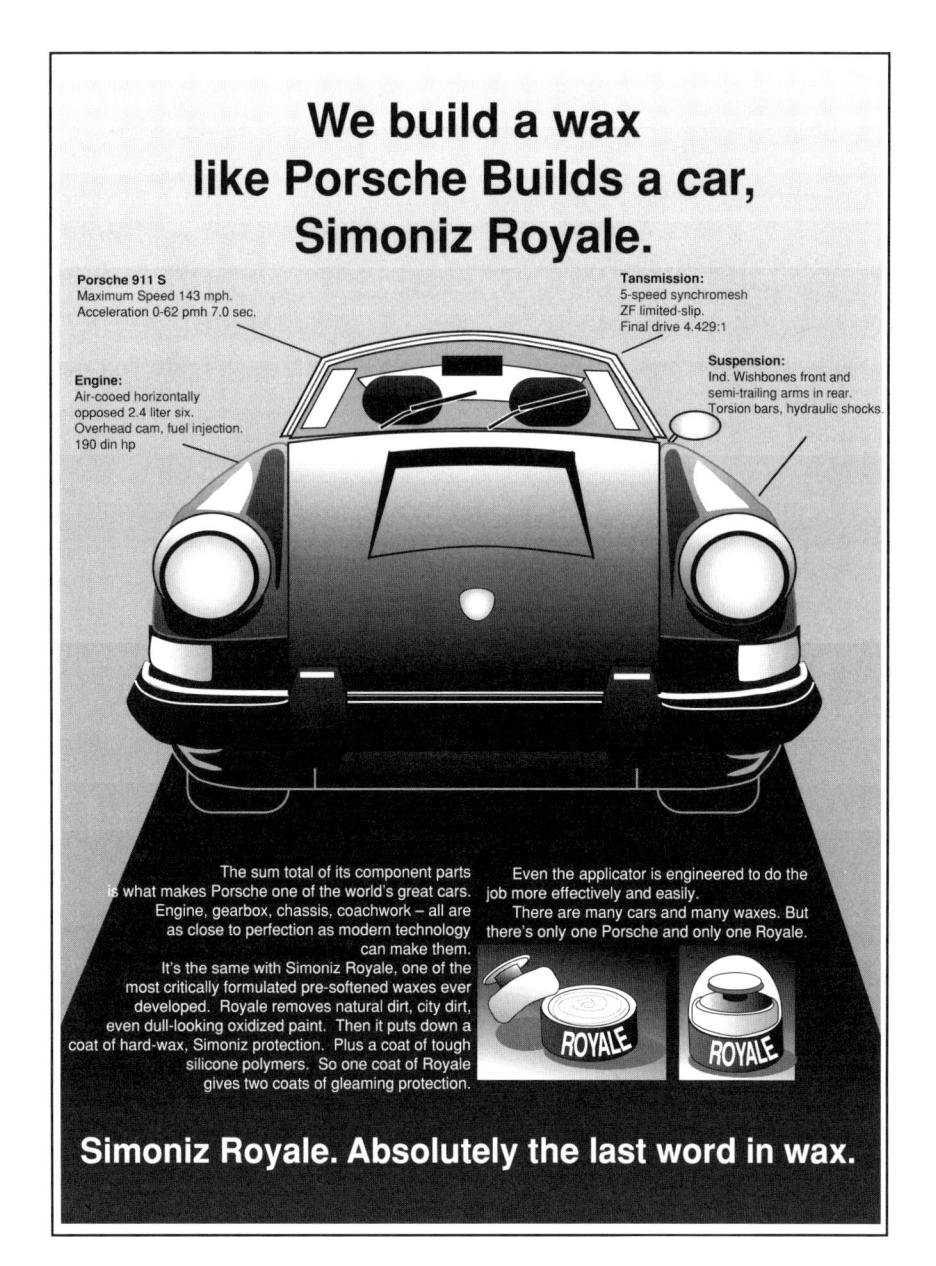

Exhibit 14.7

Comprehensive. The artwork for this comp, including the background shading, was all accomplished in FreeHand *and exported to* PageMaker *where the headline and copy were added. The small illustrations of the wax can were done in a separate* FreeHand *file and pasted onto the master drawing in a reduced format. When working in smaller sizes, it is best to work large and reduce to the size you need for the final product.*

printed off and combined for a finished product through the normal printing process. But, you don't need to go this far for comps, if (and this is a *big* if) you have access to a color laser printer.

Color laser printers can actually produce full-color comps based on your instructions in your illustration or page-layout program. The problem is that color laser technology is very expensive. The only other quick and dirty option is to try out one of the new color copying systems using your laser-printed color separations much the same way a printer would. If you limit yourself to large areas of color and don't get too fancy, the outcome can be adequate. Registration may be a problem, for there is no way to register accurately on a color copier of any type.

Even without a color laser printer, you can still execute professional color comps by simply using oil-based design markers to color your laser-printed comps. The oil-based markers won't smear the toner used in most laser printers. Or, if you don't like the smell of markers, try soft, colored pencils. The beauty

Exhibit 14.8

Comprehensive. A completed comp accomplished entirely on a computer. The whole layout, including graphics and lettering, was done using Aldus FreeHand. *For presentation onto this page, the file was placed as encapsulated postscript.*

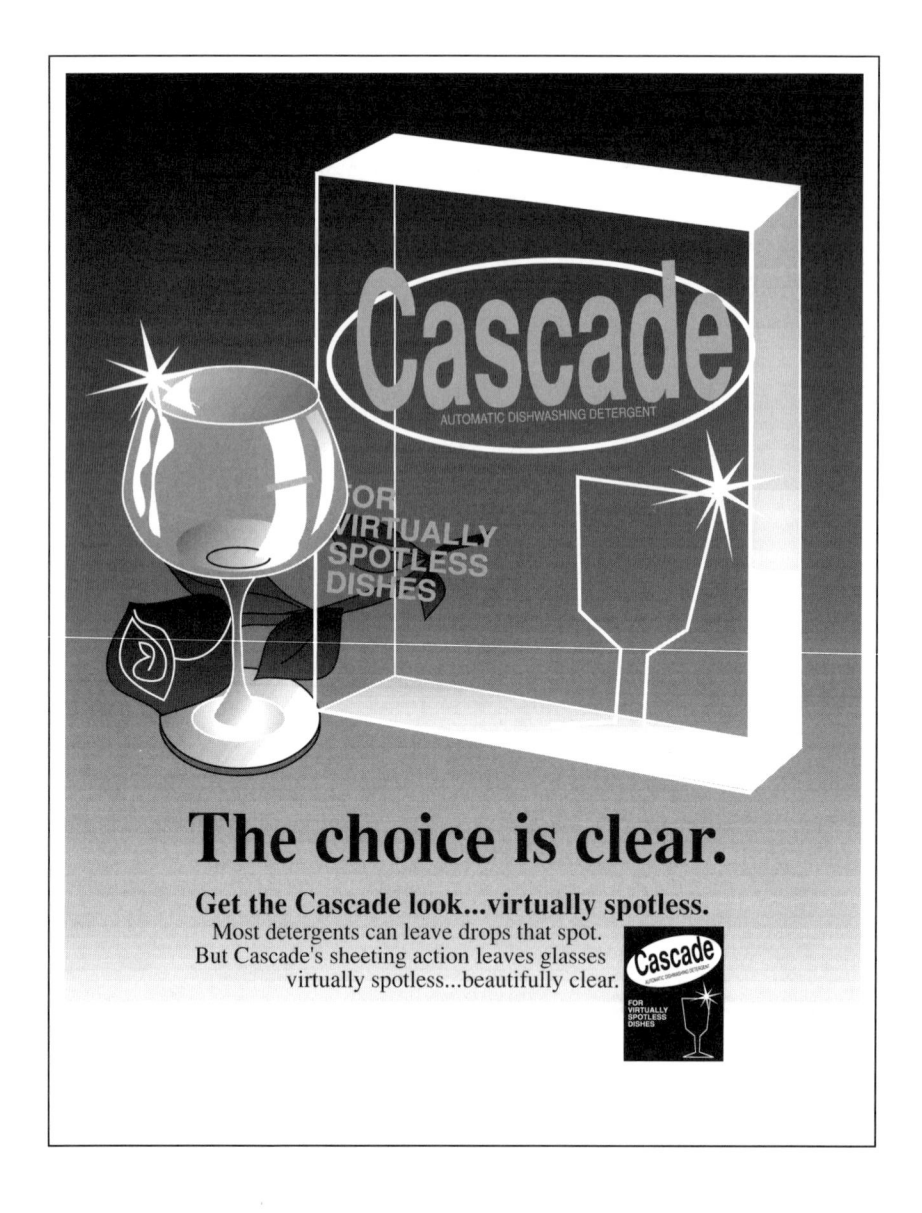

of this method is that, because *FreeHand* illustrations are already shaded, all you have to do is apply a base color to the illustration.

Preparing the Mechanical

The final stage of layout is the mechanical, the finished layout that goes to the printer. Again, the computer has revolutionized this process. If you are diligent, exact, and working with a limited range of graphics, you can literally present your printer with a mechanical in one piece—*with no pasted-up parts*! We have, in fact, sent whole ads directly to our printer's Linotronic 300 typesetter via our computer network and had the camera-ready mechanical handed back to us for inspection within a few hours. You can even go directly to negative film from a Linotronic, saving the cost of shooting negatives from a positive mechanical—but only if you are completely satisfied with your layout.

Assuming you are working in black and white, there are several ways to construct your mechanical.

Exhibit 14.9

Comprehensive. *This Crest ad was done the same way as the Simoniz ad with the copy added in* Pagemaker. *The small Crest tubes were "cloned" from the larger drawing and reduced to the needed size in* FreeHand. *One advantage of producing the body copy in* Pagemaker *(or another word-processing program and placed in* Pagemaker*) rather than in* FreeHand *is the ability to copy fit, which can't be done easily in* FreeHand.

1. You can have it run *entirely* off a Linotronic either from your computer disks or through a network or phone line hookup. This implies that all of the elements on your mechanical are computer generated—word-processed text and display type; borders, boxes and rules produced in your page-makeup program; photos scanned, cropped, and sized in either a photo manipulation program—such as *ImageStudio*—or right in your layout program; illustrations created in a paint, draw, or illustration program and imported or placed in your layout program; and any color separations already accounted for by your software.

2. You can run the basic mechanical (text, display type, rules, and boxes) on a Linotronic and have photos and art shot separately and stripped into the negative before the printing plate is made. If you don't have a scanner or access to electronic clip art, this is probably the closest you'll get to having the whole thing done in one step. Even at this level, the savings in typesetting and pasteup alone are worth it.

3. You can run your mechanical on a laser printer at either of the above two levels. This assumes you either don't have access to a Linotronic, or you

don't feel that the extra quality is needed for your particular ad. Some very nice newsletters and brochures can be offset printed directly from laser-printed mechanicals. The difference to the trained eye (or anyone with a magnifying glass) is the type. It bleeds badly at larger point sizes and can even look fuzzy at smaller sizes. But if you're on a shoestring budget, this is a great compromise.

Adding Color

Today, full color on the computer is tedious and fairly imprecise. Although there are color monitors, full-color scanners, and photo programs to work with them, and processes to make and print the requisite separations—the end results are not as satisfying as the mechanical process now used. At the speed at which computer technology is advancing, however, it won't be long before full-color photography can be handled cost-effectively and with good results.

Many page-layout programs support spot color, and many more are developing color capabilities. Both page-layout programs like *PageMaker* and illustration programs like *FreeHand* have the ability to add color and make separations for printing. In fact, at this writing, *FreeHand* contains a complete Pantone library of colors as well as the ability to mix your own, and the newest version of *PageMaker* will have full-color capabilities including the Pantone library.

The only drawback is the exactness of the color separations—they are *too* exact. If you opt not to have your colors overprint (a wise choice unless you're intentionally trying for a special look), both *FreeHand* and *PageMaker* "knock out" the shape of the colored object on the object beneath it. Ideally, this allows one color to print in a white space designed exactly for it. In reality, printers usually provide for a tiny overlap between the knockout and the color printed over it. Without this overlap or shadow, and if registration isn't absolutely exact, you'll most likely end up with tiny slivers of white space where the top object didn't quite fit into the knockout below it.

If all you're doing is adding some spot color, both programs, and many others, will do just fine. Just remember, working with color has always been a difficult proposition. Working with it on a computer can be rewarding and exciting, but it is also confusing and occasionally frustrating.

One final word of warning. If you are thinking of investing in color capabilities for your computer, be aware of the WYSIWYG problem (what you see is what you get). Color monitors are the greatest thing since sliced bread, but they're hardly accurate. Don't expect the color you see on the screen to replicate on your new $8,000 color printer or look the same in your finished job hot off the press. One problem is that color monitors use light-mixed colors that just don't look the same as colors mixed with real ink. What can you do?

- First, set up your monitor with a color card. They are usually provided with the monitor. Some software programs, such as Aldus *FreeHand*, provide a color card based on the Pantone system. Get as close as you can to these color cards and check the adjustment every so often to make sure it hasn't wandered.

- Once you have set up color in an ad, check it against what your printer is using. Don't expect a color comp run on a color printer to match anything the printer has. Be ready to get a close match, or re-spec your color based on printer samples. If you use Pantone or another coded system, you can easily check out what you thought was Reflex Blue on your screen by taking a quick look at your printer's Pantone book.

- Finally, be prepared for disappointment if you rely too heavily on your color screen for the final word. Use your monitor and software programs to their fullest, but be sensible and talk over your choices with your printer and *look at samples.*

Remember, the closer you can get to a finished mechanical on a computer, the more cost effective your production process is going to become. With the possible exception of scanned photos, the rest of the process saves money. Once scanned photos reach the quality of photographic halftones and the printing process quickens, prices will drop. Then you won't see any more traditionally done photos in ads.

Chapter 15

Printing

When computers were new, we were so happy to be working on them instead of typewriters that printing was just gravy. It wasn't long, however, before we began to appreciate the nuances between such terms as *letter quality* and *near letter quality*. If all we did was churn out correspondence, then either would suffice, so long as the end product didn't look like it had been hand-lettered by someone suffering from a caffeine overdose. Then, along came the desktop publishing revolution, and choosing the right printer became serious business.

Roughly speaking, printers can be broken down into three types:

- **Daisy wheel** printers use a type element that looks like a wheel. Each character is present on the wheel which rotates into place as it is chosen by the computer/printer memory. Daisy wheel printers provide letter-quality printing but are slow—usually somewhere between 15 and 70 characters per second—and limited as to type size, weight and style. Bold, for example, is accomplished by simply striking over a letter several times.

- **Dot-matrix** printers also form letters by striking an inked ribbon; however, the letters consist of a series of dots rather than a single character. Most dot matrix printers allow you to run everything from extremely rough drafts to near letter-quality jobs. They are faster than daisy wheel printers (between 60 and 300 characters per second) and have the added advantage of being able to produce type in different weights, styles, and sizes. They can also print graphics—a giant step above daisy wheel printers.

- **Laser printers** are the desktop publisher's answer to typesetting. They are quieter than impact printers (there is no ribbon to strike) and faster, printing lines per minute rather than characters per minute. At upwards of 600 lines per minute, laser printers typically print six to eight pages every minute. These printers literally assemble entire pages in memory before they print them. The real breakthrough, however, is the laser printer's ability to print documents that are near-typeset quality.

Most laser printers today are based on one of two technologies—the Apple LaserWriter or Hewlett-Packard's LaserJet. The basic difference between the two is that the LaserWriter (and printers based on its technology) uses *PostScript*, a programming language that allows entire pages of both text and graphics to be sent to the printer at one time. Type can be produced at any available size and even extremely complex graphics can be printed out, restricted only by the resolution of the printer. Software/hardware packages that will turn a printer based on LaserJet technology into a printer that accepts *PostScript* are now available, and new LaserJet printers are now coming on the market with built-in *PostScript* capability.

Keep in mind that, although prices have come down considerably, laser printers can still cost you quite a bit—ranging roughly from $1000 to $5000 depending mostly on the amount of memory the printer comes with.

Some of the newer laser printers—especially those that accept *PostScript*—come with at least 1 megabyte of memory. These are variously upgradeable to as much as 12 megabytes or more and some accept external hard drives boosting the memory even higher. The greater the memory, the less time it takes to print, the more pages the printer can store at one time, and the more printer type fonts it can handle. For example, upwards of 30 type fonts now come packaged on some laser printers, and with expanded memory, dozens more can be added. In fact, some font manufacturers sell hundreds of fonts on their own hard drive ready for installation on your system. The difference in printer memory size can mount up in dollars, however, so be ready to pay for what you get.

Although laser printers are definitely the ideal, you can get along without one. Many quick printers and photocopy stores carry the most common software applications, and can run laser copies files right off your disks. If you're in doubt, just call. It pays to at least have a dot matrix printer, however, to run drafts. These won't exactly match your laser output copies, but they will give you some idea of what to expect.

Pre-mechanical Printing

The kind of print job you need depends on where you are in the layout process. Word-processed documents or manuscripts can be proofed from almost any type of printer. If cost per page is a factor, consider drafts run on a dot matrix printer. With toner cartridges running over $100 each, every copy you run off a laser printer just to edit manuscript pages will cost you more than it's worth.

For the same reason, don't use your laser printer to run multiple copies of multi-paged documents. On the average, toner refills for a photocopier are cheaper than toner cartridges for laser printers. And the wear and tear on a laser printer (which runs hotter than a photocopier) should be taken into consideration. It is much simpler, and cheaper, to take your original laser copy and run multiple copies on a photocopier.

Exhibit 15.1
The laser-printing process.

A. As the paper enters the printer from the paper **tray**, it is given a positive charge. As the paper moves along the **paper path** to the **transfer drum**, the rotating drum receives a negative charge from the **charger**.

B. Meanwhile, the computer image is transferred to the rotating transfer drum from the printer's memory via the **laser light**. The laser light bounces its image onto a **rotating mirror** and onto the drum. The light "draws" a picture by neutralizing the spot where black will be, leaving the surrounding area negatively charged where white will be.

C. The **toner cartridge** provides a negatively charged powder. As the drum rolls through the toner powder, the negative toner avoids the negative surface of the drum, but sticks to the neutralized dots created by the image drawn on the drum's surface by the laser light.

D. Since the toner is negative and the paper positive, when the paper passes over the drum, the dots stick to the paper.

E. The **fuser unit** "fuses" toner onto the paper using temperatures of up to 400 degrees Farenheit.

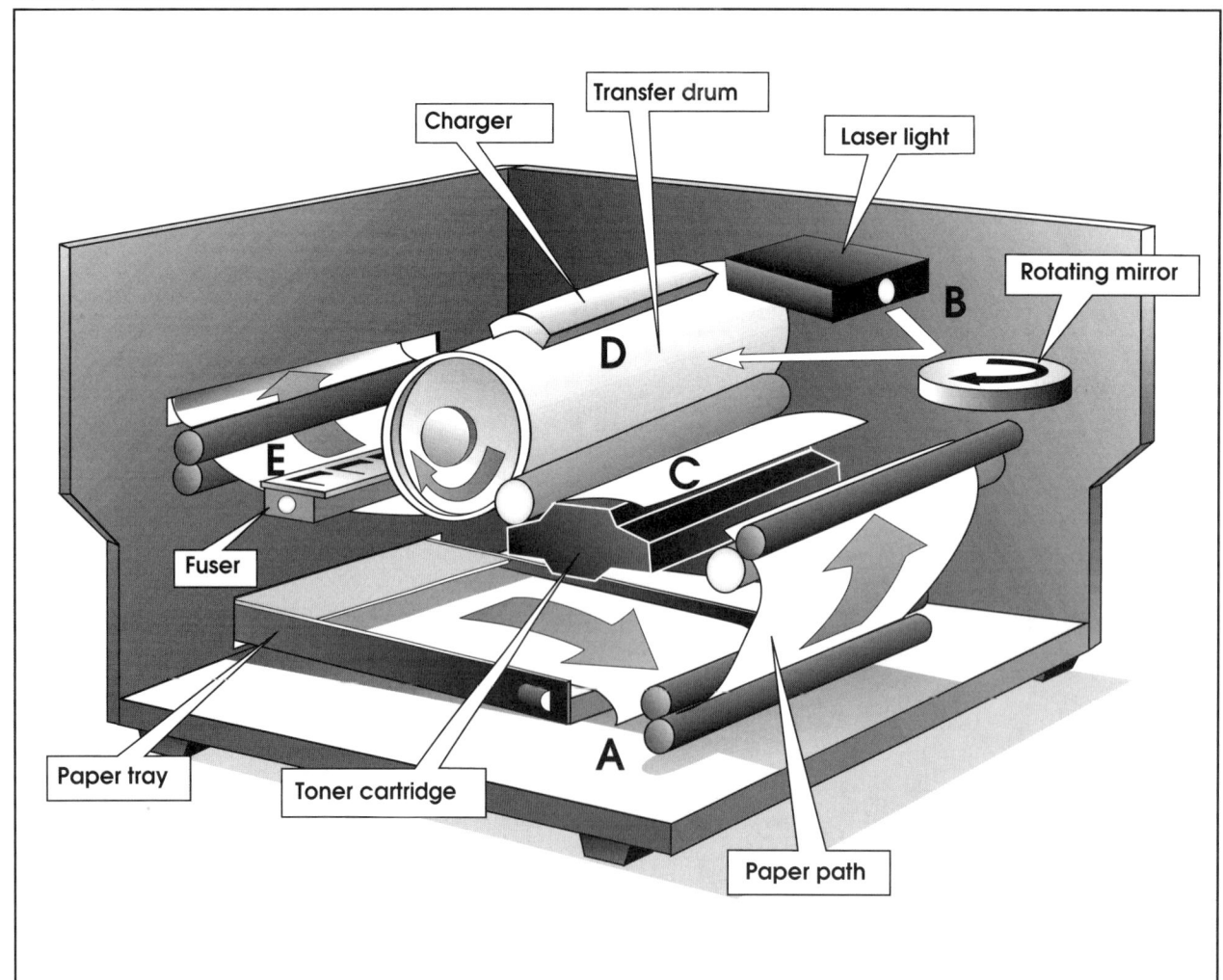

Illustration by Thomas H. Bivins © 1990

Save the laser printer for drafts that need to be checked for page layout, type alignment, and design considerations. You're going to be running quite a few. Here are a few tips for running drafts on a laser printer based on *PostScript*.

- If you've run previous drafts on a dot-matrix printer, don't count on the laser-printed version being the same. Alignment is a good bit different on these two types of printers, as is letterspacing, sizing, and so on. Get your original draft in the best shape you can before you run a copy on the laser printer. Be prepared to make adjustments.

- Prior to running a second laser draft, make as many adjustments to your first draft as you can. For example, don't just adjust the kerning and run another copy when you could have also reset the column width and changed the headline type. Learn to economize and make each copy count.

- Don't expect completely clean copies from your laser printer. These printers are temperamental. Toner quality and distribution vary from cartridge to cartridge, new cartridges take a few copies to "kick in," lightness versus darkness adjustments are tricky, and larger black areas are just not going to print out solid, no matter what you do.

    Some printer manufacturers recommend removing the cartridge and shaking it to spread the toner more evenly. This often works. Don't try it unless you know how to remove the cartridge and put it back. And don't do it in white clothing.

- Read your printer software manuals' sections on printing. Each program deals a little differently with print specifications. Don't assume that each program will use the same commands or even the same menus. Be aware, for instance, of paper size limitations. Many printers will run letter- and legal-sized documents only. Some allow for different paper trays for each size, while others require hand-feeding anything other than letter-sized paper.

    Some software programs allow you to *tile*. Tiling breaks larger pages, such as 11"x17", into four overlapping pieces. You can cut and paste these together for a rough layout. Other programs limit the actual area on a given paper size that will be printed on when using a specific type of printer. For example, *PageMaker* reduces the print area of legal-sized pages to 6.8" x 12" when printing on a LaserWriter; however, when printing to a Linotronic typesetter, it will run full size pages including bleeds and crop marks to indicate trim size (more on this below).

    Most laser printers will only print to within a quarter-inch of the paper edge. This limits your ability to use bleeds, or at least see them on drafts printed on laser printers. But it doesn't restrict your final copy if run on a phototypesetter.

- If you are using bleeds, or if you want to run a tabloid-sized page so you can see it whole—without tiling—try reducing it. Most page-layout programs will allow you to set a reduction value before you print. For instance, an 11"x17" page can fit onto an 8.5"x11" page at a 70 percent reduction. In most cases, it will still be legible. When reducing, indicate the edges of your document with crop marks, or simply add an unshaded box around the outside edges of your page before you print.

Selecting Paper for Laser Printing

Paper is probably the least thought about part of laser printing. Most of us simply opt for whatever is handy. The fact is, some papers are made specifically for laser printers, and some papers definitely should be avoided.

Ask yourself three questions when you pick laser printer paper.

- Will the finished product be used as a finished piece or for reproduction?
- Does the paper say what you want it to say? In other words, what is its look and feel?
- Does it run well in your printer?

Keeping in mind the paper specifications presented earlier in this chapter, the following rules of thumb should help you select the proper paper for your needs and your printer.

- Brighter paper reproduces well on laser printers. (This doesn't mean *whiter* paper. There are varying degrees of brightness even among white papers.) Brighter papers are also good for reproduction masters. In fact, several paper manufacturers make papers specifically for laser printer output that will be used for reproduction. Also, since it's hard to predict the degree of darkness of your printer, the brighter the paper, the more contrast you're likely to have between the print and the paper. In general, avoid colored paper; however, some interesting effects can be obtained with lighter colors such as gray and beige.

- Stay away from heavily textured paper. The heavier the texture, the more broken your type will look, because it will be harder for the toner to adhere to the paper's surface. Texture also affects any large, dark areas such as screens and display type. Some texture, like that found in bond paper and linen stock, is fine. The trick here is to experiment.

- Avoid heavy papers like cover stock, generally 90 pounds or more, unless you like removing jammed paper from your printer. On the other hand, extremely light papers, such as onion skin, may stick to the rollers or jam as they feed into the printer. Don't experiment much here. Just settle for a text-weight paper (generally around 60 pounds) and consign covers to your commercial printer.

- Use a fairly opaque paper, especially if your laser-printed copy is to be your final version. If you use a paper with high opacity, be sure it isn't also heavily textured.

- Don't expect heavily textured papers to retain their texture. Unlike offset presses, laser printers flatten the paper as it moves through the printer. In most cases, any texture will be lost.

- By the same token, don't use embossed or engraved papers in your laser printer since they might jam the mechanism and will flatten out anyway.

- Make sure your paper is heat resistant. Since laser printers work in temperatures of around 400 degrees Fahrenheit, certain letterhead inks may melt or stick and any metal or plastic will certainly ruin your printer. Above all, don't use acetate in your laser printer unless it has been specifically designed for your particular printer.

Printing the Finished Piece

Printing specifications vary greatly depending on whether you're printing a draft or a final product—a mechanical that will be reproduced by a commercial printer, or a report or presentation. Depending on your particular needs, a mechanical might be printed right off your laser printer. For quick-print jobs this is probably the cheapest way to go. Remember, though, that a LaserWriter only prints at 300 dots per inch. This is okay for body copy and most display type below 64 points, but for complex gray-scale photos and very large type, you might consider another method.

If you do go with laser-printed originals, the following tips might be helpful.

- Make sure your printer's toner is new or in good shape. If you can't get truly dark originals, try having your laser originals re-copied on a good photocopier. Just remember, each generation of copying deteriorates the image further.

- Use a strong typeface with solid serifs or sans serif and a good x-height. Pick a size that's easily readable (generally 10 or 12 point). And don't work with display type larger than 36 point, since it will tend to show the ragged edges even at 300 dpi.

- Large black areas and wide rules will tend to "gray out" on a laser printer, even one with a new toner cartridge. Try to avoid them.

- If you must use photographs, select those with few heavy black areas and a good contrast level. Remember, they are going to print out at 300 dpi, which will give you only about 33 shades of gray. If possible, work with line art or high contrast photos instead.

- Use a bright, fairly slick paper for your reproduction master.

To get the best possible camera-ready pages, run your mechanical on a computer-compatible photo typesetter or page compositor, such as the Linotronic 300. At 2500 dots per inch, the quality rivals (some say surpasses) traditional typesetting methods. Display type that looked ragged on your laser printer will look crisp and black; shaded areas will look dense and smooth; large, black areas will be uniformly black; illustration will be crisp; and photos will appear in a full range of grays. Clearly, there are advantages to using this method; and now that the price of a page of copy on a Linotronic is roughly five dollars, cost is one of the major ones.

If you are going to use a Linotronic, here are some tips.

- First, consider whether you need a positive or a negative run. Negatives will save you a step in the printing process, although they can't be checked for accuracy easily. In fact, positives containing photos are best run as negatives since the photos will probably muddy if shot a second time.

- Understand the parameters of your output device before you send anything to be run off. Are you running your pages on a Linotronic 100 with a 1250 dpi capability or a Linotronic 300 with a 2500 dpi capability? If you are using a Linotronic 300, is it actually set for a 2500 dpi default or has it been set down to save running time? In most cases, printing at 1250 dpi produces more than enough resolution and your final product will run in less time than if printed at 2500 dpi. Lower resolution does mean fewer gray levels; however, this usually isn't a problem since most of us can't easily distinguish between 95 levels of gray and 256 levels of gray anyway.

Also, ask about the default line screen. It can be variously set on many typesetters. If you don't designate a line screen with your software, your gray-scale images will default to the typesetter's settings. If you're running magazine-quality photos, use 120-133 line screen setting. For newsletters and newspapers, use 85-90.

- Although you can obtain extremely fine reproduction by printing scanned images on a phototypesetter, many images will need further adjustment. In fact, you will often find it cheaper to have halftones shot separately and stripped into your negative. See **Chapter 12** for more information on scanning.

- Remember, the limitations of print area imposed by your laser printer don't necessarily apply here. The Linotronic 300, for example, can print widths up to seventeen inches and any length. This allows for bleeds and over-sized pages. Don't forget to indicate that you want your pages run with crop marks, however.

- If you're running color separations, be sure to request registration marks—and carefully check your final output for proper registration.

- Make sure you include the type of program you used, copies of the original scanned photos on disks, and anything your printer needs to know to run your pages for you. Printers are likely to charge you even if the pages don't look like you thought they would—especially if it's because of something you didn't tell them.

- If your final product doesn't look like what you laid out, trace the problem to its origin. Computer programs are notoriously flukey, and trading disks between your machine and your printer's machine and thence to the Linotronic allows for many a slip. Among other things, make sure that you are both using the same version of your page-layout program. If you've included any illustrations to be placed by them, make sure they have that program as well. Specify any screens or other vital photographic information. And make sure the typefaces you used are carried by your printer or typesetter. Nothing is more frustrating than having to completely reset your ad because your Linotronic operator doesn't have Helvetica Narrow.

Color Printing

For most of us, in-house color printing is beyond our wildest dreams—and certainly our pocketbooks. There are basically two ways to consider color: as used in creating a comprehensive and, thus, produced in house, and as a final print job. In the latter case, color separations are developed, either through your software program and run on an output device, or by your commercial printer in the traditional way. For our purposes, we will discuss only the possibilities of in-house color printing.

There is a great deal of difference between what you see on that $2000 color monitor and what comes off your color printer. That's because screen colors are light mixed. That is, they produce virtually all the visible colors the human eye can behold by varying the amounts of red, green, and blue with light. The better color monitors now available can apply up to 256 shades to each of these primary colors, giving us a possible color palette of nearly 17 million combinations. Most color printers (as well as commercial printers) replicate this palette by mixing yellow, magenta, and cyan (yellow, red, and blue) inks or pigments; and what you mixed with light just isn't going to look the same when mixed with ink.

The issue is further complicated by the technology itself. Just as monochrome laser printers print with cells instead of dots, so color printers are limited by their inability to vary density. In traditional color printing, variations in density are implied by variations in dot size. Color printers, like monochrome printers, use dithering to produce either colors or shades of gray. As we saw in **Chapter 12**, the greater the number of gray levels, the lower the resolution. For the same reasons, the greater the number of colors, the lower the resolution. Since each color is *simulated* by printing dots of various colors next to each other to form a specific color or shade, the more colors you indicate, the more dots you require, thus lowering resolution.

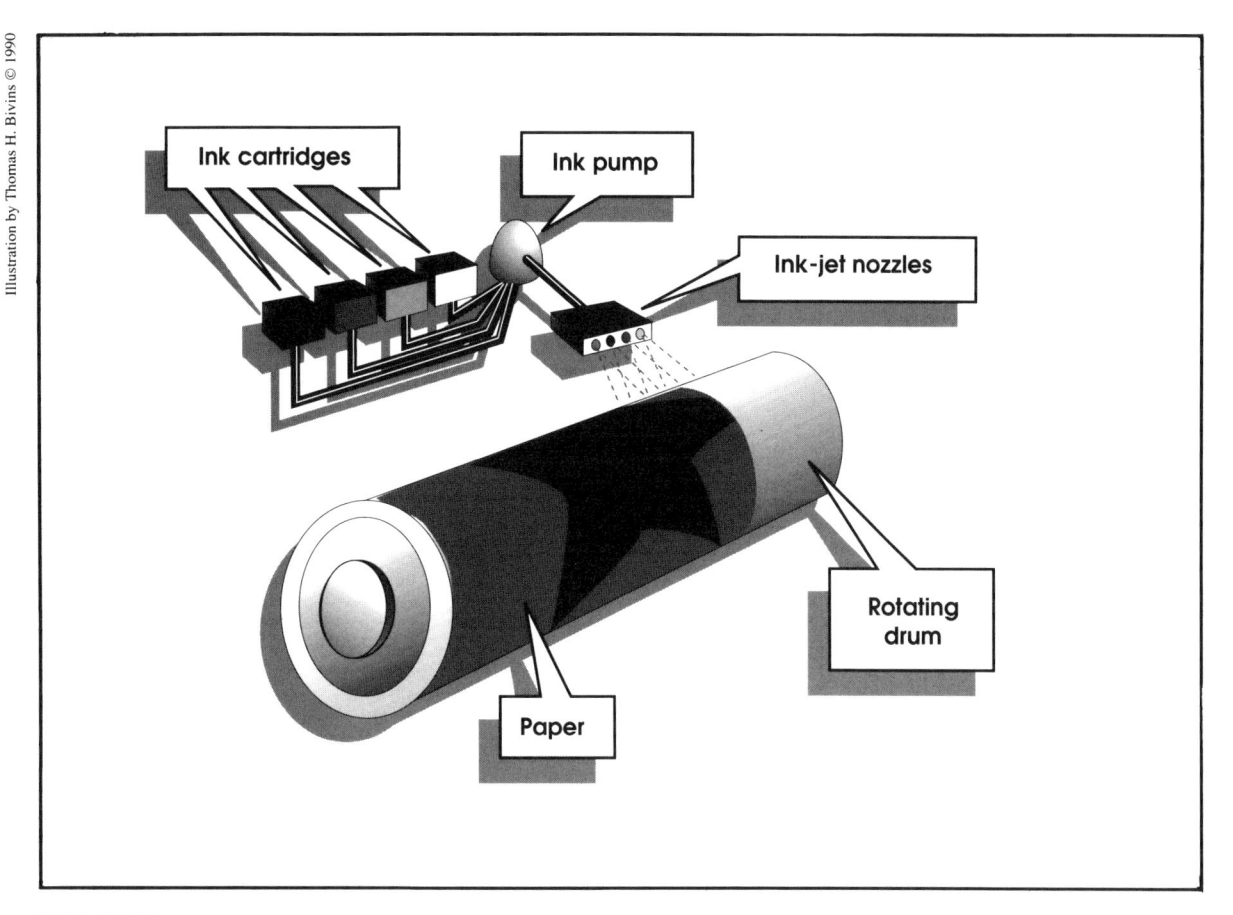

Exhibit 15.3

Ink-jet printing. During this process, the paper adheres to a rotating drum onto which four colors of ink are sprayed by a head moving parallel to the drum. The ink is drawn by a pump from ink resevoirs or cartridges holding yellow, magenta, cyan, and black pigments.

Now, let's go over the three most common types of color printers available today: **ink-jet printers**, **thermal transfer printers**, and **film recorders**. Of course, most dot-matrix printers can also print in color, but the range and quality is very limited.

Ink-jet Printers

Ink-jet printers are great if all you want to do is add some spot color to a presentation and don't care much about high quality. These printers use small jets to spray colors from bottles or cartridges inside the machine onto paper spinning on a rotating drum. The colors are mixed from yellow, magenta, cyan, and black and reproduce best on special paper. Although at the bottom end of the line these printers are relatively inexpensive, the best quality comes from those in the $60,000 to $70,000 range. In the $1500 to $2000 range, you can find several models that are useful for rough color comps and limited presentations.

Thermal Transfer Printers

Thermal transfer printers literally transfer color to paper via a transparency film and lots of heat. They also provide pretty good resolution (200-300 dpi). But they

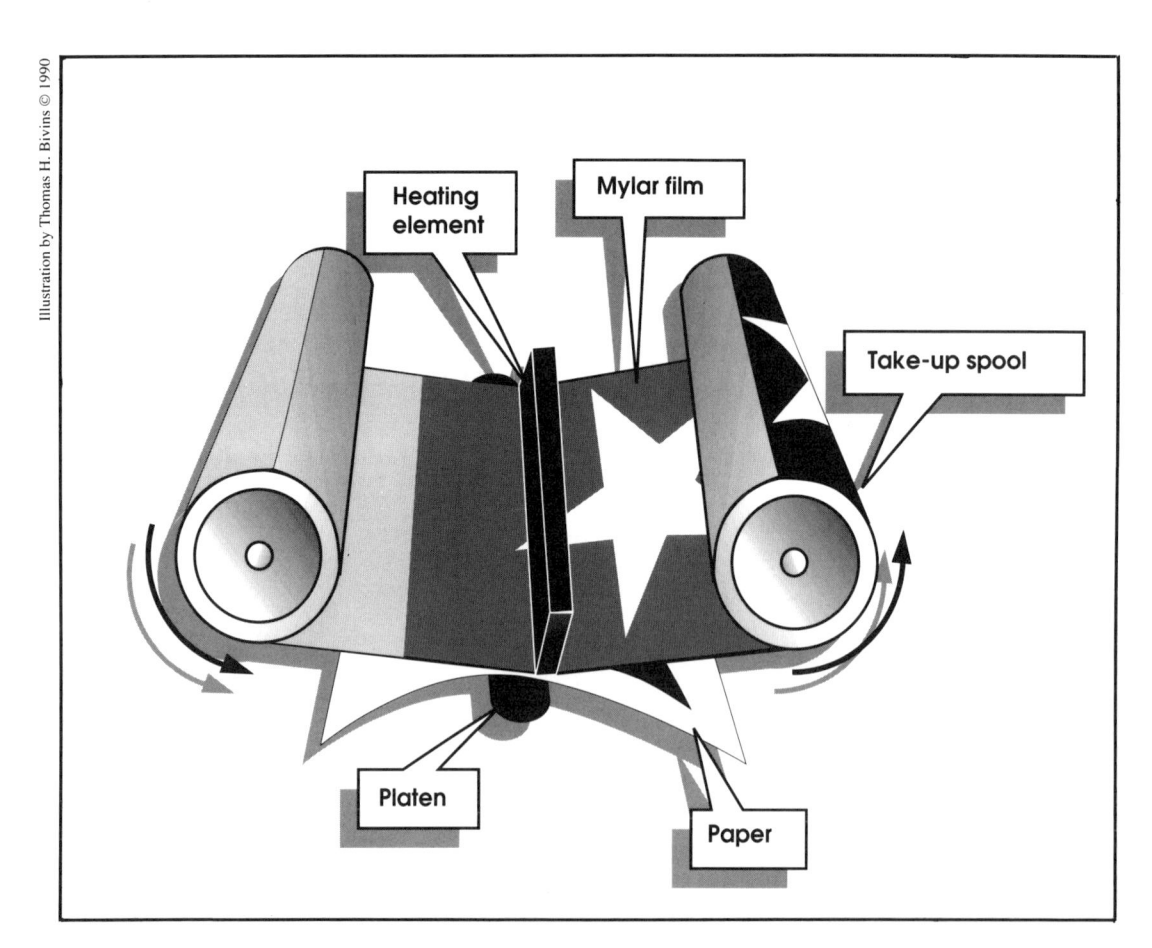

Exhibit 15.4

Thermal transfer printing. Thermal transfer uses sheets of Mylar film coated with yellow, magenta, and cyan pigments. A thermal head scans the page, transfers the proper sheet into place, and melts small dots of color onto the page. The result is very good for comps but the dithered appearance isn't camera-ready and the finished layout is very slick (light reflective) because of the transfer method.

dither the output much the same as a dot-matrix printer would, making it unsuitable for camera-ready art but certainly good enough for most comps. Thermal printers are relatively fast (about a minute a page) and relatively inexpensive (about fifty cents a page).

Although at around $8,000 the Tektronix color printer is already quite an investment, you still only get bit-mapped images—passable for graphics but not so good for type. On the other hand, you can get *PostScript*-type images (no jagged, bit-mapped edges) for a mere $20,000 plus by investing in something like the QMS *Colorscript 100* (although, at this writing, QMS has just introduced a *PostScript* color printer for *just* under $10,000). If you need to proof color separations before sending them to a Linotronic, for example, a *PostScript* compatible color printer could be very helpful. Whether you use one or the other, the basic problem of WYSIWYG still applies. The disparity between your monitor, your color printer, and your commercial printer's inks is going to make you crazy if you depend on your layout and output devices to provide you with accurate colors.

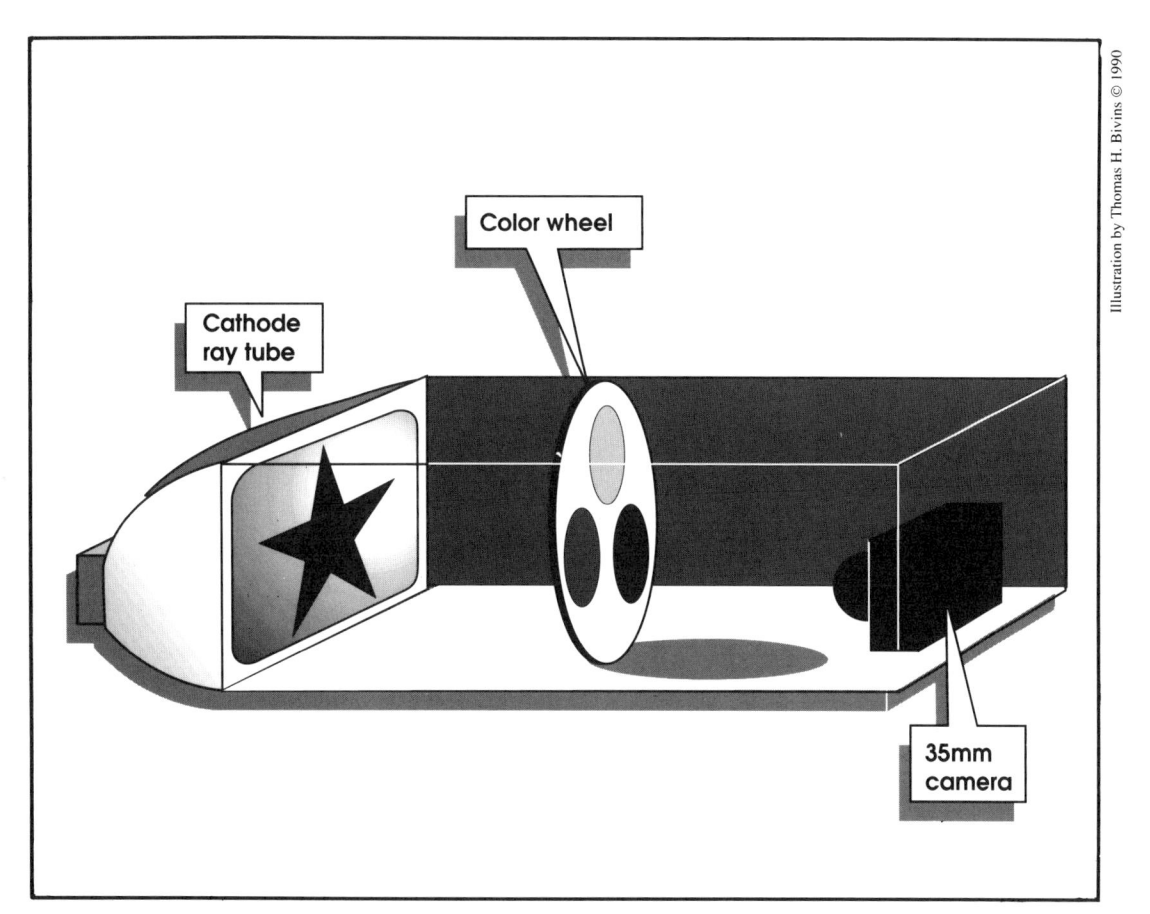

Exhibit 15.5
Film recorder. From the outside, film recorders look like a simple, plastic box. That, in fact, is exactly what they are. Inside the box, a 35 mm camera takes a series of multiple exposers of a CRT (cathode ray tube) through a color wheel—one exposure for each of the red, green, and blue filters on the wheel. A light beam eminating from the CRT exposes the film as the filter wheel moves into place for each color.

Printing 155

Film Recorders

Film recorders actually take a picture of what's on your monitor. At $6,000 to $12,000, they'd better be good photographers! They use a 35mm slide format to record exactly what you set up on your high-resolution color monitor. The output is excellent for generating color separations but not as good for color comps.

In short, in-house color printing hasn't reached the point at which it's worth the investment to *most* people. However, if it's like the rest of the computer industry, it won't be long before it's cost effective and aesthetically satisfying.

Appendix

Setting Up a Desktop Publishing System

So, you're ready to set yourself up with a desktop publishing system, but you don't have any idea where to start. It wasn't all that long ago that the choices were amazingly simple—you just bought a Macintosh and a copy of *PageMaker* and you were set. Today, the choices for hardware and software are far more complex, and depend on at least two factors: what you intend to publish and how much you have to spend. Even the most basic ads require some fairly sophisticated hardware and software, and it behooves you to make the right choices now so that you can expand later with the least amount of trouble and cost.

Your hardware choices are especially dictated by your needs and your pocketbook, although personal preference is undoubtedly a factor. For example, if you have already been working on a PC (IBM or compatible) don't assume that you'll have to switch to Apple Macintosh just to get involved in desktop publishing. Software layout programs such as *Ventura Publisher* and Quark *Xpress* can turn your PC into a superb desktop publishing system. And, with the advances in special add-ons to non-*PostScript* laser printers, you can now rival the output of a standard *PostScript* printer with your PC system.

Hardware

Whether you're starting from scratch or adding to an existing system, at the very minimum you'll need the following hardware.

- A computer with enough RAM to handle the larger layout and art programs. For example, *PageMaker* 4.0 requires 4 MGBs to run efficiently.

- At least a 20 MGB hard drive. The fact is, most layout programs now require a hard drive to work, and you're going to need the storage space and room to work.
- At least one floppy disk drive for backup file storage.
- A monochrome monitor.
- A printer. For the beginner who will be sending, or taking, final output to a Linotronic, a dot-matrix will do for rough drafts.

If you aspire to a more advanced system, you'll probably be considering the following as either basics or add-ons:

- A high resolution monitor. Although you can certainly get by with less, if you're going to be working with photographs, you'll want a monitor that will show you a complete range of grays.

And, if you're going to be working on ads with large page sizes, double-page spreads, or just want to see an entire page at once and still be able to read the body type, look into a large-screen monitor. These vary in price (none are cheap) and configuration. The most typical large-screen monitors come in either landscape (wide) or portrait (tall) configurations. If you work on magazines and newsletters, a landscape orientation would be best.

If you are working in color (either for printing color comps or for creating separations for Linotronic printouts) you'll eventually want a color monitor. Again, be prepared to pay the price.

Exhibit A.1
Basic configuration. A single-person operation can get by with a computer and a printer—preferably, a laser printer.

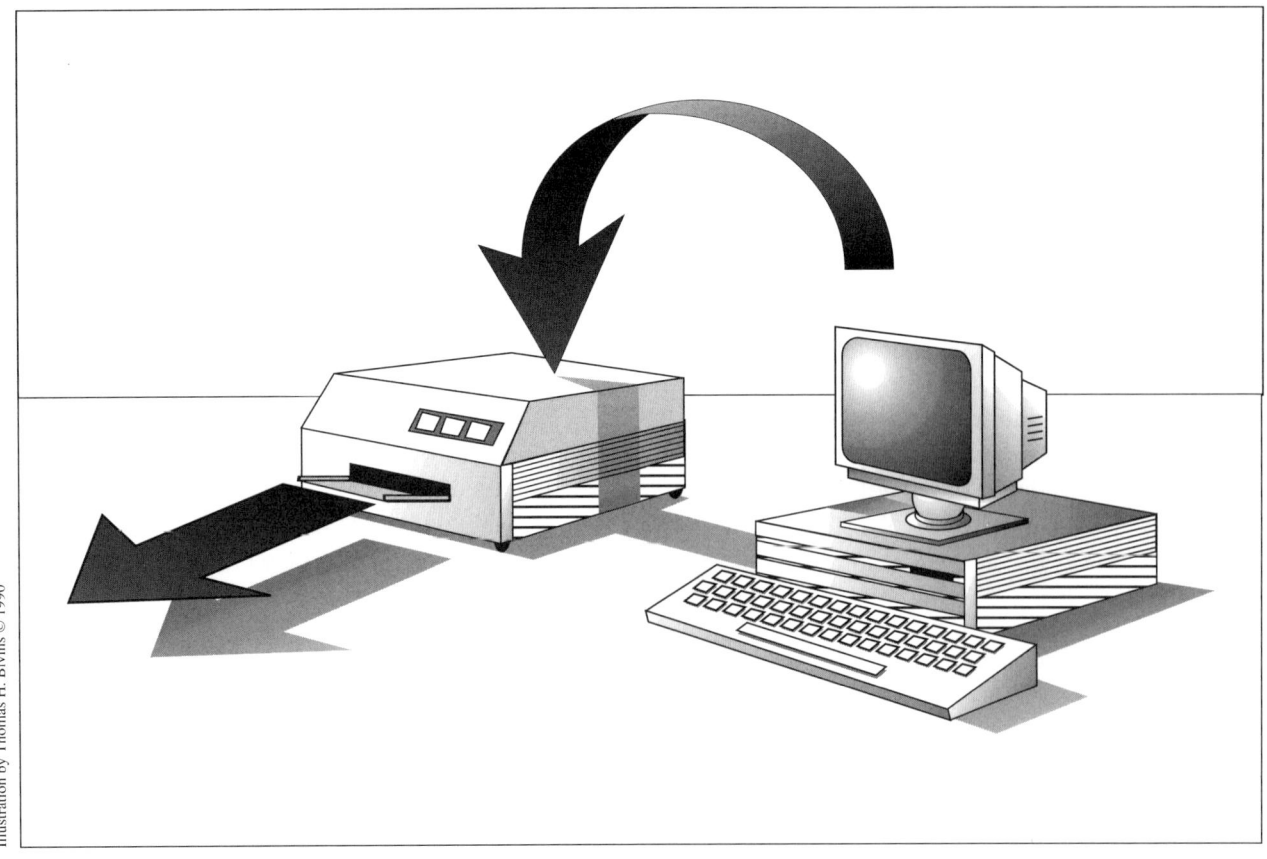

- A laser printer. Although you can get by with a dot-matrix printer for drafts, you'll want the kind of precision a laser printer can deliver. Many of your less prestigious layouts can often be run right from laser-printed masters.

- A scanner, especially if you want to use photographs or if you're tired of trying to calculate just where your artwork will fit in your computer layout by holding it against your screen.

- A color printer, especially if you want to run color comps or proofs. For most art directors, a color printer isn't necessary; however, if you're trying to impress your clients, nothing works like a color comp.

There is always something you can add—a more expensive computer, expanded memory, a better laser printer, a graphics tablet, and so on. Just make sure that you will get your money's worth out of that fancy, new piece of hardware before you buy into it.

Exhibit A.2
Advanced hardware configuration. One of the most common desktop publishing setups includes some sort of input device (keyboard, mouse, stylus) as well as peripheral devices such as a scanner which feed into the computer itself. From there, the infomation is sent to an output device such as a laser printer or, for finished work, a phototypesetter such as a Linotronic.

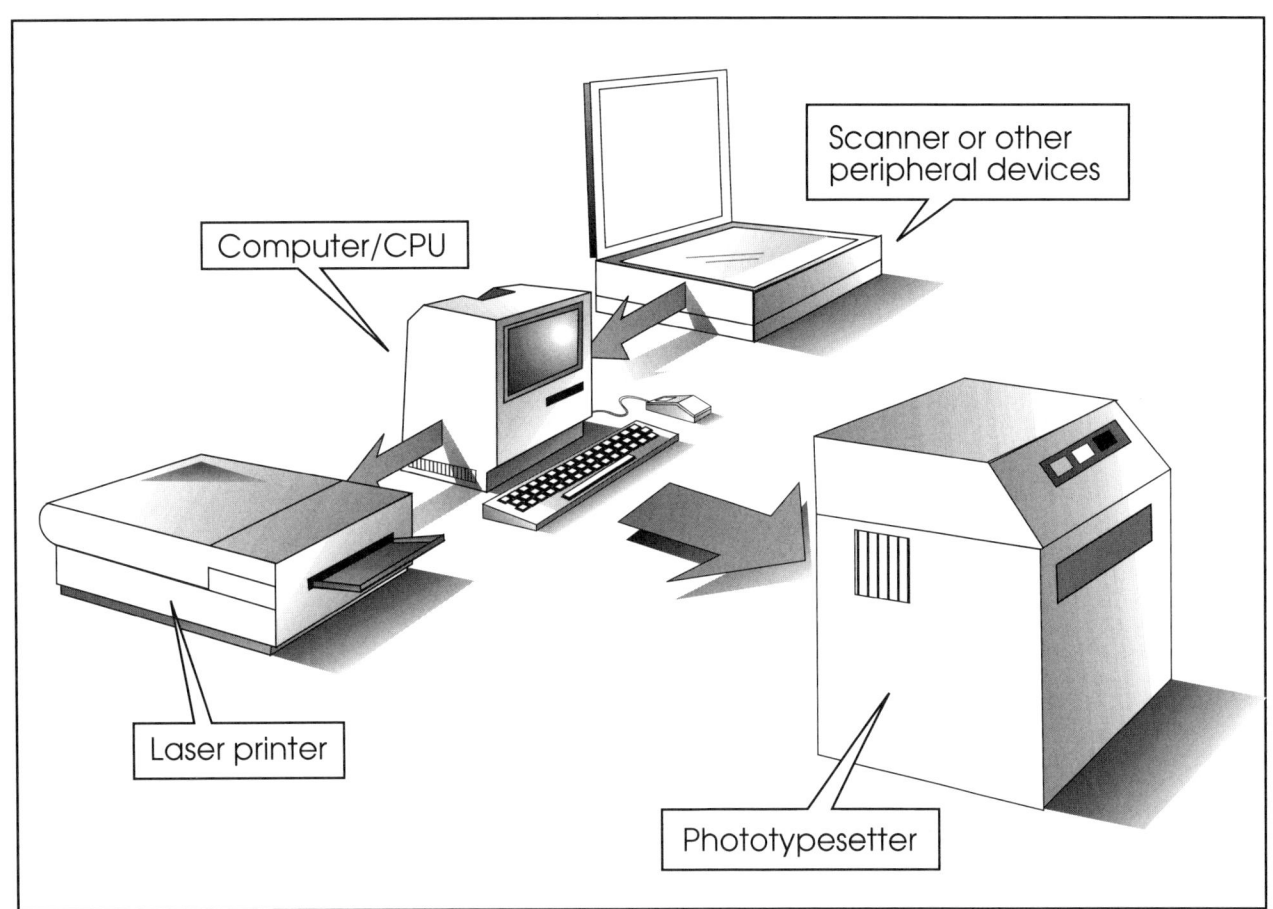

Software

These days, you can purchase a word-processing program that will do a bit of page layout (simple blocks, columns, lines, etc.), or a layout program that will do a bit of word processing. But, what you really want is the best of each, since no one program can yet deliver in all areas.

As with hardware purchases, buy what you need to do the job, but be aware of your future needs as well. Software, unlike hardware, isn't easily extended by adding a peripheral device. If you buy into a word-processing program that will only do short documents because that's all you do right now, you'll just have to buy a whole new program later if you decide you need greater capabilities. Plan ahead and purchase software that you can use both now and in the predictable future.

Again, there are basic needs and more elaborate needs. For the beginning desktop publisher, the following types of programs are recommended at a minimum:

- A good word-processing program—one that will serve your current *and* future needs. The industry standards are relatively expensive, but programs as *WordPerfect* for the PC and Microsoft *Word* for the Mac have become leaders in word processing for good reason. These, and others like them, have limited layout capabilities and can sometimes even use imported graphics. The key to their success, however, is the fact that they can adjust to longer and more complex documents easily. For example, both *WordPerfect* and Microsoft *Word* can perform various indexing, sorting and text calculation functions as well as execute excellent spell checks.

  Remember, word-processing programs are also a matter of taste; however, don't assume that your favorite PC-based program will be as good in its Macintosh version. It's been our experience that there are good PC word-processing programs and good Macintosh word-processing programs, and *they are different programs entirely*. Read some reviews, try out sample programs, and, above all, project your needs as far ahead as you can.

- A page-layout program. As with the word-processing programs, what's good for the goose isn't necessarily good for the gander. What works well on a Macintosh doesn't necessarily work well for a PC desktop publishing system. Industry standards such as *PageMaker* (for the Macintosh) and *Ventura Publisher* and Quark *XPress* (for the PC) are your best bet. Don't skimp on quality. A low-end page layout program will give you low-end results—if you survive the frustration factor.

Aside from these basic requirements, the serious art director will want access to various add-on programs that will enhance the job and reduce the number of intermediaries involved in the publication process. Take a look at these software extras.

- A graphics program (or programs). This is an area in which your talent is the deciding factor. For those with little or no artistic or design talent, some basic (but fairly inflexible) programs are best. Object-oriented programs such as *MacDraw* and *Cricket Draw* provide you with clean, *PostScript*-printable lines, but are limited to basic and somewhat static forms. Of course, bit-mapped images can be created on a number of paint programs including *MacPaint* and *FullPaint*, but they aren't for polished ads.

Judging by the multiplicity of newspaper graphics being generated using *MacDraw*, you might think it is a superb artist's tool; however, programs such as Adobe *Illustrator* and Aldus *FreeHand* are actually the software of choice for experienced designers and artists. Be warned, these programs are not for the inexperienced designer. They are complex to learn and use, but the results can be astonishing.

- A color graphics program. If you work in color, can be useful. However, the two most popular programs mentioned above, *Illustrator* and *FreeHand*, can also be used in color and can produce color separations. Although a color graphics program such as *PixelPaint* or *Modern Artist* can be fun to use, especially if you have a color monitor, they are truly luxuries if you already own an illustration program. And, since they produce bit-mapped images, they are of limited use in ads.

- A photo manipulation program such as *Image Studio* or *Digital Darkroom*. If you have a scanner and work with photos on a regular basis (either as finished art or simple placeholders for the screened art) you'll want one of these programs. They allow for the kind of fine tuning many scanners don't provide including brightness and contrast adjustments, gray-scale manipulation, photo retouching, and myriad other tasks. These programs are not toys; they are serious graphics tools that, as they become more sophisticated, may actually replace the traditional methods of working with photographs.

- A font editing/creation program such as *Fontographer* or *Letra Studio* allows you to create your own type fonts. These are terrific fun for novice and experienced type designers alike, but they can be difficult to learn if you know absolutely nothing about type. They are especially good for developing logotypes and creating special letters for illustrations.

The Proof Is In the Pudding

There's a lot to be said for that old saw. Ultimately, your final, printed ad is going to determine how successful your desktop publishing system is—and a lot of that success depends not on your hardware and software, but on you.

You are the final ingredient in this system. Your energy, talent, interest and organizational abilities will determine the success or failure of your ads. Truthfully, you can get by on a lot less than you think you can if you possess the right attitude and the requisite abilities. Fancy hardware and expensive software only enhance and streamline a process you should already have down to a fine art.

The fact is that many excellent ads are still laid out the "old-fashioned" way. There is no substitute for being able to accomplish the task this way. (For instance, what happens when the power goes out or your only computer breaks down?) Don't get the wrong idea—computers have made and are continuing to make a huge difference in publishing. Just remember: that multi-thousand dollar system you sit down in front of every day is only a tool. Simply holding a brush in your hand doesn't make you an artist, the same as sitting in front of a typewriter doesn't make you a writer. Dedication, hard work and talent will.

Take a hard look at your ads and ask yourself a few questions:

- Are they already the best they can be without the addition of desktop publishing? If they are, you probably already know the basics and are ready for desktop publishing. If they're not, why not? Will the technology help the look or simply add to the clutter? Be honest. Don't expect desktop publishing to give you something you don't already possess.

- What, exactly, do you expect desktop publishing to add to your layouts or the process of developing them? Again, if you're looking for an answer to your design problems, check out your own abilities first. On the other hand, if you're expecting the technology to streamline the process and save you some money—you're probably right.

- Will the savings you accrue be offset by the cost of the system? It takes a lot of savings in typesetting to counter balance a $25,000 investment. On the other hand, a basic setup might pay for itself in the person-hours normally used up to do the same thing by hand.

- Are you willing to take the time needed to make yourself an expert on your system. If you aren't willing to become an expert, you're wasting your money. Anyone can learn the basics (or just enough to cause trouble). If you're serious about desktop publishing, you'd best dedicate yourself to the long haul. The authors of this text aren't exactly beginners, yet they both learn something new almost every day. Be prepared to immerse yourself in the process, the programs and the machinery. The more you know, the more streamlined the publications' process becomes.

Above all, don't set yourself up for frustration. Realize the limitations of your system and of desktop publishing in general. Understand how it works and why it does what it does. You don't have to become a "computer nerd" to gain a fairly complete understanding of your hardware and software. The more you know, the less frustrated you'll be when something does go wrong. Most of the frustration of working with computers comes from not knowing what's happening in software or hardware problem situations. Keep those technical support hotline numbers close at hand and use them. Don't be afraid to ask questions, but read your manuals first so you'll know what to ask.

Finally, take it all with a grain of salt. Don't talk to your computer. You probably don't talk to your typewriter. They're both just tools of the trade. Misuse them, and your shortcomings will become apparent to everyone who reads your ads. Use them wisely and they'll show off for you.

Colophon

How This Book Was Put Together

This entire book was written, designed, and laid out using desktop publishing. We have learned a great deal during the experience that will serve us in the future. We have explored new avenues and developed techniques that are invaluable to any desktop publisher. Many of these techniques are shared within the chapters of this book. Some, we will introduce or reinforce here.

The Tools

A number of software and hardware considerations are important to any desktop publishing endeavor. These are usually dictated by the complexity of the job as mentioned in the preceding appendix on setting up a system of your own.

Hardware

For our purposes, we needed the most powerful hardware available to accomplish such a large publication effectively. For starters, we used a Mac II (the earliest model) with an 80-MGB hard drive and 4 MGBs of RAM. Storage space for such a large publication is always a problem. Fortunately, we also have access to a 275-MGB file server on which we kept backup copies of all our chapters and stored the scanned images for **Chapter 4** on photography. The 4 MGBs of RAM were needed to run such memory-eating programs as *Image Studio* and the latest version of *PageMaker* (4.0).

We couldn't have begun to do justice to our layouts without a large-screen monitor. We have a high-resolution Radius two-page monochrome monitor capable of displaying 256 shades of grey. Many of the images seen in **Chapters 4**, **5**, and **6** were scanned in using a Hewlett Packard ScanJet Plus.

Drafts were printed on an Apple LaserWriter II NTX, a powerful and speedy machine. Final, camera-ready copy was produced on a Linotronic 300 at 1270 dpi. Scanned photographs in **Chapters 4**, **5**, and **6** were run with 90 lpi screens to increase contrast. As pointed out in **Chapter 4**, scanned photographs increase in clarity with lower resolution. Efforts to run photos at the standard 133 line screen produced high resolution but extremely dense proofs which muddied when printed. The rest of the examples, not produced originally on the computer, were halftoned the traditional way using a 133-line screen.

Software

PageMaker has always been our layout software of choice. Version 4.0 came out just in time to accomplish our final layouts and includes a number of time-saving functions designed specifically for book production. Chief among them is an automatic indexing function that keys to page layouts instead of word-processing files (eliminating the very tedious step of matching indexed word-processed files to page layouts). The index can be viewed at any time and includes all documents linked under the *book* designator. The table of contents was also generated in *PageMaker* 4.0 simply by designating all chapter heads and all subheads as entries. This can be done from the *define styles* menu for each chapter/file. Both indexing and compiling a table of contents are generated across documents stored in separate files but linked as a single publication under *PageMaker's* new *book* function.

In addition, the new version comes with a built-in word processor. All final spell checks and those tedious global search and replace jobs can now be done in the page-layout program. This was especially handy when we decided to raise the point size of the bullets that appear so often throughout this book. We simply called up the word processing editor in each chapter, searched for bullets and replaced them with a larger point size.

Style sheets, a fixture in *PageMaker* 3.0 and now in version 4.0, are still the mainstay of any long publication. Without them, we couldn't have laid out this book. Our style sheet became quite lengthy. Here is what we eventually settled on.

- **Body Text**—11-point Times, leaded 13, justified, first indents .25 inches.

- **Chapter Number**—18-point Avant Garde, normal face, flush left.

- **Chapter Title**—24-point Avant Garde, normal face, flush right.

- **Chapter Section**—14-point Avant Garde, bold, flush right.

- **Captions**—9-point Times, italic, leaded 11, flush left.

- **Drop Caps** (for chapter title pages)—48-point Avant Garde, bold, pasted to the scrapbook and placed in *PageMaker* as a graphic element which then permitted textwrap.

- **Examples**—9-point Bookman, leaded 11, flush left, indented .50 inches.

Sub Points (bulleted and numbered items)—11-point Times, leaded 13, justified, indented .25 inches. Space between bulleted items was leaded 6 points to tighten up the lists. This leading was also saved as a style called "bullet leading" so that the leading could be clicked and set quickly.

- **A-level Subheads**—13-point Avant Garde, bold, flush left with 1.5 spaces following between it and text.

- **B-level Subheads**—11-point Avant Garde, bold, flush left with .5 space following.

- **C-level Subheads**—11-point Avant Garde, bold, indented .25 inches, body text leading.

- **Figure Numbers**—9-point Avant Garde, bold, flush left with a .5-point rule following to the right edge of the copy block. (This new function in *PageMaker* 4.0 allows you to set ruler lines anywhere above or below a beginning paragraph. We simply designated a baseline placement for a .5-point line and indented it .65 inches so as to follow the figure number. Several had to be created due to the varying lengths of the figure numbers.)

A number of other software programs were used for specialized work. For photo manipulation, we used *Image Studio*. For illustration, we used Aldus *Freehand*. Several illustrations were traced using Adobe *Streamline* and then further enhanced in *Freehand*. We also used Adobe *Type Manager* to spec our type for alignment in critical places.

And, finally, all our word processing was accomplished in Microsoft *Word* 4.0—for our money, the most efficient program on the market for the Macintosh.

The Layout

We worked from a template we developed early on using a 30 pica text column thrown to the inside leaving a 12 pica margin on the outside for captions, small illustrations, and overflow illustrations from the text column. Running feet were 9-point Helvetica with 10-point Avant Garde page numbers. These were set on the master pages along with the column guides.

During the later stages of the layout process, we purchased a brand new book called *Real World PageMaker 4.0: Industrial Strength Techniques* by Olav Kvern and Stephen Roth. This book proved to be invaluable in speeding up the final layout. It contains hundreds of shortcuts, many not mentioned in the *PageMaker* 4.0 documentation. Probably the most helpful hints were directions for setting up several *Quickeys* that take the place of tedious and repetitious mouse movements or multiple key strokes. *Quickeys* is a program developed by CE Software that allows you to assign key strokes to commonly used functions so that you don't have to go to the menus. For example, since we used the text wrap function of *PageMaker* constantly, we simply set up a single key stroke that would automatically outline selected items, saving us having to go through several menu manipulations. And, even though PageMaker has key strokes designed to change *toolbox* icons, they are double strokes involving the shift and function keys and requiring the finger spread of a concert pianist. We consigned the most frequently used icons—the pointer and text icons—to single keys which we could reach with ease.

On the whole, this entire project has been an incredible learning experience. As desktop publishers, we have at least doubled our own proficiency. The moral, of course, is practice, practice, practice.

Chapter number—*18 point Avant Garde, normal face, flush left.*

Chapter title—*24 point Avant Garde, normal face, flush right.*

Drop caps *(for chapter title pages)—48 point Avant Garde, bold, pasted to the scrapbook and placed in PageMaker as a graphic element which then permitted textwrap.*

Sub points *(bulleted and numbered items)— 11 point Times, leaded 13, justified, indented .25 inches. Space between bulleted items was leaded 6 points to tighten up the lists.*

166   Colophon

Body text—*11 point Times, leaded 13, justified, first indents .25 inches.*

A-level subheads—*13 point Avant Garde, bold, flush left with 1.5 spaces following between it and text.*

B-level subheads—*11 point Avant Garde, bold, flush left with .5 space following.*

Figure numbers—*9 point Avant Garde, bold, flush left with a .5 point rule following to the right edge of the copy block.*

Captions—*9 point Times, italic, leaded 11, flush left.*

C-level subheads—*11 point Avant Garde, bold, indented .25 inches, body text leading.*

Glossary

Account executive. A person in an ad agency in charge of advertising for an account. May be called *account supervisor*.

Advertising awareness. A research and marketing term used to indicate how familiar the target audience is with the advertising for a given product.

Advertising concept. An idea that quickly communicates the most important product benefit to the relevant target audience.

Audio. Refers to the sound portion of a TV commercial.

Bi-level scan. A bi-level scan produces bit maps at roughly 300 dpi. Although bi-level scanned images look okay at greatly reduced sizes, they plainly show the bits when enlarged. They don't print well on a Linotronic since the 300 dpi is "locked in" during scanning and will print at that figure regardless of output device.

Bit-map. Font characters or illustration constructed from individual bits presenting a jagged appearance at larger sizes.

Bit. The smallest unit of information in a binary system.

Body copy. Text material set in blocks in relatively small type. Distinguished from display copy (headlines and subheadlines and other larger type).

Body type. Type set 12 points and smaller, used for body copy. Distinguished from display type, 14 points and larger.

Border. Rule (line) or design art that surrounds an ad and defines its edges. All ads do not have to have borders.

Brainstorming. A group meeting in which spontaneous ideas are randomly presented as a means of solving problems or developing plans.

Brand name. The name given to a specific product, i.e., Chevrolet.

Bugs. Unplanned problems within software programs that cause data to be misinterpreted.

Byte. A unit of information, used mainly in referring to data storage. A group of eight bits used to represent a *character*.

Campaign. Planned advertising through several executions in one or more media.

CD ROM. A compact disk allowing only reading (no recording) via laser scanning.

Cell/dot. The "dot" produced by a computer output device that replicates a halftone dot. This cell is itself composed of smaller *printer dots*. These smaller dots determine the number of grays in an image by their configuration and by how many are turned on or off. When you send your image to a printer, it determines how many gray levels will be produced by dividing the number of dots per inch (dpi) the printer can print by the number of lines per inch (lpi) in the image (as defined by your software or the printer's default setting).

Character. Standard 8-bit unit representing a symbol, letter, number, or punctuation mark. Generally means the same as *byte*.

Cliche. A word or phrase used too often to be effective in either headlines or copy.

Clip art. Pre-packaged illustration, usually obtained through purchase of thematic sets.

Color separation. Process of breaking down full-color art into its primary color components.

Commercial. An announcement or spot. A radio or television sales message.

Compatibility. The degree to which different types of either hardware or software interact successfully with each other.

Comprehensive (comp). A layout prepared to resemble the finished ad as closely as possible.

Copy platform. The statement of the basic ideas to be used in an ad or campaign and their relative importance. Listing of selling points and benefits and instructions regarding policy in handling elements in the ad(s). Also called copy policy, copy outline, copy plan.

Creative blueprint. A systematic means of analyzing an advertising problem completed before the creation of any advertising.

Daisy wheel printers. Printers utilizing a circular type element that rotates into place as each letter is chosen by the computer program.

Demographics. The statistical description of prospects in physical terms, such as age, sex, occupation, marital status, education, household income, etc. See psychographics.

Derivative. A term used to describe ideas, language, or symbols used in advertising that are attributable to others or that first gained widespread recognition elsewhere.

Desktop publishing. The creation of publications utilizing computer hardware and software.

Digital fonts. Computer-designed and -generated typefaces.

Digital. Referring to communications procedures, techniques, and equipment by which information is encoded as either a binary one or zero.

Display type. Type larger than 12 point, used for headlines and other emphasized elements.

Dot-matrix printers. Printers utilizing a fast-moving head to strike an inked ribbon, compiling letters and forms from individuals bits.

DPI. Dots per inch. This figure represents *resolution*. The greater the dpi, the higher the resolution. Some typesetters, such as the Linotronic 300, are capable of producing up to 2500 dpi while the most the LaserWriter can produce is 300 dpi. Since resolution decreases as the number of gray levels increases, an output device with an ability to produce 2500 dpi is about the only way you're going to get anything approximating 256 levels of gray. Dpi can be set on most scanners as *sampling rate*. For magazine-quality images, scanning at 150 dpi seems to be adequate. For images that will be enlarged later, scanning at a higher rate is recommended.

Drop shadow. A shadow created, usually behind a box, in a page-layout program.

Dummy. A mockup of the finished product, showing where the elements will be placed.

Element. Any one of the distinguishable components of an ad: headline, subheadline, body copy, illustration, logo, border, etc.

EPS. *Encapsulated PostScript*. The format in which graphics created in illustration programs such as Fr*eehand* are transported into page-layout programs such as *PageMaker*. EPS creates large and unwieldy files when used to save photographs. It is best to avoid this format for anything but illustration.

Execution. All elements of an advertisement in any medium—all symbols including the use of type, the type of artwork chosen, and the space in which they appear.

Face. The style or design of type.

Font. A complete set of type characters of a particular typeface and size.

Formal balance. In design, the symmetrical arrangement of elements on both sides of a vertical line in the middle of an ad.

Formatting. Setting up guidelines for the placement of text within word-processing or page-layout programs. Indents, line length, spacing, etc. are examples of formatting.

Four-color process. A printing process that reproduces a full range of colors using red, yellow, blue, and black. *Full color.*

Grayscale scan. Depending on the scanner, a grayscale scan can produce up to 256 levels of gray. Although many scanners allow you to set resolution as you scan, grayscale scanned images depend on the output device for their final resolution. A LaserWriter, for example, can only produce images with a maximum of 48 levels of gray; while a Linotronic 300 can give you in excess of 256 levels of gray in addition to excellent resolution.

Halftone. The traditional method of rendering a continuous tone photograph into a series of dots of varying sizes that can then be printed. This process is replicated on a scanner by the creation of *cell/dots*.

Hardware. The machinery of computing comprised of the computer itself and all physical peripherals attached to it.

Headline. Also *head*. Larger type lines used to get attention in an ad. Usually at top of ad. See *subhead*.

Illustration. Usually a drawing or a painting.

Importing/exporting. Transferring data from one software program into another.

Initial caps. Upper case characters, typically bold and larger than text, set either above (raised cap) or below (dropped cap) the first line of a body of text.

Ink-jet printers. Printers utilizing small jets to spray colors from bottles or cartridges inside the machine onto paper spinning on a rotating drum.

Jingle. A musical signature used by advertisers or radio stations to identify themselves to listeners. Jingles vary from complete songs that tell the story to a brief (but memorable) musical intro with an open middle for live or taped copy and perhaps a short musical close. Jingles are frequently prepared in a variety of lengths and seasonal variations for maximum flexibility.

Kerning. The space between text characters or the act of reducing or expanding that space.

Laser printers. Printers utilizing a laser-read photo transfer method for reproducing text and graphics.

Lay out. To put the elements of an ad in a pleasing and readable arrangement in a given amount of space. *Layout* is the noun form, the resulting physical "blueprint."

Line art. Illustration without gradations of tone.

Line screen. The frequency at which dots (or cell/dots) appear in a printed image. This figure is controlled by the number of lines in the screen used to produce a traditional halftone or the setting of the output device in a scanned photograph. Most output devices have a default setting: LaserWriters default to a 53 lpi screen at a 45-degree angle. The Linotronic 100 defaults to a 1250 dpi screen at a 45-degree angle. A typical newspaper photo uses about an 85 or 90 lpi screen while a typical magazine photo is run at 133 lpi.

Live copy. The copy read by an announcer in contrast to taped commercials.

Live tag. A message added by the announcer to recorded commercial giving local address, local price, etc. Often used when a manufacturer's radio commercials are aired by stores locally.

Local area network (LAN). A hardware and software configuration allowing a small number of computer workstations to operate as a unit.

Logotype (logo). The name of the advertiser in art or type form that remains the same from ad to ad. See s*ignature*.

LPI. Lines per inch. This is normally representative of the screen you use in the halftone process; however, lpi is a determining factor in scanned image quality as well. See *line screen*.

Market profile. A description of prospects in terms of demographic. psychographic, and geographic characteristics.

Market segmentation. Dividing the market into homogeneous subsections in order to treat each more appropriately.

Marketing. The entire system of business activities used to plan, price, promote, and distribute products and services to prospects. Advertising is only one factor in the marketing process.

Master pages. In *PageMaker*, the initial pages on which elements to be repeated from page to page are created, such as page numbers, headers, etc.

Medium. A means of communicating: newspapers, magazines, television, radio, direct mail, outdoor, etc. Plural: *media*.

Megabyte (MGB). 1,048,576 bytes, equal to 1024 kilobytes.

Moire effect. A shimmering effect resulting from scanning an image previously halftoned, such as an image from a magazine. You can reduce this effect by scanning in the negative mode (if your scanner allows) and returning the image to a positive in a photo manipulation program such as *Image Studio*.

Output device. The device by which you print your document. It can be any type of printer (e.g., LaserWriter) or typesetter (e.g., Linotronic) or any number of graphic plotters or other such instruments.

Pasteup. A layout in which all types and illustrative material are combined for reproduction as a single unit.

PC (personal computer). A generic term for a single-user microcomputer, typically an IBM or IBM clone.

Photostat (stat). A photographic copy. See *PMT* and *Velox*.

Pica. A unit of horizontal type measurement. Six picas equal one inch.

PICT. A picture-type, object-oriented format common to many draw programs. It uses PostScript to print out on most output devices.

PMT (Photo-mechanical transfer). A photostat produced without a negative (like a Polaroid process). Faster than *Velox*. Screened print.

Point. A unit of vertical measurement of type: 12 points to a pica; 72 point to an inch.

PostScript. Computer language developed by Adobe Systems allowing outlines to be constructed according to mathematical formulas resulting in smooth contours.

Premise statement. A brief statement that includes all aspects to be communicated in the advertising.

Product attributes. Qualities not inherent to a product but ascribed to it by a prospect.

Product benefits. The advantages product features offer a prospect.

Product concept. The quality, performance and features inherent in the product and its use.

Product features. Special qualities or functions inherent in a product.

Product positioning. A marketing strategy which takes into consideration how consumers perceive a product relative to competitive offerings.

Psychographics. Refers to describing prospects according to their personality and lifestyle traits. See *demographics*.

RAM (Random Access Memory). Storage device into which data can be entered and read.

Repro proof. A reproduction proof. Clean, sharp proof made from galley ready for pasteup so it can be photographed.

Resolution. Resolution is determined by *dpi* or dots per inch and can be set as you scan (see *sampling rate*), reduced during importation into a photo manipulation program, or enhanced or limited by your output device.

Retouching. Correcting or improving photographs or other artwork by using art techniques. Getting ready for making plates.

RIFF. *Raster Image File Format.* The working format in Image Studio, it takes up less room than a standard TIFF file and can be converted to TIFF, or other formats, if need be. At this writing, it can't be used as-is in many other programs.

Rough. A preliminary sketch showing where type and art are to go.

Sampling rate. The number of dots per inch scanned into your image file (sampled) as a result of your scanner's setting. Many allow up to 300 dpi while newer models are offering 400 dpi. Theoretically, the higher the sampling rate, the better the resolution (see *dpi*). Lower settings (such as 72 dpi) are sufficient for locator graphics used only for placement in your layout. Most high-quality publications can use 150 dpi images quite well. Line art and images that will be enlarged later should be scanned at 300 dpi or higher.

Sans serif. In typography, a type that has no cross strokes or serifs at the tops and bottoms of characters.

Scaling. Enlarging or reducing an element in some increment of its original size.

Serifs. The short cross strokes at top and bottom of characters in certain typefaces. especially those in Roman face.

Signature. The advertiser's name in an ad. Abbreviated as *sig*.

Slogan. Sometimes called a tagline. A cleverly written statement that communicates quickly everything a particular product represents.

Software. Computer programs.

Stat. A photographic print. Velox or PMT are two types. *Photostat*.

Stock. Art, music, or photos on hand in files or libraries for immediate use.

Storyboard. An artist's rendition of a commercial, usually drawn on paper in separate frames.

Strategy. An approach to problem solving aimed at defining the target audience, the competition, the product/service benefits, and the advertising message.

Style sheets. Electronic menus allowing preset designations for text formatting. Some software allows style sheets to be transferred from one program to another.

Subhead. May be (1) a display line enlarging on the main headline, usually in smaller size, or (2) a short heading inside the copy used to break up a long patches of gray.

Tagline. A statement, often cleverly written, that quickly communicates what a particular product represents.

Target audience. Those prospects to whom the product you are pitching is most relevant. The relevancy may be determined given any number of criteria: current use, future use, newly discovered use, etc.

Teaser. An ad or series of ads purposefully designed to promote curiosity about advertising to come.

Tens. 10-second commercials.

Text files. Typically, word-processed files transferred to another software application as characters only, often without formatting.

Thermal transfer printers. Printers utilizing extreme heat to transfer images to transparency film of different colors.

Thirties. 30-second commercials.

Thumbnail. A rough layout in miniature, at the doodling stage.

TIFF. *Tagged Image File Format.* One of the most common file formats for saving scanned images. It is useable in almost all page-layout programs, photo manipulation, and illustration programs. Its major drawback is the amount of file space it takes up. An image scanned in TIFF can be reduced by lowering the resolution as you scan or as you import it into a photo manipulation program.

Tint block. A shaded rectangle created in a page-layout program into which text is inserted.

Tone. An attitude or expression natural to the product and the people who manufacture it.

Tracking. A means of connecting thoughts within body copy through which each copy point is tied to a central theme.

Typography. The field involving designing, setting, and using type.

Velox. A photostatic print that has been screened. Less expensive than regular halftone process. Also see *PMT*.

Visualization. The process of mentally picturing how an ad will work before it is produced. Also, getting an idea into visual or graphic form.

Voice-over. The off-camera voice of an announcer who is heard but not seen.

White space. The space in an ad not taken with any other element, type, pictures, etc. An important design element in itself.

Word processing. Creating text with a computer. Word-processed documents may be used as is or imported into a page-layout program.

NOTE

The Glossary includes some terms selected from Albert C. Book and C. Dennis Schick, *Fundamentals of Copy and Layout*, 2nd ed., NTC Business Books, Lincolnwood (Chicago), 1990.

Index

Ad format 134
Adobe *Illustrator* 124, 140, 161. *See also*
   Illustration programs
Advertising
   problem 5, 6, 8-16
   process 4
Advertising Age 39
Aldus *FreeHand* 124, 131, 140, 161. *See also*
   Illustration programs
Art direction 53–64
   print media 55-64
   television ads 73
Art director
   motivation 40
   responsibility of 7, 53, 55
     television 73
   training 5
Art Director's Annual 39
Audience 65
   target 10, 18
   motivation 10
   ratings 38

Balance 56
Bernbach, Bill 6, 18
Bleeds 149
Blueprint, creative 23-26, 42, 43
Boxes 133
Brainstorming 29–30, 43
Brand name 38
Broadcast advertising 65–80
   development 65-66
   portfolios 88

Broadcast advertising (*cont.*)
   radio 75–80
     music 77
     production 79
     script writing 78–79
     using celebrities 76
     voiceovers 77
   television 67–75
     commercial formats 72
     film versus video 73
     reach of 66-67
     script writing 70
     storyboards 73
     terminology 72
Brochure 49
Buying patterns 14

Call-to-action 49
Camera-ready copy 131
Campaign 32–38, 83
   big ideas 33
   continuity 33-35
   extendable versus limited 33
   portfolios 87
   single versus multi-media 38
Cartoon 62
CD ROM (Compact Disk Read Only Memory) 128
Client
   budget 11
   research 9
CLIO 39
Clip art 127-129

177

Close 49
Collateral piece 49
Color 63, 63–64
    computer comps 144
    monitor 144
    separations 63
    use of 63-64
Communication Arts 39
Comprehensives 58, 130, 139
Computer
    clip art 127
    copy fitting 106
    kerning 107
    layout 130-39
    magazines 99
    page orientation 136
    photography 109-20
    printing 146-50
    revolution 97
    typography 100-103
Concept 27, 43, 47, 53, 74
    campaign 33
Consumer
    buying patterns 14
    classification 14
    motivation 10
    recall 38, 39
    research 8, 11-14
Copy 46
    platform 42
    points 47, 49
    selecting visuals for 61
    tracking 48-49
    writing body copy 46–47
Copyfitting
    computer 106
Copywriter
    broadcast 73, 75
    motivation 40
    responsibility of 7, 53
    training 5
Copywriting
    body copy 46-47
    close 49
    clustering 41
    copy platform 42
    headline 43
    lead 47
    print ads 41-52
    radio scripts 78-79
    style 51

Copywriting (*cont.*)
    subheads 49
    TV scripts 70, 72
Creativity
    effect on persuasiveness 38
    recognition for 40
Cricket Draw 161
Crompton, Alastair 82
Cropping
    of photos 119

Demographics 11
Design
    print ads 56–57
    balance 56
    emphasis 58
    proportion 56
    sequence 56
    unity 58
Desktop publishing
    putting a system together 157–60
Digital Darkroom 118, 161
Director
    television 74
Display type 106-107. *See also* Copyfitting
Dithering 110-11
DPI (Dots per inch) 110
Drawing 62
Drop shadows 133
Dropped caps 108
Dummy 58

EPS (Encapsulated Postscript) 110, 117, 140

Film
    versus video 73
Font
    bit-mapped 101
    digital 101
    outline 101
    screen 102
    printer 102
FreeHand. *See* Aldus *FreeHand*
Format 134
FullPaint 161

Grammar 50
Graphic elements 131
    boxes 133
    drop shadows 133
    lines 133

Graphic elements (*cont.*)
   tint blocks 133
Gray levels. *See* Scanning
Greeking 138

Halftone 109
Hardware
   selecting 157
Headline 43–45, 47
   blind 44
   complementing visual 43
   tied to lead 47
   types 43

Idea 36, 47. *See also* Concept
   campaignable 32-33
   generation 11, 29-32
   matching visuals to 62
   radio 76
   rules for checking merits of 82
   selling 81-86
Illustration 123–128. *See also* Visual
   cartoon 62
   drawing 62
   program
      object-oriented 124
      scanning line art 125
      tracing 125
   repro 62
   type 62-63
Image Studio 116, 118, 122, 125, 161
   cropping photos 119
Impulse purchase 46
Initial caps 108
Inspiration 4

Jingles
   radio 78
Job search 90–94

Kerning
   computer 107
Klauser, Henriette 41

Lamination 89
LAN. *See* Local area network
Lasker, Albert 81
Layout 57–59, 58
   comprehensives 58, 139
   computer 130–39
   dummy 58

Layout (*cont.*)
   mechanical 58, 142
   rough 139
   thumbnail 58, 136
      headline 137
      body copy 138
      scaling 136
      size 136
      visual 137
   types 58
Lead 47, 48
Line art 125
Linear thinking 41
Lines 133
Linotronic 113, 151, 152
   negatives 122, 151
   running mechanicals 143
Local area network 99
Locator 111, 127
Logotype 45

MacDraw 123, 161
MacPaint 117, 118, 123, 161
Macwrite 104
Market
   niche 22
   saturated 22
Master pages 133
May, Rollo 4
Mechanicals 58, 131. *See also* Layout
Media 11
Mediamark Research, Inc. 11
Message 43, 65
Microsoft *Word* 104, 160
Mock-up 58
Moire effect 110. *See also* Photography
Music 77-78

Needle drop 78
Nelson, Roy Paul 54, 56
Nonlinear thinking 41

Objectives
   writing 42
Ogilvy, David 89
One Show 39

Page orientation
   computer 136
PageMaker 98, 104, 160
   image control 118

Index 179

PageMaker (cont.)
  linking photos 119
  placing graphics 131
  placing text 131
    greeking 138
  scanning photos for 115
  sizing graphics 132
  text wrap function 119
Pantone
  used with *FreeHand* 144
Paper 50
Persuasion 38, 39, 49
Photography
  computers 109–120
    halftones 109
    moire effect 114
  print ads 114
PICT 110
Planned purchases 46
Portfolio 87–94
  case 89
  compilation 88-89
  content 87-88
  presenting 90
Positioning 22–23, 28, 42, 46
PostScript 124, 147
  clip art 127
Power, John E. 81
Premise statement 34
Presentation
  to clients 85–86
  to colleagues 83–85
Printers
  color 154
  daisy wheel 146
  dot-matrix 146, 158
  laser-type 101, 146
    LaserJet 101, 147
    LaserWriter 112, 113, 115
    postscript 157
    print area 149
    toner cartridges 147
  memory 147
Printing
  computer 146–50
    color 152
    paper 150
    tiling 149
    using bleeds 149
Produce
  broadcast 74

Product
  attribute 22
  benefit 38
  as hero 67
  positioning 22-23
  profile 9
  research 8-10
Promotion 22
Proportion 56
Psychographics 11
Puns 50
Purchase
  decision 46
  impulse 46
  planned 46

Quark *Xpress* 98, 157, 160

Radio. *See* Broadcast advertising
RAM (Random Access Memory)
  on printers 101
Recall 38, 39
Redfern, Walter 50
Repro 61
Research 8–10, 83
  client 9
  conducting 15–16
  consumer 11–15, 49
  libraries 9, 15
  syndicated sources 11-12
  product 9
Resolution 110. *See also* Scanning
Resumes 90
RIFF (Raster Image File Format) 110, 117
Rough 58, 130, 139

Sampling rate 110, 118 *See also* Scanning
Scaling 136. *See also* Scanning
  scanned images 118, 119
Scanner 120
Scanning 109
  bi-level and grayscale 109, 110
  dithering 111
    cell/dot 110, 111
    printer dots 110, 111
  gray levels 110
    formula for determining number of 112
  procedure 113
    sampling rate 114
  scaling of images 118
  scanned art 127

Screens 109, 110
Script writing
   radio 78–79
   television 70–73
      formats 72
Self promotion piece 90-92
Selling ideas 81–86
Selling point 47
Sequence
   design 56-57
Signature cut 46
Simmons/Target Group Index 11
Slogans 34, 45
Software
   capability 99, 104, 106
   selecting 160
Speculative work 87
Spot color 63
Starch INRA Hooper 63
Stereotypes 55
Storyboards 73, 74
Strategy 3, 17–26, 83
   defined 17
   development 17-20
   structuring 23–26
Style
   in writing 51
Style menu 106
Style sheets 106
Symbols 55

Tagline 45
Target audience 10–11, 18
   radio 75
Teamwork 6-7
Television. *See* Broadcast advertising
Thumbnails 58, 130. *See also* Layout
TIFF (Tagged Image File Format) 110, 116
Tint blocks. *See* Graphic elements
Tone
   concept 28, 42, 47
   photographic 109

Tracking
   copy 48–49
Type
   classes 59
   computer 104-104
   display 106-107
   families 60
   legibility 60
   measurement 60
Type face
   standard printer faces 103
Type-only ads 61
Typography 59–61
   computer 100–103

Unity
   design 57

VALS 12–13
Ventura Publisher 98, 157, 160
Video
   television production 73
Visual
   complementing headline 43
   illustrations 61
   logical 54
   photography 61
   print ads 43, 54–55
   selecting 61
   surprise 54
   symbols 54,55
   tied to lead 47
   types 54
   vague 54
Voiceover 77

Word processing
   picking a program 97–99
WordPerfect 160
Writing. *See* copywriting
WYSIWYG 102

Yankelovitch Monitor 12
Young, James Webb 11

**TITLES OF INTEREST IN
ADVERTISING AND SALES PROMOTION
FROM NTC BUSINESS BOOKS**

Contact: 4255 West Touhy Avenue
Lincolnwood, IL 60646-1975
800-323-4900 (in Illinois, 708-679-5500)

SALES PROMOTION ESSENTIALS by Don E. Schultz and William A. Robinson

SALES PROMOTION MANAGEMENT by Don E. Schultz and William A. Robinson

BEST SALES PROMOTIONS, Sixth Edition, by William A. Robinson

SUCCESSFUL DIRECT MARKETING METHODS, Fourth Edition, by Bob Stone

SECRETS OF SUCCESSFUL DIRECT MAIL by Richard V. Benson

STRATEGIC ADVERTISING CAMPAIGNS, Third Edition, by Don E. Schultz

WHICH AD PULLED BEST? Sixth Edition, by Philip Ward Burton and Scott C. Purvis

STRATEGY IN ADVERTISING, Second Edition, by Leo Bogart

ADVERTISING IN SOCIETY by Roxanne Hovland and Gary Wilcox

ESSENTIALS OF ADVERTISING STRATEGY, Second Edition, by Don E. Schultz and Stanley I. Tannenbaum

THE ADVERTISING AGENCY BUSINESS, Second Edition, by Herbert S. Gardner, Jr.

THE DICTIONARY OF ADVERTISING by Laurance Urdang

THE ADVERTISING PORTFOLIO by Ann Marie Barry

PROCTER & GAMBLE by the Editors of Advertising Age

HOW TO BECOME AN ADVERTISING MAN, Second Edition, by James Webb Young

BUILDING YOUR ADVERTISING BUSINESS, Second Edition, by David M. Lockett

ADVERTISING & MARKETING CHECKLISTS by Ron Kaatz

ADVERTISING MEDIA SOURCEBOOK, Third Edition, by Arnold M. Barban, Donald W. Jugenheimer, and Peter B. Turk

THE DIARY OF AN AD MAN by James Webb Young

ADVERTISING COPYWRITING, Sixth Edition, by Philip Ward Burton

PROFESSIONAL ADVERTISING PHOTOGRAPHY by Dave Saunders

DICTIONARY OF TRADE NAME ORIGINS, Revised Edition, by Adrian Room

HOW TO PRODUCE CREATIVE ADVERTISING by Thomas Bivins and Ann Keding